SEALED ORDERS

SEALED ORDERS

Agnes Sanford

LOGOS INTERNATIONAL
PLAINFIELD, NEW JERSEY
1972

Standard Book Number: 0–912106–37–9
Library of Congress Catalog Card Number: 72–76592
Logos International, Plainfield, N.J. 07060
© 1972 by Logos International
All Rights Reserved
Printed in the United States of America

To my daughter Virginia

1.

MY first recorded words, written down by my mother in 1898, were spoken (or rather screamed, for I was a little over one year old) at a railway station full of loud trains. I was terrified by these howling monsters. My mother informed me that God would take care of me, an explanation which seemed at the time somewhat inadequate.

"Where *is* God?" I demanded. "Baby want to *see* God!"

So do we all, so do we all. And this book is the story of a searching and a seeing.

Up to this point, my travels had been by sedan chair, mule cart, canal boat, and steamer, and had taken me from my Chinese home in Hsuchoufu all the way to my home state of Virginia. My father, Hugh Watt White, a minister and missionary, was at home on furlough, and destined to remain there for three years due to the Boxer Rebellion in China. My only memory of these years was not of my parents nor of a baby brother born during this time, but of my grandparents.

I remember my grandfather Henry Martyn White, tall and beautiful with snowy hair and beard, preaching in his little Presbyterian church in Kernstown, Virginia, where he had semi-retired after a long pastorate. I remember sitting between his knees in the buggy and driving over the gentle rolling Valley of Virginia, while he pointed with his whip and said, "The Yanks came right over the brow of that hill . . . ."

It was hard to imagine him fighting "Yanks" or anyone, and indeed he was Stonewall Jackson's chaplain, and the amount of fighting he did was probably negligible.

There is a book about my great grandfather and his two brothers, who were professors at Washington and Lee University at Lexington, Virginia, the original family home. It is called *Samuel S. White and His Times*. I read it once and found it very dull, but anyway there it is. Certain vague rumors would seem to suggest one ancestor who had to do with horse racing, but concerning him, the less said the better.

I remember my grandmother, tiny and adorable in her black silk dress of a Sunday morning. I remember on weekday mornings taking her hand and going to the barn with her, with thrills of delicious excitement, to hunt for hens' eggs in the sweet-smelling hay. For this she wore a vast blue-checked apron and a straw garden hat, and she would whistle in a meditative manner between her few and terse remarks.

When I was four years old, China had settled into its normal uneasy peace, interrupted only by the spring-fall wars of various warlords, and of course by flood, drought, and famine. It must have been winter when we returned, for one memory stands out sharp and clear in my mind. My father wept. He shed tears, sitting alone in a mule cart in the bitter cold of that ghastly frozen plain of North China. I did not dare to say a word. I longed to comfort him, but did not know how. Fathers were people whom one adored from a distance. I adored him, and without fear, but I never knew how to break through the wall of reserve that surrounded him, nor did it ever occur to me in all his life that one could break through. There he was, beautiful, with black brows and eyes of brilliant blue, regular features and sensitive mouth, surrounded, to my childish mind, with an aura of holiness that was almost majestic.

My mother had no such aura. She was vivacious and strong of personality, with curly black hair and sparkling brown eyes. She was more human, more approachable, but also more terrifying. "The Bible says, 'Children, obey your parents in the Lord,'" she would proclaim, and would see to it that one did so. Her parents I never knew, for old Colonel Graves and his lovely, wistful, second wife both died before my mother was married. Many a story she told me, however, about them and about her five half brothers and sisters and her three full sisters whom I came to know very well on various furloughs and visits.

Best of all, it would seem, the little Augusta who was my mother had loved her stepbrother, Charles Graves, a grown young man when she was a child. "Brother Charlie," she called him, for it was considered discourteous to speak to the half brothers and sisters without a prefix, such was the difference in age. (My mother even called my father "Mr. White" until such time as she called him "Dada.")

Indeed, so devoted was the little brown-eyed girl to her half brother that she entertained a desire to marry him when she grew up, and as celebration of this happy event, Brother Charlie promised to give her a diamond ring and a barrel of sugar. Unfortunately, small Augusta confided her matrimonial plans to an older child, who callously informed her that girls could not marry their brothers. Augusta rushed to her mother in tears of anguish, inquiring whether this was true. My grandmother Agnes pondered it for a moment and then wisely replied, "If you *want* to marry your Brother Charlie when you grow up, you may."

I would like to have known my mother's mother. Old Colonel Graves, bouncing heavily over his plantation in a buggy and roaring at his field hands, has never seemed to me a real person. But his young wife, Agnes, with heaven-knows-what fire concealed beneath her quiet face—I would like to have known her.

It is said that before her marriage to the fat old colonel, she was in love with a young "beau" who adored the ground she walked on. Sometime after her marriage, a Negro man galloped up on a horse, delivered a small package, and galloped away, never to be seen again. Within the package was a ring of gold, heavily and beautifully chased and set with seven diamonds. Within the ring, the word "Spero" was engraved.

I know that this story is true. I wear the ring, set now with only a single diamond. I inherited nothing else from my parents, for all that they had was lost in the Japanese invasion of China. But on my finger I still carry that one word, "I hope," placed there by one whose hope, in this world anyway, is long-since dead.

I loved my other grandmother, Blanche, who watched over me and darned my cotton hose through all my college days. To my regret, I do not in any way resemble this serene and Spartan little lady. But my grandmother Agnes, whom I never knew—possibly my soul is kin to hers.

She loved flowers with a passion, as I do. She listened to them, and who knows what she may have heard, not in words but in that far-off language of the soul that is yet so very near. Perhaps she, too, was at times homesick for the pearly gates and the many-colored ramparts of Jerusalem the Golden, as I have been so often, even as a little child.

"Baby want to see God!" But we did not see God when we went back to China, thumping and lumbering in mule carts over the deep-rutted roads. Only the dead and frozen fields—only the frozen fields.

Spring came, the fields thawed, and the tenderness of winter wheat covered the land. New life awoke also in the ancient city of Hsuchoufu with its cobblestone streets barely the width of a mule cart and its fluted city wall. Our mission compound was just within the city wall and built upon uneasy land, the execution grounds being immediately beyond that wall. The region was considered to be haunted with dark shadows, but we of course paid no attention to this "heathen superstition." I wonder!

I remember the bare church with its cold brick floor, the boys' school beyond the mud wall beside our own house, plain and square. This house was not really ours at all, but belonged to the Southern Presbyterian Mission. The cook's house was behind it, and Chang Sao's little one-room home huddled beyond the one tree in the front yard, a gnarled and ancient elm set upon a little mound and full of crows at eventide. Two other missionaries' houses and a very primitive hospital made up the rest of the compound. As my memory dawns on these early years, there was much love and joy among these three families, and peace among their children, and Jesus was very real to all of us.

Every morning after breakfast we had family prayers. Dada, Mother, myself, Henry Martyn (or H.M., as he was always called), and even the little girl, Junia. We studied the Bible from Genesis 1:1 to Revelation 22:21 and then turned back to Genesis 1:1 and started through again. An occasional passage was deleted or skimmed over lightly, and when I asked for an explanation, Dada would clear his throat and look at the floor, and Mother would whisper in my ear that she would explain it later, in private.

I was also caused to memorize Bible verses every day, and to become adept in the Shorter Catechism, and surely all of this is good, for I knew Jesus—and I knew myself.

To this day, I marvel at people who join groups and classes in order to find out who they are. I never had the slightest doubt as to who I was. And why should I? There I was, alone for the most part, with the elm tree and the crows and King Whitetoes, my cat, and Chang Sao, my dear old nurse. Also, much of the time, I had one friend, Isabel, about my own age, the daughter of the Reverend Donald Grier and his wonderful wife, Dr. Grier, a tiny woman who was the only doctor for hundreds of miles. I did not have to conform to a peer group. There was no peer group, only Isabel and I, and I thought faster than she did. There were no Brownies or Girl Scouts or—anything. I considered myself too old to play with the "children," my younger brother and sister and Isabel's. When not with Isabel, I thought my own thoughts and dreamed my own dreams, no radio or television to interfere with them.

I do not remember learning to read any more than I remember learning Chinese. Nobody taught me Chinese. It just happened, and I can still speak it, though I cannot read or write it.

Although much of the above is inference, there are three memories which stand out sharply in the first six or seven years of my life. One is the picture of my father holding the baby Junia in his arms and lifting her up to see the little mimosa tree in bloom. I was too big a girl, of course, to be held up in his arms . . .

And I recall discovering in very early spring a tiny white flower of the speedwell type—just a weed really, smaller than my smallest fingernail, but the first thing to open its face to the new spring. And I still remember with what rapture I stooped over and touched it.

Then, third, when I was a wee bit older, someone gave us a little branch of a blossoming pear tree. It rested in a vase in the living room, and I could not sleep all night for the excitement of knowing that it was there and waiting until daylight when I could see it again.

So much for the early years. They were good years on the whole. We did not in any way suffer from being a minority group, nor did we resent it. We *were* different. No wonder they called us "foreign devils" and spat at us occasionally on the street (but usually missed). Everyone was different—all peoples and races, all men and women within the races, all animals and plants and growing things. No one had ever told us that all people were the same, so we were spared the stultifying effect of that false doctrine. We accepted inequality and thought nothing of it. When placards were posted on the city gates saying that all the foreigners would be killed by morning, we did not really believe it—and it did not happen.

They were good years, these early years in Hsuchoufu. We had a house in which to live, and a yard, rather bleak and sere, for it was difficult to grow flowers in that hard alkaline soil, but still a yard, with an elm tree and a mimosa bush and maybe a few nasturtiums painfully grown by my mother, who loved flowers as had her mother, Agnes. We had the Chinese servants, who cheated us cheerfully but loved us tenderly. And although Dada and Mother both were away on the streets or in the chapel all of every long afternoon (while I kept an eye on the little ones and wondered a bit about the placards on the city wall), they returned at evening time, and we had supper, as we had every meal, all together. Maybe Dada was withdrawn and absentminded, with the burden of his work upon him. Maybe Mother's nerves were worn by exhaustion into irritation. But they were there, and it was beyond any bounds of possibility that anything except death would ever separate them.

This, a child needs, that its soul may live.

Then life changed, as it does from time to time, all life being a succession of changes—the spiral staircase by means of which we mount the heavens. There entered into the seventh year of my life the most unbelievable beauty and the most troublesome fear that I have ever known.

It was a change in my father's life that occasioned a change in my own, swinging it into a new orbit of beauty and of terror. He became weak and thin, his face so gaunt that he let his beard grow to cover it. No one told me the cause of this, for I was still a child, going on eight years old, and to a child, one did not explain grave matters such as life and death. Very likely no one knew the cause of his collapse, referred to vaguely as a nervous breakdown. Looking back now from the vantage point of many years, I can see a cause that they never saw: he was doing the work of the Holy Spirit without the full power of the Holy Spirit.

We are told in the Bible that the Holy Spirit does not testify of Himself but He testifies of Jesus (John 15:26; 16:13). This, my father did. He both preached and lived the love of Jesus with such warmth and faith that many of the Chinese heard him gladly and gave their lives to this foreign God who was also their God. The Holy Spirit worked *through* him, yet not quite in him, just as for many years while I did the works of prayer and healing in Jesus' name, the Holy Spirit was obliged to push His way, as it were, through all the burdens and fears of this world. I did not know then that the outburst of power called the baptism in the Spirit was available today just as it was on the Day of Pentecost, and so I had not received this infilling of power that awakens within one the wellspring of life. Yet the miracles that God did through me, as recounted in *The Healing Light*, were real and true, and their results remained. And the healing of souls and the forgiveness of sins that Our Lord accomplished through my father were real and true. But since the wellspring of God's power had not been awakened within him, the toll on his own strength was great, and the nerves of his body could not stand it.

We were ordered, therefore, by the mission, to take a year off from work and to rest at our own little stone cottage in Kuling, an estate bought from the Chinese and administered as a summer home for missionaries.

All the houses in the Kuling Valley were built of stone hewed by hand out of the mountainside. There was no other material with which to build. The mountains had no trees, only rocks and low bushes, and in the valleys, the feathery and whispering bamboos. From far away one could hear the stonecutters' song as they carried the great swinging blocks to their appointed sites. It made a wistful music filling the air, together with the rush and roar of the Big Stream that flowed through the valley and the birds that flew and nested in the steep, rough slope of the front yard. The house was almost as rough and simple as a cottage might be in old Ireland, without heat or water, screens or rugs. But I loved it and still love it more than any place on earth, for there the earth was my own, and it communed with me and I with it.

Never have I seen such beauty! The winter was a miracle of snow and ice: weird shapes of bushes bowed to the earth with glittering white snow, and miracle balls of gold made of the velvet blooms of an early daphne encased in balls of ice. There was a loneliness upon the steep hillsides, for all but four of the little houses were empty, their windows like closed eyes waiting to wake in the morning of spring. Dark came down early, and fear began to move in me like a low wind, as I watched the last rays of golden sunlight fade away and the shadows creep down the mountainside, engulfing the valley in blue stillness.

My father and mother would go out in the afternoon for a walk or for a cup of tea with other families marooned upon this island of coming darkness. Our faithful servants were with us, but for some strange reason, I felt myself vaguely responsible both for them and for "the children." I must never let them know that I was afraid, lest they should be disturbed. As evening drew on, I would watch at the front window for the darkening figures of my father and mother to come slowly up the road, my father strangely weak and thin, my mother big with child. Fear would grip me with such a strangling hand of terror that I would be actually sick, and even my body would react with nausea and diarrhea. Yet I thought that I could not speak of this to anyone, for I must be strong. I had been taught from infancy that one does not cry when one is hurt. . . .

What did I fear?

Surely the mission station with its excitable crowds and its placards on the city walls was far more dangerous than this peaceful mountainside, haunted only by darkness and cold! I did not know what I had feared until it was revealed to me long afterward in a prayer group.

"I see a great fear coming into your mind when you were seven years old," a friend said to me. "And it is still with you."

That was true. I have always been rather free from reasonable fears: I never minded sleeping alone in my hillside house in New England, the nearest neighbor half a mile away. I do not fear to go anywhere alone by day or by night. I have no terror of mice or men or thunderstorms. But waiting for a loved one to come home has been the agony of my life, and only now is it being healed— only now when I know what it is and whence it came and know the power of the Lord to cover it with His love and take it away.

What then did I fear? I feared that my father would not come home at all, but would die in the snow on that lonely road.

In spite of this fear, however, the seventh year of my life spent on the Kuling Mountains was one of my happiest years. April came, flower-crowned and robed in green and gold and tawny brown as all the mountainsides came back to life. The tops of the high mountains were not long content with the grey of rocks nor the saffron and emerald of new leaves but burst gloriously into red and purple—for lo, the scrawny bushes that covered it were wild azaleas! The near hills rioted and flamed in shades of crimson and flame, of cerise and scarlet. The distant mountains, brooding in gentle folds under the springtime sun, were no longer blue, but purple and lavender.

By the sides of stream and road, wild flowers bloomed amid newspringing grass: anemones and tiny orchids and violets in every shade of blue and lavender and shining fragrant white. And all through the valley, overhanging the Big Stream and festooning themselves over every stone, bloomed a riot of pink and white blossoms: deutzias red and pink, daphne and mock orange and bridal wreath in snowy white, the whole earth breaking into waves of bloom as the ocean breaks into white spray upon the golden sand.

There was nothing to harm or to hurt upon those mountains: no poisonous snakes, no poison ivy, no evil-thinking man. In great freedom I roamed where I pleased, intoxicated with beauty, so caught up in the ecstasy of life, that I was living, it seemed, in another dimension, not that of earth.

Amid all this beauty, my little sister Sara was born and was a comfort and joy, a pledge, as it were, of new life to the family. And new life did return to my father, the strength of resting and of the healing earth—but not completely.

We returned to our mission station, and my lessons continued as briskly and vigorously as ever. H.M., being four years old, was added to the school. My Aunt Junia, a truly remarkable woman whom I later came to love, was a teacher in public school and kept my mother supplied with the proper school books. My mother, teacher par excellence, swept through them with ease and added to them that which seemed to her good, particularly the Bible. Frankly, my heart goes out in pity to children who must attend public school and endure the boredom of sitting idly while others recite, doodling and dawdling while slower pupils catch up to them. It is, I suppose, inevitable, but one of the greatest blessings in my life I count to be that except for a few brief months on furlough when I was nine years old, I never went to school. (And those months have completely gone from my memory, blotted out, I presume, by a boredom beyond belief.)

During the next two summers we spent our vacation time, not at Kuling, but for reasons that I do not know, at Chefoo, a seashore resort in North China. I remember attending some sort of a community church with my parents and seeing the children of the China Inland Mission march in and take their seats, tiny people even as young as five years old, the girls in flat straw hats with ribbons down their backs, the boys in little jackets and very short shorts and caps which they removed on entering into the courts of the Lord with joy—or was it with joy? I grieved for them and I still grieve for them. In New Zealand I met a doctor of about my own age who told me that he was sent to this school at the age of five and did not see his parents again until he was fifteen. Even more do I grieve for those stalwart and really devoted parents who gave up their own children that they might go far inland and tell the love of Jesus to a strange and wild people.

Compared to the life of these little ones, sitting so stiffly and meekly, without father or mother, my own life was a bed of roses.

"Do you remember," asked that doctor, for we were playing the game of long ago, "do you remember that whale that was washed up on the shore?"

"That whale!" I exclaimed. "He was seventy feet long and he stayed there for ages. We used to climb up and slide down his slippery back . . ."

Yes, I remembered the whale, which I enjoyed apparently without being troubled by a sense of smell. And I remembered the Second Beach, over a bluff, where one might find cat's-eyes, little conch-shell stoppers pretty enough to set in rings. And I remembered the Japanese gunboat that hid in the harbor and the Russian gunboat that pursued it there into supposedly peaceful waters. Cannon reverberated through the night before it once more escaped. And I remember the searchlights that swept the harbor nightly even though the Russo-Japanese war had come to an end in 1905.

It was shortly after this that my little world crumbled and fell apart. The glory of sunset and morning, of tiny flowers in the grass, and laughing crows holding a caucus in the elm tree faded away and was gone. The flowers no longer spoke to me of God's love, nor did the crows rejoice my heart. For the peace of our little group was darkened and put out by bitterness and anger. This break in our loving relationship was caused by a difference of opinion about the work itself. My father, who was in charge of country work and the training of Chinese ministers, wanted to give them more freedom and more authority. He even said that the time would come when the Chinese church, if it survived at all, would have to stand on its own feet.

The other missionaries did not share his vision. The Chinese, they said, could not be entrusted with authority, and a time such as my father proclaimed would never come at all. For who could imagine the church persecuted and the missionaries driven away?

None of this was told to me at the time. But night after night, I lay awake and heard low, heartbroken voices in the living room below and trembled at the sound of my mother's sobs. Before this, I had never known her to weep. Neither flood nor famine, illness nor death, could shake her . . . nothing but this breaking of the bonds of love. Not even to Isabel did I speak of this, for my grief was too great for the release of words. We still played together solemnly, but our old spontaneous overflowing joy had disappeared.

Somehow I lost faith not only in those missionaries who had been my father's friends and closer than brothers and who now appeared as his enemies—I lost faith also in God. For these people were "completely Christ-centered and Bible-centered," as they loved to say. Their God was real, and Jesus was their loving Savior. Therefore, Somebody Up There should have been able to help them. My parents would have said that I had no right to think this, but I knew that I did have such a right. I, too, knew Jesus. I had been converted while on furlough at the age of nine. Though remembering nothing of the public school to which I had presumably been subjected, I did remember very well the gentle Presbyterian minister who had made sure of my salvation and who had given me the right hand of fellowship and received me into the Southern Presbyterian church. The experience was real, moving me even to those tears that I never dared to shed at other times, being taught from birth that big girls do not cry. Jesus was real—as real as anyone whom I could see with my eyes. In fact, never in my life do I remember doubting His reality.

But there was something wrong. And if it was not in Jesus and not in the Bible, then it must be in the church.

I hit upon it one morning while my mother was curling my hair while I, as usual, recited those Bible verses that I had been caused to learn.

"Verily, verily I say unto you," I recited, "He that believeth on me, the works that I do shall he do also" (John 14:12). And I asked my mother, "Then why don't we do them?"

"Because the age of miracles is past," she told me. "This is a new dispensation."

I made no reply. One did not argue with one's mother who was also one's schoolteacher, and thus had total authority. But I thought, "Either the Bible is lying—or she is, she and all of them —these missionaries . . ."

God bless them, for they were as good and as completely consecrated people as one could find. They were not consciously lying. But they had been misinformed. The age of miracles is not past. This is not theory, but is a matter of absolute knowledge; I have seen miracles. I myself, small as I am, have learned to do the works of Jesus even as He said.

So *that* was the trouble. These missionaries did not know that they themselves were the children of God, and if children, then heirs—heirs of God and co-heirs of Jesus Christ. And when they thought that God could no longer do the smaller miracles of the healing of the body, how could they believe that He could do the greater miracle of the reestablishing of love? Thus the ancient enemy defeated them. For he could not tempt them to steal or to kill or to commit adultery. But he could tempt them toward hate and anger, and so could break their hearts.

As the cloud deepened over the mission station, it rested upon the children of these missionaries, especially upon Isabel and her brother and sisters and upon my own.

There was one other family in the station, a new family not long married and blessed with babies spaced about a year apart. I heard low murmurs between my mother and our lady doctor, and between Chang Sao, my dear old nurse, and Isabel's nurse. On the basis of these murmurs I gathered that men were by nature cruel and that they did by night evil deeds that brought into the world all these too-numerous babies. I do not remember whether these little ones were affected by the shadow of the station's agony or whether they were not. But all the rest of us—first, one of my three little sisters (the fairest one of all was born about this time)—became ill with diphtheria. We were all quarantined in our own house. Thus Isabel was lost to me. All this, I was told, was necessary in the interest of health, but one could not help a feeling of being rejected by God and man . . . especially as about this time, I contracted trachoma in its virulent Chinese form and was forbidden to use my eyes in reading, writing, or drawing for three months, after which they were completely well. Even school was not held, for Mother was stationed as nurse in the room with the little sick girl, shielded from the rest of the house by a sheet which was drenched with carbolic acid and hung over the door.

About the time our little one recovered, Isabel's only brother fell ill with diphtheria. We were cut off from the world by flood or drought, I forget which—for either the drying up of the Grand Canal or the flooding of its adjacent fields brought all travel to a stop—and the necessary antitoxin did not arrive from Shanghai in time to save the little boy. He died and was buried by night in the boys' school yard, for we, outcast foreigners that we were, had no other place to lay our dead.

The quarantine was lifted, but the shadow deepened.

Then all of us, five in my family and the remaining three girls in Isabel's family, had measles one after another. Each case lasted three weeks and was followed immediately by another one. Spring dragged on with its "wang-mei" of hot drizzle and mold, and still we were not able to arise and go to Kuling, which had now become our heaven and our promised land. Finally, toward the end of the summer, the measles had worn itself out. It being too late then for the long trip to Kuling, we took rooms for a few weeks at the temple guesthouse on Yuin Long San (Cloud Dragon Mountain), outside the city gates. Temples had small brick-paved rooms or cells, even as monasteries did in the Middle Ages, for the comfort of the traveler. We had been to this temple often on little trips or picnics, and I remember it well: the rocky hill, covered with stones of yellow and pink, not unlike our California hills; the paved walk of smooth, shallow steps where beggars sat and pilgrims climbed to the cave where was enthroned the huge Buddha —third largest in the world—his legs gravely intertwined and his serene eyes cast down as he contemplated his gilded navel. The walls on either side of him were lined with smaller deities or holy men, while at the yawning mouth of the cave were the temple guardians, vast snarling devils, blue-faced and furious.

Isabel and I, in better days, had thought this temple to be fun and had even climbed gaily up the Buddha's folded legs and the hands that rested upon them, and had sat, each of us on a toenail. We laughed as we did so, because these were only idols of wood and stone and had no feelings. We would not have treated a peach tree that way, for it had life.

Days passed slowly in this ancient retreat. But it was a relief from the overpowering smell of the city and the fields, where the human excrement used as fertilizer stewed in the boiling sun and where cholera and amoebic dysentery took their yearly toll of human lives.

One day I entered the temple alone. No monks were there, droning their "O-me-to-fu" with half-shut eyes and vacant faces. No pilgrims happened at the moment to be burning incense before the great Buddha or muttering prayers to the goddess of mercy near to his right hand. And a thought came to me—What if these idols had some power after all? How could I know whether my parents knew the truth about them? What would happen if I myself were to worship the great Buddha? Would God smite me dead? I hardly thought He would, but it was an interesting possibility. So, in a spirit of high adventure, I decided that I would just try it and see what happened.

I folded my hands together, bowed before the serene gilded idol, who apparently paid me no attention whatsoever, and murmured "O-me-to-fu" as the monks did.

Nothing happened. Or did it? I wonder. For gradually there came to be within me another voice, sneering, despising, scorning me. I thought little of this inner dialogue, assuming that everyone as they grew older had within them two voices, one of which continually denied or derided the other one.

The summer ended, and we went back to our home just within the North Gate of the city wall. What few flowers remained in the yard had withered and died in the summer heat. And my baby sister, Virginia, the tiny, blue-eyed fairy with hair of red gold, having survived the diphtheria and the measles, now fell ill of amoebic dysentery. Emetine was the specific for this disease, but there was no emetine. There was no doctor. And like the flowers in the garden, the little one, then one year old, withered and died. I had loved her with delight almost as a mother would, being old enough now to feel within me the first stirrings of a mother love. All night long we sat beside her, Dada and Mother, Chang Sao and I, while her little life ebbed slowly away.

I will never forget my father's last words to her, his trembling hand on the little red gold head, "Oh, little girl, little girl," he murmured, "if there was only something we could do for you."

There was. For I have seen many such an illness healed almost instantly by the prayer of faith. If he had only known to give himself as a channel for God's power, laying both hands on the child, praying for her the prayer of command—the miracle-working prayer—she could have recovered as Peter's wife's mother recovered when Jesus rebuked the fever and it left her. The miracle-working prayer: "Lord, enter into this baby and destroy with Your might all germ and infection within her and fill her with new life. Thank You, Lord, for it *will be so.*" A child can pray thus if he only believes! I have known a child to do it, and her baby brother to be instantly healed of polio. Or a woman can thus say the word of power, or a man—anyone wholly given to Jesus and believing that He lives and that the age of miracles is now and that at the word of faith His power leaps into life and works through us as channels to create life even as it did through Peter and John and all who followed Him.

But my father did not know.

Later on, he found out that he could do an equally great miracle: exorcism of one possessed. Toward the end of his life, he read *The Healing Light* and was quite fascinated by it. But it was too late then.

Shortly after this tragedy, Isabel's parents decided to send her to Shanghai to Miss Jewel's School for English Missionaries' Children. This school was precisely what the name would suggest. The manners and morals of the children were very carefully guarded, their deportment was at all times extremely proper, and their souls were tended with anxious care lest they go down into hell. Even though that year was long and lonely, I am glad that my parents held me at home until the new American School was established.

After the normal barricade between child and parent had been redoubled and made firm by the overhanging sorrow that was never discussed, Isabel had become my whole life. There was nothing emotional in our relationship. We were simply part of each other, closer than sisters, playing together those games that we made up for ourselves—endless adventures with the paper dolls that we drew and painted and cut out; excursions veiled in secrecy out onto the street with pennies borrowed from the cook to buy sugarcane; flying kites on the city wall; the erection of an elaborate house under the elm tree for King Whitetoes, who looked upon it with consummate disdain . . . With instinctive wisdom, we did not speak of the cloud that hung over the station. How could we, without rushing to the defense of our embattled parents? So for a little while, for a little while, with the joy of our own inventive and creative play, we could forget it.

I remember standing outside the North Gate and watching the lumbering wheels of the mule cart take Isabel forever away across the dry, dusty land. But not really away, I said to myself, for she would write to me . . . often. Day by day I watched for a letter, my heart in my throat when I heard the cook's soft padded footsteps reentering the kitchen after his "ascending the street" of a morning. I would envision in his market basket the little bundle of mail that from time to time made its way to us by junk and sampan, mule cart or swift runner, and among it a letter for me. It never came.

It might be expected at this point that in my loneliness I turned to the Lord. No, I didn't. I was rather fed up with the Lord, if the truth must be told, although I would never have said it or even admitted it to myself for fear of being cast into hell. Not that I ceased to believe in Jesus! I do not remember a time when I did not believe in Him. But I felt that He had rather forgotten me and my family and that He was a bit careless about fulfilling His promises of giving us His peace and joy. Nevertheless, my favorite hymns were still "Jerusalem the Golden" and "Ten thousand times ten thousand in sparkling raiment white . . ." and "I'm but a stranger here, heaven is my home."

Even today they are my favorite hymns, and I sing them to myself while driving the car down the San Diego Freeway, with that same wistful, heart-choking tenderness that I felt as a child.

What was it? What is it? Is it possible that one remembers?

Meanwhile, the shadow in the station lightened. Somewhere along the way the decision had been made—my father would go forth next year to start a new station, and others would come to Hsuchoufu to take his place. I did not grieve about that overmuch, for the mission station had lost its glory. I grieved for a whole life that was past, but particularly for that rather gaunt front yard with its one elm tree. The yard had long been the home of my soul, much more than the house, too often filled with the echoes of sorrow. However, the Lord had not completely forgotten His promise, for He sent a cheery presence into the house in the person of a new missionary, a warm and delightful young lady who came into our home like a ray of sunlight and there abode. Perhaps my bedroom was given to her, for I slept for some months on the upstairs porch. Or possibly my sleeping there was for purposes of health, for I remember the solemn examination of the doctor to ascertain the reason for my thinness and weakness, and her recommendation of fresh air and mild exercise. And I recall thinking within myself that she was looking in the wrong place for the reason, for it was not in my body.

On the whole, I rather liked lying beneath my mosquito net and looking out at the far stars, and, for a while, at Halley's comet, sweeping night after night like a great broom across the skies. I even rather liked the eerie sound of the watchman's ram's horn on the city wall, and the incessant howling through the darkness of faraway dogs, although it made me shiver. I do not really think it was my airy bed that caused sleep to depart from my eyelids. But it was true that night after night I lay awake until one or two o'clock, and when I did sleep, strange thoughts and pictures were apt to float up into my mind and start me quaking and perspiring in utter terror. One of these horror pictures was most strange, because it was not based on anything that I had seen in real life. It had popped into my mind full-grown, a composite mental picture, when I was studying the history of the ancient Greeks, particularly their methods of human sacrifice. It was as if I had slipped back through time and seen this particular episode. And it was more real and more completely devastating than anything I had ever seen in China. I could feel it coming before it came. My throat would constrict and my stomach would turn sick and I would think, "Oh no! Oh no!" But then it would come, and I could not stop it.

Nevertheless, I remember during this time one weekend that was full of light; it illumined my life for weeks to come. Two or three men visited the mission station, to help, I suppose, in resolving its problems. Out of one of them, the light shone. I could not see it with my eyes, but I could sense it in his presence. It gave me a feeling of comfort without words and, as far as I knew, without reason. I never understood this nor did I even speak of it to anyone until this day. But looking back now, I wonder—Was he one of those shining ones into whom the Holy Spirit had come as this light came upon the Day of Pentecost? He must have been. And he never knew that through him that light had illumined a lonely child in a city far away.

Help came to me also from another source, and this one, deep within myself. Being forced to depend upon myself to fill the hours of the long day, I began at that time, when about twelve years old, to consider what talents were within me and to use them. In my intense love of beauty, I tried to paint. In themselves, my efforts were worthless, being mainly painstaking copies of pictures that spoke to my soul. But there was in them a bit of good. They brought forth in me the beginning of a skill that has been, and still is, one of my greatest joys.

I remember the picture of a full-blown yellow rose that I copied with great care from a gardener's catalog. It was impossible for me to reproduce the glory of the photographed rose, but in giving my whole attention to it hour after hour, I sensed some of its perfected glory enlightening my inner being. It impressed upon my subconscious a picture of perfect beauty that I have never forgotten, just as memorizing Bible passages (part of my daily study assignment) implanted in my subconscious, feelings of the reality of God's being, surrounded by the numinous aura of the beauty of words.

As I sit in my California home looking out upon my own roses glowing in perfection before a background of wild and glorious mountains, I marvel again at the goodness of God who has returned to me a thousandfold all that beauty for which my starved heart yearned in childhood. I did not know Him then. I had heard of Him with the hearing of the ears, and I had given my heart in love as best I knew how to His Son Jesus Christ, but I did not know Him.

How wonderful that even then He knew me and sent me a yellow rose on a garden catalog to comfort me!

Only the surface of my mind, of course, was comforted by the shallow beauty of a painted rose. There were depths into which I did not look. There in the depths there grew a fear, very common, very natural, very real—the fear of death.

My release from this cold fear came during a journey that my family took. We were resting between steam launch and house-boat at the city of Haichow and spending a few days with our missionary friends. I was sharing a bed with Miss Josie Woods, a delightful young woman missionary. Before going to bed, I knelt as always and said my prayers, and it suddenly came into my mind to ask God to take away the fear of death. So I did, quite simply and naturally.

I slept and dreamed that I was dying—the most real and vivid dream that I ever had. I simply awoke in that bed in the dream, and knew that I was dying. And I was filled from head to foot with a radiation of God's power that I have since come to know. Then, I had no idea what it was; my whole body tingled in a thrilling manner, and I was filled with unbelievable joy. I thought, "I wish I could go and tell Dada and Mother that I'm dying," but of course I could not move. And I thought, "But surely they will know how happy I am, so it doesn't matter."

This dream was not as other dreams are, for in other dreams, things are displaced, or there is an element of unreality or of fantasy. This dream was absolutely literal, and I can still see in my mind that square room with moonlight coming in the window, and the shadows of the ivy leaves making patterns on the walls. I can still hear the gentle ticking of the clock, and I remember every aspect of the dream, both emotional and physical. But I have never from that day to this feared death. I do hope that no well-intentioned person, medical or otherwise, will interfere with this transition when it comes for me, for I would like to be conscious and aware, to see whether it feels as it felt when I was eleven years old and dreamed . . . (or did I dream?).

2.

J owned four tiny rosebushes—three pink "cabbage roses," and one velvety red "General Jacqueminot." They represented my first business venture. The money was earned by collecting used bottles and selling them for a penny (or even for a "cash," one-tenth of a penny) to the schoolboys next door, whose loud study periods filled the house with rhythmic chanting as they recited at the top of their lungs. Having acquired certain assets, I then "ascended the street," according to the Chinese idiom, accompanied by the cook, purchased these small, scrawny bushes, and from that time forth tended them carefully, even persuading the cook to save for me the water in which he washed the chickens, that I might pour it on the roses for their nourishment. And by a miracle, I was allowed to take these rosebushes with me when we went to our new home.

The time of our departure was long in coming, for a home had first to be found for the new missionary who would replace my father. Then he must arrive and be trained in the intricacies of the Chinese language and of the country ministry. He must also meet and be accepted by the colporteurs and country ministers whom my father had taught over the years. Indeed, another child was born to my parents in Hsuchoufu—a boy, greatly to the delight of everyone and especially of the Chinese, who had not hesitated to express their woeful pity for a couple bringing forth four daughters and only one son.

So at long last, we departed forever from Hsuchoufu, but not in desolation. The Lord had turned our minds forward to the new station; therefore, we did not grieve overmuch for the home and the work that was lost. Nor did we go alone, for thirty of my father's church friends and helpers went with us out of their love for him. In a long procession, we lumbered and thumped along the deep-rutted roads, the dust rising in clouds about us, mule cart after mule cart, wheelbarrow after wheelbarrow, and ahead of all, mother swaying along in a sedan chair carried by four bearers and holding in her arms the beautiful blue-eyed boy who did much to fill the empty place within her heart. And amid pots and pans and bedding and furniture, there jolted along on a wheelbarrow my four small rosebushes.

There was no "foreign house" for us in the city of Yencheng whither we went. Chinese friends going ahead of us had rented a dwelling in the native style: three small buildings around a brick-paved courtyard. On one side was a living room and a bedroom; opposite to it, across the courtyard, two other bedrooms; at the end of the quadrangle, a kitchen and dining room; and across from that, wall and gateway opening out into other shacks and buildings, where dwelt Chinese friends and servants.

There was no heat in these buildings. When the temperature dropped below freezing, we carried charcoal braziers from room to room. There was no passageway from one building to another except across the brick-paved courtyard. Worst of all, there was no place for my rosebushes. But with infinite charity, my parents permitted me to gouge the bricks from one corner of the courtyard and to shove the bushes into the dank soil. They survived. So did I.

In fact, I have no traumatic memories of this period except the gradual dying of the nerves in two front teeth too roughly screwed apart by a somewhat inadequate dentist in Kuling. In Yencheng, an outpost in really primitive, waterlogged country north of Shanghai, there was no dentist. One simply endured the toothache as best one could.

It is rather natural that I should have retired from life at this time into a dreamworld wherein I was princess and heroine, undergoing untold pain and danger in order to save and rescue prince and hero. Before this dreamworld became more real to me than the real world, however, some inner sense of rightness warned me that I should give these dreams flesh. I should write them down and weave them into stories that might someday be published. My first efforts were naturally terrible, but this creative effort not only saved my mind from utter extinction but also brought forth in me whatever talent for writing was latent within. As I grew a bit older, I found poems more fun than stories, and I still find them so. A grief when swung into poetry and written out becomes a cathartic and leaves the mind washed clean.

The bits of stories and poems that came to me were utterly worthless, and I knew it. If I had taken for granted that I had perfectly heard the inspiration of God and therefore needed not to change a single word, much of their value would have been lost. Yet in a sense, they did come from God, for through them God was saying to me, "These talents lie buried within you. Study and learn, and they can be brought forth." Therefore I studied in college every kind of writing except journalism—essays, short stories, poetry, and drama. My patience is extremely short with those who think to attain perfection without study. God does not, except with an occasional genius such as Coleridge, Mozart, or Handel, "give" a work of art whether in paint or in words, without requiring the instruction, the effort, and the concentration that the mind needs in order to achieve real worth. And this is for our good.

In these particular lines I had no teacher, for although my mother was a wonderful music teacher as well as a general instructor, she was not skilled in the teaching of painting or creative writing. But even then, in my childish efforts, there was formed the habit of concentration and of expectancy which brought into my lonely life that zest of creativity which is the very light of life.

At this point in my life, I defied my mother's dictum for the first time. I had been writing little stories for the children's page of the Shanghai *Mercury*. The children used pseudonyms, and my mother decided that mine should be "Sweet Olive." These words to her meant a shrub with a pleasant odor. But to me they meant a scrawny dark-skinned girl named Olive, and I was not going to identify with her. I utterly refused to accept this name and chose my own, which I have forgotten. But I have not forgotten my mother's displeasure, detectable for about three days in a certain lofty coldness of demeanor. Nor did I forget the effort of will that was required for me to make this decision.

Another hobby of mine at this time was photography. A small

Brownie Kodak and a developing and printing kit afforded me great delight. There was also reading. A small church in the South had closed its Sunday-school library at this time and sent us a truly wonderful "missionary barrel" of old books and magazines—many years' collections of the *Youth's Companion* and *St. Nicholas* magazine, long-since defunct, and many books of an extremely improving and uplifting nature. One of them was a collection of deathbed scenes in which drunkards were converted and saved just before their last breath. Then there were several touching stories of children: Little Prudence who took a kettle of hot water to a poor family, carrying it carefully that she might not smirch her frock; and Little Dotty who was so holy that she spent her time in the graveyard dropping daisies into graves as they were dug—until finally she died, and someone dropped a daisy into her grave.

But along with these touching idylls, I read Dickens and Scott and other adventure novels, which I greatly preferred to the holy books of the Sunday school. In fact, there gradually developed in my mind a certain cynicism concerning piosity, a cynicism which lasts to this day.

We come into life, I am quite sure, with sealed orders. Even at this time the Lord was preparing me to be an explorer and a way-shower along the paths of healing and of miracles. From the very beginning until now, I prefer deeds to words and I am not delighted by the saccharine smiles of those who bear down upon me to report a "mountaintop experience" concerning some "precious soul."

This attitude of cynicism, indeed, tended to spread to Christianity in general. I did not doubt the reality of Jesus Christ, nor the devotion and consecration of my missionary parents. But *something was wrong somewhere*. There was Jesus, and He had said, "The works that I do shall ye do also"—but they were not being done. I had analyzed this when I was eleven years old, and my mother had told me that the age of miracles was past. But I forgot my own analysis and knew only that here was this thing called Christianity, but it didn't work.

I would look at our dear and wonderful Chinese helpers, those who had left all that they loved—family, friends and livelihood—and had followed my father to a strange land, and I would try to convince myself that Christianity must have meant to them all that it is supposed to mean to anyone. They must have seen in my father and through him a light from beyond that they followed, as the Wise Men followed the star. "Bok Ching Tien" was my father's nickname: "White Clear-Skies." What did they see beyond those clear skies? Love, certainly—his love and the love of Jesus and the hope of heaven. The foundation stone of their teaching was that Jesus came to save their souls so that they could go to heaven and not be lost forever in the troubled realm of demons and devils.

Those won by this good news were not the scholars and the sophisticates. They were the simple ones to whom the realm of evil spirits was so real that they lived from birth to death in fear of them. They pasted bits of colored paper over their doors to frighten the devils away. Having a theory that demons could move only in a straight line, they built their cities with a walled area beyond each gate and within it a gate at an angle, hoping to keep the devils out of the main part of the city. They hired their Buddhist priests to attend a deathbed in order to drive away both the demons and the soul of the departed one by means of firecrackers and gongs and loud lamentations. A mother who could not afford a priest was even known to put her daughter out of doors to die alone, lest her ghost remain forever in the house.

We called all of this "heathen superstition," and when our friends and servants told us that they *saw* these apparitions, we did not believe a word of it. I remember sitting on the woodbox in the kitchen, drinking tepid tea from the cook's teapot and laughing heartily as he seized a kitchen knife and charged about the room to show me how he had driven away a most unpleasant ghost who had appeared as a bloody head popping in the window.

It was good that I did not believe these things, but set them down entirely to the Dah S-fu's imagination. Now I wonder.

"We Orientals have an advantage over you Occidentals," a tiny Japanese hairdresser once said as she put up my hair. "We can *see* these things and you can't." To her it was an advantage, for she was a Christian, and the power of the Holy Spirit was alive and active in her so that she delivered many oppressed people while she curled their hair. My father, although he did not see them, had come to know the terrible reality of these thought-forms and had learned from a country minister how to exorcise them.

One did not need to labor in order to convince the Chinese peasant of the reality of a hell or hades. He knew it, and he feared it, both in this life and in the continuing life of which he had no doubt whatsoever. Did he not burn incense and paper money and bamboo replicas of manservants and maidservants at the graves of his departed, hoping that their essence might in some way ease the dark journey of the soul through the terrors of that life beyond death?

That Jesus Christ should have emanated from a higher plane and come to earth and given His life so that He could free both the living and the dead from an ever-living death—that to them was easily comprehensible.

Moreover, they had evidence of the fact that Jesus Christ set them free from the terror and the danger of evil spirits even while they lived here on this earth. Had not one old ex-bandit, Mr. Tai, demonstrated this power of deliverance to the whole countryside around Hsuchoufu? Not only that, but they perceived, in a way that we are unable to perceive, that those who accepted Jesus walked in a circle of light that protected them from evil spirits. Knowing this, a heathen family would sometimes invite a Christian family to live in a haunted house rent free for a few months, believing that after a while the Spirit of Christ abiding there would make it untenable for evil spirits.

Up to this point, then, Christianity *did* work. And I felt rather guiltily that I should be satisfied with this quite real and evident salvation.

But I was not.

Into the drabness of life at Yencheng, our Kuling vacation burst like an explosion of light. The mountaintops shimmering in the sun and the deep green valleys laced with roaring streams and rapids over shining rocks; white cascades sparkling into emerald pools; clean and fragrant air; blue folds of mountains, dimming into the distance, and below them the great plain of the Yangtze River stretching to the far horizon; the crisp bamboos crinkling in the sun; and from far away the haunting song of the stone-carriers, "Ay-yah, ho-yah-h, *ay-yah-h,* ho-yah . . ."

Going to Kuling was truly entering into heavenly bliss. After ten months of total loneliness, to have my friends again: Isabel (rather more grown-up and young-ladylike than the rest of us), and Ellen Drummond, and Grace Sydenstricker (younger sister of Pearl Buck, nee Sydenstricker), and the boys whom I had known from infancy—the three Woods boys and James Graham—these were the center of the little group who played together in sun and in rain every day except Sunday. Sunday was kept holy unto the Lord, as in the words of Scripture.

On sunny days we ranged the mountains and the deep valley from end to end. We rolled rocks down from the Wave Range to see how high they would bound into the air before they finally crashed in a cloud of splinters into some deep chasm out of sight. We played tennis, at which, alas, I never could excel due to a certain imbalance of eye and hand. (Could it be because I am by nature very left-handed, but was trained contrariwise?) We would tramp the two miles to the swimming pool at the end of the valley, but there, while I delighted in the beauty of the deep water-filled ravine, I simply could not learn to swim. I had been told that if one jumped off the dam into deep water one would automatically swim. I tried it—twice. It did not work.

When the tennis courts were not in use, we played other games upon them, pom-pom pullaway and prisoner's base and king-of-the-castle. We invented a wild game of paper chase that went the whole length of the valley. Sometimes we tramped with older people on all-day picnics to far, wild bits of mountains where I loved to terrify others by scaling high cliffs and standing on them with my toes over the edge. The only sport in which I excelled was rock climbing.

Even our rainy days in Kuling were filled with delight. By some unspoken law, the gang would always gather at my house. And during a three-day typhoon, while the rain crashed on the tin roof of the house and the Big Stream roared through the valley below, my parents would take to the bedroom with typewriter, knitting, and Bible, and we would surge through the house playing every sort of indoor game, learned or invented, with or without dominoes or cards. (We used flinch cards, not bridge cards evilly bedizened with kings and queens and jacks. If one played with such as those, one would in all probability go to hell.)

Mother suspended school during the Kuling vacation, so that

I could forget Caesar's Gallic wars and the intricacies of algebra. Every day was a holiday. Except Sunday.

On Sunday, all five children must at the same moment be properly clothed and sashed and brushed and hatted, and must walk up the winding road by the Big Stream to the Union Church. There, for a season, one sat with eyes glazed with utter boredom, at a thing called Sunday school. Then we filed into the pew together for divine worship. This was better—the glorious hymns and the view of mountains and clouds from the open windows, and the glimpse of friends across the church, and finally the sermon. All of this was endurable if not quite enjoyable, for I had long ago taught myself to turn off my mind when wearied of a sermon, and to tell myself a story.

But on the long homeward drag, my heart would sink, for I dreaded Sunday dinner. Conversation at dinnertime was reserved for the grown people, which was fair enough considering that we young ones had the run of the house at other times. The grown people's Sunday sport was the tearing apart of the sermon, phrase by phrase, and argument by argument. Dr. Harry Emerson Fosdick once visited China and preached at our church, and fragments of his sermon were scattered over every course brought in by our beaming table boy, Wang Er. Dr. Fosdick preached on Christian love, but he was not *sound* because he did not mention the Blood of the Lamb in about every third sentence. This went on and on until finally I burst into tears and left the table, to the utter consternation of my parents, for such a thing I never did.

What was the trouble? I could not tell them. I did not know. They were good, they were completely Christ-centered and Bible-centered, believing every word of Holy Writ from cover to cover —but *something was wrong.*

This fact, however, I set aside in a secret corner of my mind and covered with a lid. Only rarely did it pop out from under the lid and trouble me. For the most part, nothing troubled me! The days passed in a blissful glory of sunlight and wind and fun and friends and far high places where one looked down upon cloud-filled valleys that the foot of man had never trod. There were no trees upon these mountains, only the scraggly shrub that in spring blazed into the fire of azaleas. Even in the valleys there were no trees, only bushes shoulder high, and mossy rocks and rivulets of shining water. Oh, the wonder of being able to cup this water in one's hands and drink it, cold and delicious! For except in this blissful place, we drank only the brackish, alkaline water of ancient wells, boiled and filtered through cotton. Since there were no trees, one could see to the very end of the folded and fluted blue mountains, to where they descended to the rocky cliffs that edged the great plain of the Yangtze River.

The only hint of future trouble that came to me during these blissful summers of my early teens was in a recurrent dream. From time to time I would dream that I walked all the way to these last cliffs and then on down black rock steps that were very dark, into a shadowed and terrifying sea. I would awake with the shadow upon me, like a thin mist upon the mountaintop, soon blown away by the lovely light of day.

I loved to seek, out upon these far mountaintops, a certain height or rock that I could reach, simply setting out toward it without benefit of path. It amazes me now to remember the great freedom that my parents gave me. True, there were certain galling rules concerning bedtime, and Wang Er would be sent with a lantern to escort me home from a party at the untoward hour of ten, much to my shame and embarrassment. But on a sunny day, I was allowed to roam the mountains alone. There was nothing to fear upon those mountains unless it might be a snake hidden under the bushes or in the high grass. I made a decision in those early days from which I have never wavered: I would not go all of my life in the bondage of treading only a known path lest I step upon a snake. I would go through untrodden country toward the goal of my choice, whether or not I trod upon a snake.

During the summer the wild flowers did not crown the mountaintops with ruby and amethyst nor drape the valleys with gold and pearls as they did in the spring. The first outburst of ecstatic bloom ceased, and nature rested. Yet even in this summer rest, flowers bloomed here and there, clematis and lilies hid among the bushes in the valley, bluebells and Saint-John's-wort among rocks and crags. These I would gather with reverence and love and bring them home, never to waste them, but to cherish them in beauty as long as they would live. One rule I made for myself: I would never sit down and rest on returning home, no matter how weary I might be, until I had arranged the flowers and cooled them in water and set them in vases about our living room. It was a plain, square room, roughly whitewashed and unadorned. But it needed no other beauty than the green glory of the nearby mountains shining through windows and door, and the loveliness of trumpet lilies and clematis breathing sweetness from the mantelpiece, or a bowl of fringed white grass-of-parnassus and club moss on the dining-room table.

Twice during these two summers of my early teens, God spoke to me, though I did not know at the time that it was He, for He did not speak in any way that one would expect—not on Sunday morning, no matter how hard the minister might strive to say His words. Nor was it on a Sunday afternoon when, after our walk (for we were allowed to walk on Sunday, but not to run nor toss a ball), we settled in a circle in the living room to study the Bible, and for lighter reading to immerse ourselves in the *Christian Observer* and the *Sunday School Times.*

Only now, looking back, do I realize that it was God who met my spirit when my spirit met Him in faraway places quite alone. One time I had climbed to the highest valley, a shallow trough between waves of shining silver gray rocks breaking upon the hilltops. Tall rough grass filled the valley, and I lay upon it full in the sun, and what I thought about I do not know. But in some way that I could never recapture, I entered into a state of indescribable dreamy bliss wherein I was one with the tall crisp grass, and with the tiny creatures that lived within it, and with the high blue sky whence sunlight drenched my body with pure joy.

There was no more time. It was yesterday and today and forever. And there was no more *me* as a separate being. I was part of the tall grass, and the tiny sounds when it crinkled in the sun sounded within myself also, as truly as did the beating of my heart. The wee grasshoppers were part of me, and the ripples of warm breeze that flowed through my being, and the far sky—the far, ever-reaching blue of the sky.

What was it?

Surely—although the mind and the tongue of man had not been able to describe Him to me—surely at that moment (or eternity) His Spirit communed with mine. And possibly this is why, in spite of all the dullness and cynicism with which "religion" became encrusted during these unawakened years, I never once doubted that God was real.

One other time I felt this indescribable presence of God the Creator. Again I was alone, but this time active, exploring a rocky slope where the bushes grew high and thick, and wild flowers hid among them. Many a time I had thus explored, but this time was different. While leaping and scrambling over the rocks, I entered into a state of high ecstasy that was not entirely of this world. Was it Jesus standing invisibly beside me, saying, "Lo, my child, I am with you always"?

As far as I can tell, it was not. It was rather the uncreated essence of the Creator, His ever-living creativity, flowing into me from bamboo and from rock, from ferns and moss and tiny orchids hiding in the grass. I did not know this at the time, for I had no idea that sentient life of any kind could be in things inanimate. But it *can* be—it *is*. The life of the Creator is in every created thing, for it is made of the very essence of His being, and His word from whence it came still speaks through grass and grasshoppers to those attuned to Him.

Primitive people, sensing this, have worshiped nature as their God. We know that sun and moon and earth do not have kingship over us. They await the kingship that we should have over them, through Jesus Christ who burst through from God into man to be the King of all of us.

3.

IN my fourteenth year I was sent away to the Shanghai American School, newly established in rented houses far out on Szechuen Road. This to me was the gateway to heaven. Here the joyous companionship of Kuling was simply moved to another setting: three tall narrow dwelling houses in rows of similar dwelling houses such as one can see today in the residential section of practically any old city on the waterfront in the Far East, in the United States, or in England. In front of each house was a tiny apron of lawn surrounded by a high brick wall. One went out of its gate and across the narrow street to the opposite house, its bedrooms turned into classrooms, its basement into kitchen and dining room. And somewhere behind this building was another sedate three-storied house used as the boys' dormitory.

There was no playground. We walked down Szechuen Road to Hongkew Park where we invented our own games, as at Kuling, or watched the boys play rugby against a team from an English school. ("Oh I say, played!" their rooters would cry from the sidelines. "*Played*, by Jove!")

We always lost, of course. Among the games we invented was the delightful sport of making up little plays or skits or stunts and acting them in a classroom, pushing aside desks or using them as mountains, ships, or trains as the plot required. I had never seen a play in my life, such activities, even the classic Chinese drama chanted in beautiful Wen Li verse, being classed in some vague way among the works of the devil. But a group of us from the school were taken to see *Romeo and Juliet* upon a Shanghai stage, and a new world opened before me. I walked for days in the glory of that play, whose very tragedy was so bathed in beauty that it was lifted into light. Not only this, but a part of me came to life and entered into this new world. I put together bits of drama and acted in them with an abandon that I had never been able to express in real life. And it was I who was called upon from time to time to parody or paraphrase some bit of nonsense while my audience collapsed in tears of mirth. Some of these stunts remained with me for years, and even now if I see a friend from very old times, she may say, "Oh Agnes, do *The Little Ship.*"

This was a new part of me! I recognized it for the first time! I was an actress! Solemnly, I reconsidered my intent to become a writer. I had far more talent for acting than for writing, though where it came from, in a long line of Presbyterian divines, it would be hard to say. But also I was a young woman of fourteen, probably strongly influenced by the Chinese view of marriage and descendants though I was not aware of it, and I desired husband and children. (At the age of fourteen, I reckoned on some eight or nine children, later reducing it to six and finally winding up with only three due largely to my own mismanagement.) The raising of a family could be done better in conjunction with writing than with theater. Therefore I returned to my original intention of becoming a writer. (Later on, the Lord put His finger upon my writing ability and deflected it in various other directions, but He did not take it away. And I have learned that if we obey Him, He will never take entirely away something that is part of our original nature, though He may turn it into other channels than those that we had envisioned.)

I do not remember receiving any instruction in the art of writing at the Shanghai American School. As a matter of fact, I remember nothing at all about my courses or classes at this school except that they were no trouble to me. Apparently I had a fairly good mind to begin with and had learned to use it. (As I write this, I seem to note in myself a lack of the Christian virtue of humility. And alas, not too many years remain in which to cultivate this admirable quality.) At any rate, study was neither a problem nor a novelty to me. It was an unbelievable delight to live and work every day with my friends: my roommates, Ellen Drummond and Grace Sydenstricker; and my lifelong friends, James Graham and the Woods boys; others who had raced through my house in Kuling and draped themselves over the porch railings to wait till family prayers were over—the companionship of all these young people was heaven to me. I do not remember going to church at all, though I am sure that we did so every Sunday. But I remember long rickety rides on the streetcar all the way to the Bund, that most fascinating waterfront with its jinrikishas and sedan chairs and donkeys, its horses and carriages, and its magnificent Sikh policemen in scarlet and gold, their vast black beards curled upon a cord and tied under their chins, their red turbans towering over the heads of the small Chinese scurrying in every direction.

All along the Bund was the yellow Whangpoo River, black steps descending into it here and there, sampans bobbing on the muddy waves beside it, the dank odor of still water emanating deliciously from it. The Whangpoo River debouched into the mouth of the Yangtze and beyond that was the China Sea, also yellow from loose silt carried down from far mountain gorges. Far out in the harbor lay the steamers: the Canadian Pacific *Empresses*, the Dollar *Presidents*, river vessels of the Nippon Yusen Kaisha and the China Merchants, the Butterfield and Swire Company and the Jardine Matheson and ancient battered freighters from cities far away and from every country on the face of the earth. Between them and the Bund there darted back and forth like water beetles, tugs and launches, junks and sampans laden with everything from blue-uniformed ship captains to squealing pigs.

As for the square solemn buildings lining the Bund, I remember none of them. For the stores, Wing-Ons and Sincere's and Whiteaway Laidlaw's and myriads of Chinese shops—these were down another less formal street. The Chinese stores had signs in Chinese characters and also in English, and some were very quaint indeed. I remember a tailoring establishment bearing the legend, "Gentlemen suited downstairs, discreet ladies have fits upstairs." I remember also Marcel's, a teahouse where I went from time to time with a new friend, Margaret, enjoying the most delicious French pastry and marveling at the Chinese waiters ("boys" one calls them in the East), speaking exquisite French.

But I must not continue forever allowing these crisp fragments of long-buried memories to float up into my mind. Let me get down to business now and trace in this era my development in the knowledge of God.

There wasn't any.

There was only friendship and fun and the joy of discovering a new world. But since God Himself is love and is the very fountain of joy, surely these humbler gifts were also from God.

The Shanghai American School, only one year old and made up for the most part of a collection of missionaries' children, mother-trained, found it rather difficult to separate us into forms or classes. Some of my subjects were considered senior, and some junior course. But at the end of the year, I had gone as far as this delightful school could carry me, and it was time to go "home" as we fondly called that great unknown, the United States, to college. There was no question as to the choosing of this college. It was a small Presbyterian school for young ladies: Peace Institute, as then called, now Peace College, named for an eminent divine, William Peace. My mother had attended this little college in Raleigh, North Carolina, and so had her sisters. Moreover, my father's only brother, Uncle William McClanahan White, was pastor of the First Presbyterian Church in Raleigh and was on the board of the college. And my adored little grandmother lived with them, for Grandpa had died some years before. So I was truly going "home." Nevertheless, the thought of it was frightening. I knew that it would mark the end of childhood, and so it did.

Childhood nowadays would have been long behind me, for I was fourteen going on fifteen when I embarked on the tiny Japanese freighter, the *Shidzuoka Maru,* for that far country, the land of the free and the home of the brave. This small lumber vessel may seem to have been a strange choice. But our choices were always directed by economy, as we lived on the barest minimum of salary. A group of relatives of missionaries had been to China on a visit and returned on this little ship, which carried only fourteen first-class passengers. (In the second class, there was a group of Japanese brides, selected by mail and going over to marry in the United States.) To my great delight, Russell and James Woods were also vaguely attached to those relatives of relatives of friends who promised to keep an eye on us.

No three weeks of my whole life have ever been so completely given over to utter delight and glory as were the three weeks lumbering along practically awash in the Pacific upon this tiny vessel. Our made-up games on shipboard had a most nautical quality. One of our contests was to see how many times we could walk around the ship without being knocked down by a wave. Seven times around was a mile, and the one who made it without being rolled into the scuppers in a lather of foam won the game. This was not quite as exciting as it sounds. The ship was loaded heavily and rode low, that was all; the great thrilling rollers of the Pacific broke peacefully upon her deck from time to time without danger of upsetting her. It was the ocean itself that made this game, for we contested not with living beings but with the first of all living entities, the great sea, ever-heaving, mysterious, blue black in its great depths, and full of a life that one could not see— snowy white when some wandering crest broke over the ship and the spray flew high into the air.

Another one of our games was, of course, the wonderful one of exploring. In this we had always delighted. In Kuling we had explored far mountains, hidden caves, and waterfalls plunging into deep green pools; on shipboard we explored the crow's nest high up on the yellow mast, the hidden caves of engine room, coaling room, and propeller shaft, and even the space below the screw itself where hot water dripped upon us and the roar of whirling blades deafened us.

Certain of our land-games acquired added thrills when transplanted to the steamer. We played hide-and-seek upon the unlighted boat deck at night, among capstans and ventilators and coils of rope and suspended lifeboats. No one had ever told us that we were adolescent or that we were teenagers or that we were a youth group. We thought innocently that we were children—or, rather, we were just ourselves, having fun in our own way. We did not know that we were supposed to have problems, and we had none. If it ever occurred to me that I was a girl and that Jim was a boy and that his red hair had a rather nice smell to it as we hid together behind a lifeboat while Russell shouted, "Coming, ready or not!" it gave me no concern but only added a tiny fillip to the zest of life.

The need of solitude still remained with me, however. One night I absented myself from the stateroom shared with three other females (sublimely unaware of my maneuvers) and went alone up to the boat deck. The railings of the deck were somewhat informal and terminated, as I recall, where lifeboats were situated. I crawled beyond them and came to rest in the lee of a lifeboat, lying flat on my back and facing out to the black sea with its wild salt breath and the wheeling sky, spangled with a million stars— for we were in mid-ocean, far away from the heavy banks of cloud that haunt the area of the Aleutians, and the skies were clear with a clarity that I have never seen before or since. How long I lay there I have no idea, for I slipped beyond the swing of time or place. I was one with the stars—I was one with the universe. I felt in me the life of the strange creatures within the sea and beneath the waves and flying above the waves. I was not myself, I was life. And yet I was myself, and life was me. Words cannot say it nor can I now remember the actual feelings of that time between time and eternity—only that it happened. Once since then I have remembered it: when Stokowski conducted the Philadelphia Orchestra in Debussy's *La Mer*. I was listening, thinking rather sadly, "But that doesn't sound like the sea," for there were no crashes of timpani suggesting waves at this point nor any cadenza of strings with the sound of wind—when *there it was!* That feeling beyond words! That glory evanescent and unbearable in its bliss for which one would yet die that one could enter into it again! There it was!

I have tried to find it again in recordings of *La Mer*, but it cannot be thus caught. And possibly I could not experience it again under any circumstances, for one cannot command the things of the spirit. I have tried since on ocean voyages to find a dark boat deck, but there is always a shaft of pale, man-made light to blot out that light that is eternal. I have never found it again, even as I have never again found the ecstasy of that shallow valley high toward the blue sky. I have tried. It does not come. There is no use in your trying. You may lie down upon high tough grass and let grasshoppers repose upon your person, but you cannot guarantee that the skies will open to you, nor that the glory of God will pour through. Only once did God show Moses His glory in a light that cannot be seen. There is in the Creator such a passion for diversity that He cannot be standarized, He cannot be commanded. Our times are in His hands, and He will come to us as He wills, when He wills, but never in the same way twice.

We landed at Seattle, the little freighter drawing up to the waterfront almost in silence. One man in blue jeans and rather dirty sweat shirt pushed a wheelbarrow along the empty expanse of railway track and brick that formed the dock. I thought nostalgically of dockings in China: hordes of excited Chinese yelling and laughing and leaping aboard, even over the expanse of churning water yet between ship and shore. How could it be so quiet here, and so lonely? For nobody came to meet the little group of returning Americans, bound mostly for places far away. And the one man with the wheelbarrow—how strange, I thought, that a foreigner should dress so casually, just like a coolie. Then I realized that he was not a foreigner. I was the foreigner. I was, innocently assuming that I was coming "home." But I had no home. Not on this planet.

The train, trundling eastward, stopped all day in Chicago, and all day I sat in a rocking chair in the waiting room, looking out upon the street and not daring to venture thither. What if I could not find my way back to the station and the rocking chair? What if there were no one to tell me? People strolled down the street—strange, frightening people of various colors—but I was not at all sure that I would know their language . . .

So there I sat until I entered another train and headed east again. Smoke and cinders blew in the windows, and the train rocked and swayed over the Appalachians. By the time I reached my first stop at the home of an aunt, I was exhausted and almost downcast. But when I reached Raleigh, and was welcomed by Uncle Will and his charming family and my very own grandmother, my heart lifted up. Nor did the little college set atop a gentle hill daunt it in any way. To be sure, I was different from the other fifty-nine boarding students in ways that I did not at first quite understand. But this was nothing new to me. I had always belonged to the most minority group imaginable. And as I threw myself again into the delight of acquiring knowledge, I forgot the difference, and soon the other girls did, too, and we entered all together into the warm and delightful fellowship of a girls' boarding school. True, some subjects were more difficult and less interesting to me than others: physics, notably, and trigonometry, whose usefulness escaped me, as it still does. But other subjects opened the heart to new beauty and power in life and were, therefore, thrilling. In the very practical course in psychology, I learned the basis of those methods of study which to this day I use. I described them once to a father whose son faced failure in college.

"Has anyone ever taught him how to study?" I asked. And as my friend shook his head, I outlined to him those ways of memorizing, of comprehension, and of creative action that I had found useful all my life.

"Write that out and I will get it published!" he cried. "It ought to be in the hands of every college student in the United States!" So I wrote it out and it was published by the Forward Movement in a tiny pamphlet entitled *How to Learn*.

There was a splendid course in education. Peace Institute even ran a one-room primary school wherein we might practice teaching. But the studies that I loved best were poetry, art, and "expression." There was no radio and no television in those days, and it was the current thing for a young lady to sing a bit or play the piano or, failing that, to recite poems or dialogues for the entertainment of such luckless people as might be at a party and unable to escape. This sounds rather silly, but my three years of "expression" did more toward furnishing me for the Lord's work than any course I ever took, for I learned how to place my voice and how to throw it, how to stand and to walk, how to speak extemporaneously, and even how to act a bit in our small school dramas. Some people are naturally gifted in the correct use of the voice in public speaking, but I was not—and the Lord, who had His hand on me though He was not in all my thoughts, saw to it that I learned.

On Sunday, true, I did think of the Lord, for we lined up two by two and walked the seven blocks on brick-paved sidewalks under shady oaks to the First Presbyterian Church at the corner of the beautiful grounds where the ancient city hall reposed in grave dignity. There we listened to my Uncle Will proclaim the true Gospel as beautifully and as impressively as anyone could proclaim it—and I knew that he lived what he taught. He was much taller than my father, not so regular in feature, but most impressive in his morning coat and striped trousers, with blue eyes flashing—rather like an archangel, I thought, and if he had been clothed in shining robes instead of formal morning dress, he could easily have been one and flown away on golden wings. There still stands in the gracious city of Raleigh a church named for him: the White Memorial Church. And there still remain in country places under scraggly longleafed pines little country churches that he started. For he trained young men to go forth and preach the Gospel even as my father did in China.

Only one incident really broke the rhythm of my three years in this lovely city, and that was a hospital experience. From puberty on, I had suffered intense pain for about one day every month. My mother had treated it with hot-water bottles and aspirin and even an occasional sip of the whiskey that she kept sternly for medicinal use only—and *that* I found very enjoyable. But I had given little thought to this discomfort or to the migraine headaches to which I was accustomed. I had been brought up on the concept that a certain amount of suffering was not only God's will but probably also a special mark of His favor. Mother would cheer me by stories of Cousin Betty Penick who was a great sufferer and a great saint and all her life endured her migraine headaches and complained not. (I conceived an intense dislike of Cousin Betty Penick.)

However, this monthly trial became so intense that I was sent to an osteopathic physician who was also a surgeon, and upon examining me, he found that an operation was necessary. Apparently certain organs had fallen completely out of place and were jammed in where they could not function. I can easily understand how this might be, for among our made-up games was that of seeing who could jump from the highest heights, landing with a terrific thud—and that was always myself.

This seemed to me quite an adventure, and I cheerfully went to the little private hospital at the very corner of the school grounds and was prepared for the ordeal. Never having been in a hospital before, I knew nothing of proper technique of preparation and accepted the rules of no supper, no drink of water, and so forth as though they came from the mouth of God. I was somewhat surprised after all this abstinence when the nurse cheerfully brought in to me a full breakfast of scrambled eggs, toast, and coffee. But it did not occur to me that there might be any mistake connected with this, for I thought only that the ways of doctors were past finding out. So I was wheeled into the operating room and given ether.

The next thing I knew, I was not in my body. I was above it, just under the ceiling, looking down with a certain curiosity at the body lying there on the operating table. This did not last very long. Presumably, the heart momentarily stopped and the doctors brought it back, but they never mentioned this, nor did I ever mention the breakfast of scrambled eggs and toast, though from that day to this, scrambled eggs have not been my favorite dish. But there is no problem to me in understanding that there is a physical body and there is a spiritual body, for I have been *in* the spiritual body—perfectly conscious, completely myself—and out of the physical body. After this experience, I was quite ill for four days, and somehow lost the desire to live. I remember little about the days of illness, but I do remember becoming conscious and looking out of the window at a high grey sky and thinking, "All this is too much trouble," or some such thought as that. And God spoke to me through a little grey squirrel. He ran along the telegraph wire outside the window, and somehow his grace and beauty as he frisked along amused me, and the desire to live came back to me.

This operation, after its somewhat untoward beginning, turned out to be a great success. I was relieved of my monthly discomforts and to a great extent of the headaches, and after a summer's rest with certain of my relatives, entered once more with zest into college life. The summers were rather long, for I was passed from one aunt and uncle to another, and was acutely aware of the fact that I had no home on this earth, in spite of my relatives' great kindness to me (which I appreciate more now than I did then).

My adorable grandmother had an old hymn that she used to sing or whistle when she went out to feed the chickens. (For Uncle Will and Aunt Susie entertained a few hens in the backyard of the manse, and these were turned over to Grandma.) She would tie on her blue-checked gingham apron, put on her head an old straw hat of Uncle Will's, and go to the chicken yard with her bucket of feed, whistling meditatively as she went:

> I'm but a stranger here,
>   Heaven is my home.
> Earth is a desert drear,

Heaven is my home.
Danger and sorrow stand
Round me on every hand
Heaven is my fatherland,
Heaven is my home.

Even so, Grandma, even so. But I am glad you stayed in the desert drear long enough to feed me and the chickens with God's love.

She always wore a "bunnit" to church, a little black bonnet with white ruching around her face, which was dainty and beautiful. Great was her distress when one could no longer buy a "bunnit" such as she desired. She would sit of an evening beside her window and watch the people passing on the street.

"I do declare," she once murmured, "the men nowadays! I couldn't fall in love with one of 'em if I was to try."

It cheers me now to think of her and of my many aunts and uncles and cousins, a stalwart company of people as good as any who could be found upon this earth.

Most of the summer I would spend with Aunt Willie and Uncle Fletcher in their big square Southern home which overflowed continually with kinfolk of all kinds. (At the time, that seemed to me, as it no doubt did to all the kinfolks, completely natural. But I look back now and wonder how they could stand it!) There abode Auntie until she died at the age of eighty or so. Also Aunt Junia, the public-school teacher and the author and instigator of my educational process, and Miss Belle, Uncle Fletcher's sister. The others came and went.

During the summer, Aunt Junia did mission work in the mountains. She had eight nieces, all told, and we would go, two by two, and spend two weeks with her, helping with her simple cooking and housekeeping, entertaining country boys on the veranda where they draped themselves shy and speechless and drummed upon the banjo. We also attended her revival meetings up in the tiny country church, the mountaineers riding in from miles away and tying their horses to trees while they went in to be saved. One summer I must have been with Aunt Junia longer than the usual two weeks, for I remember that I taught a Sunday-school class of teen-age boys. When the time of the revival came, my spirit stirred within me, and I yearned over these boys lest they go to hell, which Aunt Junia pointed out as an immediate possibility. I decided to pray every day for one of them to go up to the altar and accept Jesus, and I did. Somewhat to my amazement, it happened that every evening the one for whom I had prayed that day went to the altar and accepted Christ.

But on the day when the mission ended, a strange thing happened: I was suddenly sorry that I had done this big-time praying. I felt uncomfortable about it, vaguely sensing, as I had so often sensed about missionary work in China, that something was wrong.

The old question came up again, the one that had knocked upon the doors of my mind when I was a child in China: "Something is lacking. *What is it?*"

Aunt Junia taught them to obey and honor God, even as I had been taught to obey and honor God and tried earnestly to do all my life. Certainly Aunt Junia taught them, also, to love Jesus and confess their sins and ask Him to forgive them. But there was an empty place in the picture. And I thought cynically, "They'll backslide again and run around fighting and cursing as usual and come back next summer and get saved all over again." And so they would, too.

Only the Holy Ghost, the Sanctifier, can keep us in the love of Jesus and protect us from the anger and bitterness of this world and bring us into the glory of the Sons of God. And we did not know the Holy Spirit nor have His power. But it was many a day before I understood this.

I recall only one Christmas vacation during all the time of dwelling in a homeland where I had no home. One Christmas while I was at Peace Institute, my family were at home on furlough, and I must have been with them. But while I recall their furlough with a feeling of contentment, I do not remember that or any Christmas save one.

Even then I do not recall the actual day of Christmas, but only the visit to the home of my roommate, Rachel Pearsall, in Wilmington, North Carolina. Rachel had several brothers. One of them went about with a bandaged hand, and the reason was that in an epileptic fit he had fallen into the fire. The epilepsy was life-long, and apparently incurable. I was halfway in love with this young man, who took no more notice of me than one would of a rather stupid puppy, and I determined to pray for him every day for seven years. This I did, and long before the seven years, he was healed, as I happened to hear—well and married and leading a normal life. I wondered whether my prayers had helped to bring this to pass, yet I could not really believe that it was so—a reaction which unfortunately is by no means uncommon. I wonder how different my life might have been if I *had* dared to believe it?

In China, Christmas had been a season of blissful preparation and wild, thrilling excitement. I painted my own Christmas cards, mostly fat English robins perching on twigs of holly, because the Madonna-and-Child theme was beyond me. We breathlessly awaited packages from home and especially the arrival of the Montgomery Ward boxes in which were Christmas presents ordered months before. We made chains of colored paper to hang on the wizened little Christmas tree obtained by Wang Er, probably by devious means, and we strung popcorn lasting from Grandma's Christmas package of the year before. True, if Christmas fell on a Sunday, it was discreetly postponed until Monday, for Sunday was the Sabbath, and on it there could be no frivolity of any kind. But this only added to the tense and happy waiting for that most glorious of days.·

During my last year at Peace College, the place had grown a bit too small for me, and when at last I graduated in a flurry of roses and a blaze of glory, I looked forward eagerly to two more years of college at Agnes Scott, a fully accredited college in Decatur (now a part of Atlanta), Georgia. I had realized that while Peace gave me a certificate to teach in North Carolina, beyond that pleasant state this worthy institution was hardly known. Therefore, with the help of family and with scholarships, I went to the larger college, intending to graduate with a B.A. degree in two years. However, I found that in order to do so, my last year there must be filled with subjects that I did not like: higher mathematics and science and French. I found also that upon the curriculum there were fascinating courses in short-story writing and the science of poetry and the theory of beauty, which I would not be able to take if my aim was graduation. So I chose to be a special student, free to study those courses that appealed to me. For years afterward, I wondered whether I had made a mistake, for if I had been forced to teach in public school for my living, a degree from Agnes Scott would have been a great benefit. But time has shown that the Lord guided this decision, for the courses that I studied there have furthered my life work of writing and lecturing, and I have not needed to teach in the public schools.

One course that I longed to take was not listed on the curriculum: astronomy. I had studied the lowly courses of botany and zoology, in order to learn more intimately the lives of little things upon this planet. But my spirit had expanded beyond this planet upon the boat deck of a little Japanese freighter one starry night long ago. I hungered to know all that I could learn about the stars and the nebulae and all the company of heaven. Was I not one with them in spirit? Was there not stardust in my soul and the lingering of a forgotten glory behind my eyes? Therefore, I put in a request for this course. The young mathematics professor claimed that he was able to teach it and would do so if I could find two others willing to enroll with me. I did, and for the only time in my life, I teamed up and studied with these two other starry adventurers. I had to do so, for the mathematics therein was utterly staggering, and I could never have mastered it alone. One of our team was a fine mathematician, the other had total recall, and I provided the creative imagination. We all entered into an expanded awareness of the universe that has been of tremendous value in my expanded awareness of God. Astronomy has so illumined Genesis for me that, like one of my young friends, I can exclaim, "Isn't Genesis the *neatest* book!"

These two years were even more idyllic than my years at Peace. Spring began in February in Georgia, and I will never forget walks in the piney woods with my roommate and first cousin, Elizabeth, finding the first sweet sprays of yellow jasmine and wood violets and columbine. Nor will I ever forget the graciousness and beauty of teachers and classmates, nor the lovely voices of the Negro cooks singing in the kitchen below my bedroom, nor the exciting ride on the "back streetcar line" (long-since swallowed up in suburbia) into the delightful city of Atlanta.

There was only one shadow on these singing days, and that was the shadow of the First World War. It had begun while I was crossing the Pacific in 1914, but at that time it had seemed far away and unreal, more so than the usual Chinese wars between warlords here and there, or revolutionary forces unseating the ancient Empress Dowager. As the months passed, it grew more real, until by the time I went to Agnes Scott it overshadowed everything, and I grieved and worried and knit khaki sweaters for servicemen and gave of my all to help the cause. My "all" being very little, I gave the last cent of my spending money; my mother was horrified, when I went back to China at the age of twenty-one, to find me with but one decent dress.

Armistice Day came while I was at Agnes Scott, and the delirium of the college was like the delirium everywhere—a relief so great that it could not be comprehended. But a strange thing happened. Even while I was shouting and singing and waving banners, suddenly the bottom dropped out of all my rejoicing. I knew that there was nothing to rejoice about. The world had not been made safe for democracy. Evil had not been banished from among men that righteousness could prevail. And all my bubbling and overflowing joy simmered into a dull and wistful confusion. I did not speak of this to anyone, for I could not understand what had happened to me. And I still do not quite understand it. Had my spirit leaped forward through time and glanced down the years to come, to the Second World War, to Communism, and to the more subtle attacks of the devil that seep through the land like creeping poison? Did I remember (even though the conscious mind did not quite permit the memory) bits of prophecy that I had heard from my father long ago? (For he knew . . . he knew. Yet his prophecy was not, as far as he realized, by divine inspiration, but from his study of the swing of world affairs.)

My conscious mind told me to rejoice and give thanks and wave banners and shout around the campus. But the spirit within me must have known that real peace could never be made upon this earth save by the peacemakers—those who are called the children of God—and they could make peace by no power save by the power of the Holy Spirit of God.

4.

I had found myself a home in the shining halls of learning beneath great oaks in a lovely land. But as every place upon this earth had been, it was only a temporary home. What was I to do next? My childhood friends were Student Volunteers or ministerial students with the intention of entering the Southern Presbyterian Mission and going back to China. I had known from the age of twelve that I could not do this. Nevertheless, I had no home save China, and I found myself yearning for that far country, its tiny villages with filthy evil-smelling streets, and its towering mountains crystal clear in the summer sun; its fluted city walls with ancient pagodas pink in the sunset light, and its yellow canals where slow junks crept through still waters and men half-naked fished with cormorants. I thought with some uneasiness of returning home, yet it seemed the right thing to do. I do not remember whether the idea emanated from my parents or from myself, but an arrangement was made with the mission: they paid my fare to China that I might take over my mother's family school and thus set her free for more missionary work.

So I embarked, alone this time, on the *Empress of Japan* out of Vancouver. This trip was as delightful as the one on the *Shidzuoka Maru*, though in a quite different way. I was a woman by this time and vaguely beginning to be aware of the fact. True, I had had two proposals of marriage while in college, but had not been interested in the least. I had only once thought myself in love and that was when at the age of twelve I developed a hopeless (and highly satisfactory) adoration for the young organist at the Kuling church and would go up to Cradle Rock of an afternoon to watch him walk home down the white street by the roaring Big Stream. On shipboard, however, with its romance of moonlight on dark waters and of a life within a life where the spirit lifts with the lifting waves and wanders free—on shipboard the heart is filled with such joy that it cannot help but fall in love. It is, however, a drifting and a temporary wandering of the emotions, and one should not take it seriously. But I did not know this. Among the several young men who showed attention to me, only one touched my heart, and he was a good deal older than I, a Scottish bachelor returning to his business in Singapore. Our friendship, for it can hardly be called a flirtation, was just a pleasant interlude, wrapped about with the breath of the great salt sea and interwoven with small excursions into Japanese ports. And, as always, I was as much in love with the beautiful little steamer as with the man. She was only 700 tons and built like a yacht, with exquisitely curving bows and a bowsprit pointing far over the ocean as though she yearned ahead of her toward the far waters yet unseen.

One foggy night, we were steaming through the Inland Sea. I donned a dark raincoat and climbed out on that bowsprit, stealing away to this forbidden rendezvous with the sea and the night and the sound of the waves. It was a thrilling experience, especially when for one moment I nearly slipped. But it did not equal that starry night on the *Shidzuoka Maru*. Something had departed, and I did not know what it was that I had lost.

We steamed into the harbor of Shanghai on a very hot day, grey and humid, and the burden descended upon me like a weight of lead. I cannot even remember being met by someone and escorted up to Kuling, though that must have taken place. And yet I seemed not to be there, for even in Kuling the glory had departed. I was alone, not a child and with none of my old friends to play with, yet not a missionary nor belonging in any way to that fellowship. But even this does not seem sufficient to account for the darkness that lay upon my soul; for were not the mountains still there, with bamboos crinkling in the sun and yellow Saint John's-wort growing between the rough stones of the mountain roads? But I looked upon them and felt nothing, and only now am I beginning to understand why this was so.

I longed to hear from my Scotchman from the steamer, but why? I did not really want to marry him and go to Singapore, of all places. I wanted *something*—some measure of joy and love and warmth—and I did not know what it was. My parents were of another generation. My younger sisters and brother H.M., the one nearest to my own age, were departing for the United States and college as I came back to China. I did not belong anywhere. I went with my parents to various meetings and concerts, but I felt always an outsider, as indeed I was. I was but a stranger there, and earth was "a desert drear," as my grandmother used to sing. But I did not know the way to the heaven that is not far away but near at hand even while we are still upon this earth.

Our mission used to meet together on Sunday evenings in someone's home for hymns and prayers and sharing. I will never forget one evening when a beautiful young wife and mother stood up to give thanks that God had healed her spirit after long darkness. As I looked at her, I thought, "But she is *not* healed! Why doesn't somebody *do* something?" I was right. She was not healed. Some months later she hanged herself from her bedroom window after trying to cut her wrists. She was found and brought indoors and did not die for several days, during which time the missionaries besought her to repent and confess her sins . . . poor dear. They desired her to say she was sorry that she had done this, but she would not say it. She was not sorry.

It would have been so easy to heal this lovely lady, even as I long afterward was healed. If only some one of God's ministers had known that he himself was a channel for God's power and had laid his hands on her and prayed for the love of Jesus to come into her and lift her out of darkness into His light! All my life I have grieved that no one knew how to pray for her. But for the first time, now, as I write this down, I wonder: could I myself have prayed for her and channeled God's power into her? I knew nothing about healing. True, I had prayed for a young man, Oscar, and he was healed. Naturally, no one ever connected me with his healing, and I did not quite know whether or not to connect myself with it. In fact, this small episode puzzled me and rather frightened me, and I decided to forget it and did so—until now. But now this incident comes into my mind and connects itself with the Sunday-evening prayer meeting and my anguish at seeing what nobody else saw, that here was a soul troubled even unto death. Could I possibly have prayed for her daily in silence and in secret as I prayed for the young man? Was that what God wanted me to do?

Perhaps the reader is thinking, "Well, of course!" But in those days it was not, "Of course." We were fundamentalists. That meant that we believed implicitly in every word in the Bible, yet we did not believe in healing through prayer. We were supposed to obey Jesus in every word that He said. Yet when He said, "The works that I do shall ye do also," we didn't obey Him, and indeed considered it heresy that anyone should try to do His works. I do not blame these good people, including my parents, for this strange contradiction, for so they had been taught. The real heresy had taken place centuries ago when people made up the idea that the age of miracles was past: that this is a new dispensation, and God no longer does miracles through His people.

No one had ever told me that I myself could channel God's healing power. Yet God Himself must have tried to tell me, for He once succeeded in so moving me by love and compassion that I had entered into a prayer pact with Him and He had answered it with healing. I should not have talked myself out of it. I should have known from that time forth that God does heal. And even though in all the church there was no one to teach me or to encourage me, I should have kept my mind open for God's further leading. Perhaps He was trying to say to me, "Look, that's why I sent you into the world." But I did not know in those days that even now one can hear God's voice as did men of old. I know now that it was indeed why He sent me into the world—because I have remembered. But that belongs far away, toward the end of this book.

God has sent many of us into the world to heal and to carry His love to those who need Him. Sometimes a person comes to me and says, "Oh, I feel such heat in my hands when I pray for someone. What is that?"

And I reply, "That is God's healing power. And if you feel it in your hands, that is because there is someone who needs your prayer with the laying on of hands."

I hope that you do not then reply, "Oh, but I *can't* do *that!*" For if you fail Him, He may put you through a hard time until you know what is His will for you. He put me through a hard time, and you have less excuse. There was no one to tell me, but you have been told. I am talking to you now.

Summer passed and we went down to Yencheng, not this time by mule cart but by a barge pulled by a steam launch through the narrow yellow canals, and when the water failed, then by a small sampan scraping along the bottom . . . and perhaps by another and another until at last we landed at Yencheng. For this was "north of the river" country—K'ang bok—part of the great alluvial plain of the Yangtze River, and there was no travel save by boat.

Here, at least, I had my work to do: teaching. Since I had been educated in a home school, it did not seem at all strange to be teaching my own brother and sisters, and I enjoyed working out my courses for them and adding any interest that I could think of through storytelling, imagination, and wonder. Beyond that work, however, there was absolutely nothing to do. Or had I lost interest in doing things? For I do not remember gardening during this dismal year. And though I tried to put into practice all that I had learned of short-story writing, the results were so sweetly false that even I knew it and lost heart.

There was now one other family in the station. Dr. Hewett was an Englishman from the China Inland Mission, loaned to our mission for some reason or other. Mrs. Hewett was a lovely lady and mother of four children who were a great blessing to my brother Hugh, who used to play with the three little girls in pinafores and the boy in very tight shorts and pith hat. These estimable people were very Chinese, wearing Chinese garments much of the time, and were not in any way accustomed even to the mild bits of American custom that I imported. They reproved me for putting talcum powder on my face, and Mrs. Hewett would gather up the neck of my middy blouse and fasten it with a safety pin close up under my chin lest I lead the Chinese astray.

The four missionaries had a social evening once a week in which they played a rattling good game of anagrams. They were all experts, and I was a hopeless failure at this game, which I still find extremely confusing: all the little squares with letters on them lying around trying to make words. Aside from this, there was no amusement whatsoever in the place. I remember walking dismally along the tiny paths through the paddy fields and looking upon the flat half-frozen land and hating China, all of it: low, brick houses with tiled roofs and dirt and dogs and smells and everything.

Fortunately, my parents saw that this was no kind of life for me, and encouraged me to advertise in the *Shanghai Mercury* for a teaching position. I received four answers. From these, I chose Saint Mary's School, Shanghai.

The next summer at Kuling, as I looked forward to a change in my life, was much better. I sang alto in the chorus of the Sacred Concert given each summer by the missionaries and "recited" in the one that they called the "Profane Concert." And I had one suitor, a somewhat rumpled little Englishman by the name of Bunce whom I had not the slightest desire to marry, a fact that I had some difficulty in explaining to him.

I was not unhappy that summer. But the deep dissatisfaction with life and with God that had begun in me at the age of eleven was growing. Something was lacking, not only in life, but in me. My dreams and daydreams should have shown me what it was, for I saw in these half-awake states myself enduring all dangers and all difficulties in order to rescue someone—of the male sex, naturally. I would climb down a cliff at the risk of my life and sit beside the wounded sufferer, unable to move because of a couple of broken legs, while the river rose and rose from cloudbursts higher in the mountains. I was rather embarrassed by these dreams and daydreams, thinking them merely a substitute for sex, which, for the most part, they probably were. Yet not entirely. I was not the princess rescued by the noble knight. I was always the rescuer. Wise people of today love to ask, "Do you know who you are?" I have always replied, "I've always known who I am." And so I have, up to a point. But I see now that this part of me, the one who risks quite a bit in order to rescue someone in trouble, this one I did not know. And who could have told me? A few hundred years ago, if I had dreamed of spiritual healing, they would probably have burned me for a witch. Nowadays, they might have me undergo deep therapy until all these wandering visions were ironed out, and I would be able to conform to my peers.

At any rate, there I was in Kuling and not unhappy. But

something had gone. I remembered the days when I would see the very air full of little dancing specks of light, and I could see it thus no more. I remembered the days when I myself had come home by the high-road, literally dancing, my feet hardly touching the ground for joy. And I thought, "That was the joy of childhood. Grown people never feel like that." Thank God I was wrong!

The next year I betook myself by ricksha down Bubbling Well Road in Shanghai and through the vile-smelling village of Tsaukato to Saint John's College and thence to Saint Mary's School. Both were run by the Episcopal Mission, which they called the American Church Mission, or in Chinese, the Sung Kong Hwei: the Holy Catholic Church, no less. This was a world that I had never entered before. There was the usual Ladies' House or home for teachers. Its four bedrooms were filled, and I was given a room in the dormitory for older girls. Actually, I felt more at home with these Chinese girls than with the four missionary ladies. They were formally kind to me although, as I overheard once, I "had no background whatsoever." This was quite true. I did not know what Septuagesima meant, nor even Advent or Lent. I did not know how to find my way through the Prayer Book, nor could I imagine why anyone should look at a book anyway in order to pray. I was utterly at sea during the course of a service. And this way of praying seemed to me as cold as ice. These people never spoke of Jesus, and if anyone did mention that word, they looked faintly shocked and pursed up their lips and murmured something about Our Lord. They never referred to the Blood of the Lamb, and while I found this a certain relief, still I could not help wondering whether they were saved.

The school work and life with the young Chinese women, however, I found quite fascinating. I had never met Chinese like these. The Chinese whom I knew and loved were our servants and the servants of my friends. Beyond these were the Chinese Christians who were, for the most part, quite simple and uncultured peasants, those who had the least to lose by "eating" the foreigners' religion. These young women represented an ancient culture in many ways far more exquisite than my own. My real relationships were with these Chinese girls, particularly one, tall and sad-faced, utterly incomprehensible but very fascinating. I really formed a close friendship with her, a friendship which I came to sense was inadvisable. Whether for this reason or for certain in-adequacies in my teaching (among other subjects, I had to teach French, at which I was very poor), I was not asked to return to Saint Mary's School.

"I wonder whether your *successor* would prefer another room?" the lady principal murmured to me one day. Thus I was informed very delicately that I was to be fired at the end of the year.

"Oh no, I think this room is very pleasant," I said, making no reference to the hidden meaning of her remark.

This did not distress me too much, for I knew I was failing in my relationships with the other teachers and in my attempt to teach French to Chinese girls.

I had an offer, however, to teach in Soochow Academy, an Episcopal school for boys. This was a glorious move. My subject was English literature, composition, and grammar, in the last three years of what would correspond to our high school. My stu-dents were young Chinese men, many of them my own age. I found them far more alert, understanding, and understandable than the girls. In fact, never in my life have I enjoyed my daily work as I enjoyed the teaching in this school.

The mission consisted of Mr. McNulty and his family, who lived next to the school grounds, and Mr. Borrman, in charge of evangelistic work, who lived in another compound about two streets away. In this compound there was also a Ladies' House with four big square bedrooms, one of which was assigned to me. The three other ladies were Mrs. Standring, tall, white-haired and beautiful, the head of the girls' school; Miss Jordan, fat and jolly, in charge of the Bible Women and their school of embroidery (To my astonishment I found that the Lord was not content until His service was adorned with fine twined linen and exquisite needle-work.); and Miss Minhinnick, new to the station and at the time studying Chinese.

There were also Presbyterian friends in the city, one of whom was my doctor. I indulged myself in those days in a num-ber of neurotic symptoms, including some migraine headaches. Therefore, I went to see Dr. Wilkinson professionally, and at times I also went socially to see his daughter Martha, just returned from college in the United States. On a certain evening I was coming home in the evening by sedan chair. It was bright moonlight, and as the chairbearers trotted down a narrow, crooked alleyway with their little chant, swinging to the swing of the sedan chair, I suddenly saw the pattern of moon-shadows of tiled and fluted roofs upon brick walls and cobbled streets and—it was beautiful! I do not know whether this was the Spirit of the Lord moving within me or whether it was the spirit of Old China that I had loved and lost. But from that time forward, I was once more a part of this ancient land so full of fear and of shadows and of a wistful and ineffable beauty woven out of the love of the ages and out of its sorrow.

When I had first returned to Yencheng after college, the weight of that sorrow lay upon me so heavily that for hours in the afternoon, I would lie upon the bed, too exhausted to move and yet unable to sleep.

"It's the climate," my mother said. "It sometimes affects people this way at first." But it was more than the climate. It was the heaviness of an ancient sorrow that bore upon me so that I could hardly breathe. Now, somehow, I became a part of all this mystery and agony—I accepted it through the beauty of patterned roofs on a moonlight night—and it no longer weighed on me. It sustained me, and I sustained it, and from that time forth I was in love with China.

Soochow was a water city, and by day I would go outside the water gate to see Dr. Wilkinson or to meet someone on the Shanghai train. I would be rowed in a tiny sampan through narrow canals upon whose sodden stone stairs women washed their rice and their chamber pots, and mangy dogs roamed in search of refuse floating upon the brown water, and little children played while the flies sat on their sore heads. And even this I loved, for I loved not only in joy but also in grief. I would wake at night and hear the rattle of the night watchman's bamboo sticks in a bamboo cup, and the faint ting-ting of the brass merchants who, for unknown reasons, always worked at night, and I would smile and sleep again, content to be a part of all of this. I would walk the cobbled street to the school, slipping sometimes in mud and ice, skirting past donkeys and beggars and the ever-present little children squatting down in some corner, their split trousers opening of themselves for practical reasons, and still I loved it. I fell in love with China before I fell in love with a man.

And then a man appeared, stopping over in Soochow on his way to the little town of Changshu where he ran a boys' school. We were having a Halloween party at the Ladies' House that evening, for we were very gay, and Gruffie (Miss Jordan, whose nickname was a complete misfit) loved to plan parties. I was on top of a stepladder, in my costume, which included a tall witch's hat, when the man appeared and stood below the ladder looking up with that expression which any girl knows: a brightening of the eyes and a sparking up of the whole person as though to say, "Perhaps this is the one."

He was a very good-looking man, though a bit grim of expression when his face was in repose: lean, blond, with straight features and most expressive dark brown eyes. At that moment they seemed to express love, and so they did, for his falling in love was immediate. Mine was almost as sudden, for it happened on the next day when he baptized the Borrman's baby, to whom he was godfather. He had on vestments, which were most becoming to his somewhat angular form. He held the baby in his arms, and as he looked down upon the little thing, all tension and grimness faded away from his face; it was beautiful with a tenderness that I was to see many a time, a tenderness that all his congregation loved, for they would sit with tears in their eyes while he carried a baby up to the altar to introduce him to the Lord—but I am getting ahead of my story.

From time to time this very shy young man (nine years older than I) would find some excuse to stop over at Soochow on his way back and forth from Shanghai. (He seemed to need to go to see the bishop or someone very often.) He was extremely cagey about his maneuvers when he arrived at Soochow and rambled with his Yankee mountaineer's loose-hung stride up to the Ladies' House. In fact, there was even some conjecturing among the ladies as to his motives and whether they concerned me or Miss Minhinnick. I knew! Had I not lain awake for hours the night before, imagining his footsteps coming up the brick walk to the front door? Had I not taught school that day with my heart beating like a hammer as I thought of his coming? For I was desperately in love with him and he with me, though he had not as yet summoned up the courage to speak of it.

We went on long walks together, the better to be alone, with only Chinese glancing curiously at two foreigners shamelessly walking together—for if they were married, then the woman should have been at home cooking and tending her children and not appearing brazenly with her husband in full daylight; and if unmarried, then they should not have been together in any case. This however was better than sitting in the living room of the Ladies' House where three other ladies, not to mention cook and gatekeeper, were likely to dart in at any moment. Ted loved to tell of our rambles through the countryside where, as he would say, we would push the goat off the grave so we could sit down. In the evening we strolled on the city wall, for within its fluted parapets there was a wide and pleasant walk. I have never felt such ecstasy as upon those evenings! Once we sat upon the rampart beyond the Dry North Gate and swung our legs over the edge, looking down at the narrow street where by lantern light, people and donkeys and sedan chairs surged to and fro, unaware of the still haven above them where two people sat very close together, hand in hand.

Summer came, and Sandy (for that was his mission nickname, and only after our marriage did I call him Ted) had not yet proposed. He was, after all, thirty-three years old. He had been hopelessly in love twice before and totally lacked finesse or confidence in his relationship with girls. As for me, I was still in the Victorian era wherein my parents had established me.

Sandy was wont to go to Mohkanshan for the summer rather than to Kuling. This summer, however, to Kuling he went, appearing shy and beautiful, his brown eyes shining, at our small square house on the mountainside. Every day he came, and we roamed the mountains together, to my delight and his discomfiture, for though he did not admit it at the time, I frightened him. I loved to climb cliffs and stand on the edge of precipices, and these things made him feel quite ill, though he never told me so until years afterward. Since I simply could not learn to play tennis or to swim, I compensated by showing off in the only outdoor sport at which I was anywhere near adequate.

Sandy was as different from my parents as any person could

be. They stood somewhat in awe of him, and he of them, but they respected each other. My father gravely studied the Prayer Book and said that at least Episcopalians were "sound," for that book showed that they definitely believed in the Blood of the Lamb. I remember nights I did not sleep from the sheer excitement of the blissful and tormenting feelings that swept through me, but I do not remember any disharmony between my parents and Sandy and me. That was a miracle.

Still, he had not spoken to me of marriage. But I knew that he would do so when we met again at Soochow. And so he did, having paved the way beforehand by hinting in one of his delightful letters (they were very funny) that he had something of import to say when he next came. This way, as he explained to me later, he had to say it, which he did, with considerable formality and great shyness. Needless to say, I accepted—he should have known quite well that I would!

Up until this time, I had been a conscientious teacher—heart, soul, and mind absorbed in my work. I loved the English language, and I adored my delightful young students with their grave courtesy and comical use of English. I loved everything connected with teaching: the regular routine and the actual imparting of knowledge, for I could explain English not only in the Wu dialect spoken in Shanghai and Soochow but also in the stately Mandarin, the language of my childhood. This would tickle the boys no end. Their bland, impassive faces would break into dry grins when I exploded into Chinese, and their eyes would twinkle behind their almond-shaped lids.

But about the time that Sandy entered my life, I am afraid that I taught with only half my mind and less than half of my heart. As for Sandy, who had lived thirty-three years as a bachelor (and I do mean really as a bachelor), and who was very high-keyed by nature, he was commanded by the bishop to marry at once. His orders must have been passed on to Mr. McNulty, for with commendable Christian patience he arranged for a substitute, and Sandy and I were married at Soochow on the third of April, 1923, immediately after an early Easter. Travel to Yencheng was impossible for our friends and for Sandy's best man and ushers, as well as for many others who came up from Shanghai for the occasion. So my three friends of the Ladies' House gave the wedding feast as their present to me. My own family made the trip to Soochow and were entertained by the missionaries.

It was a unique wedding, held in the Chinese church with the schoolboys present as well as the missionaries and friends. In the middle of the ceremony, a peasant woman from the street ambled up to the altar, her market basket on her arm, to see what it was all about. According to Chinese custom, I rode to the wedding in a red satin sedan chair completely enclosed in heavily embroidered hangings, and Sandy rode in another one almost as elaborate. We returned thus to the Ladies' House, as beautifully decorated as the church had been with all the early-blooming spring flowers and shrubs. After the wedding reception, we were escorted to the train and put in our private compartment for the trip to Shanghai and thence to Kashing, where we spent a honeymoon in the midst of the most idyllic beauty imaginable.

Ted, as I soon learned to call him, had rented a house on a hill overlooking beautiful Hangchow Lake: a house complete with seven bedrooms, cook, boy, and amah! They did everything for us, even hiring sedan chairs or sampans for our trips to the pagodas and teahouses of this most lovely spot in all China. The chairbearers grinned at us appreciatively, and made little jokes that fortunately Ted did not understand. However, I was secretly amused, for I had been to many a Chinese wedding, both as an invited guest and (more informatively) sneaking in with Isabel and the servants (uninvited), which was considered quite proper. I had seen the little bride, gorgeously appareled, sitting demurely on the wedding bed with eyes cast down while the bridegroom's friends made bawdy jokes around her to try to make her laugh.

How different everything would have been if we had been Chinese! I would not then have grown to the advanced age of twenty-five in single abandonment nor would my husband have become a bachelor of thirty-three. Long before his puberty, Ted's parents would have sought a marriage counselor or "middleman," and a suitable marriage would have been arranged for him. The marriage counselor would have looked up Ted's kinsfolk and gone into the family history. There he would have seen the kind of wife acceptable in such a family and would have chosen a single-minded housewife type, a good cook and careful housekeeper, and one apparently capable of having and tending children and incapable of being interested in anything beyond those children and their father.

I would not have been considered.

My parents, on the other hand, would have been interviewed by another marriage counselor, who, seeing their restless natures and their wide interests and their lack of a binding home-involvement, would probably have beat his breast in dismay and given up the job of finding me a suitable husband—unless he could have married me to some wealthy man with a foreign education, wide interests, and many servants.

On the whole, I am glad I was not born a Chinese girl.

I explained to Ted before we were married that my consent presumed that we would remain in China. There, I felt qualified to be a competent wife and housekeeper, knowing from birth all the intricacies of servants and the squeeze system and the other subterranean activities that had to be either coped with or discreetly ignored. There also I could continue in the work I loved— teaching—while the servants prepared meals and cleaned house and looked after the babies. Ted agreed to this, though a bit dubiously. He was sincere in his promise, but the exigencies of life willed it otherwise. Did not Job say long ago, "The thing which I greatly feared is come upon me"? (Job 3:25).

Oh, Job! Even now I grieve for you. May we have a date as soon as it can be conveniently arranged after my entry into the heavens that we may commiserate together upon this matter.

I loved being a married woman in the Episcopal Church Mission in Changshu. True, the church itself was a puzzle to me. I had joined this church, being duly prepared for confirmation by a long-suffering Mr. McNulty. But I did not conceal the fact that I was joining only because I was marrying one of its priests. And while Mr. McNulty endeavored to impress upon me the age, value, dignity, and righteousness of the church, I thought of the said values in the Presbyterian church and from time to time introduced this thought into the conversation. If my school principal and minister made any attempt to tell me the real purpose of the rite of confirmation (that the Holy Spirit should come within me and the grace of God be increased in me more and more), I do not recall it. Actually, I do not think he mentioned such numinous matters as the Holy Spirit. He expounded rather the manner and methods of the church: her seasons and colors, her rituals and ceremonies. And I listened indulgently, holding, meanwhile, my own opinion concerning these things.

Ted himself had designed and caused to be built a very handsome though simple church upon the compound. His schoolboys used it as their chapel. The Christians of the town, however, preferred to go to the small crowded building in the middle of the town, and there they went, looking up at the gentle, loving face of Mr. Wilson, the head of the station, towering head and shoulders above them in his imposing six-foot height.

Mr. and Mrs. Wilson and two of their four children lived across the compound from us and, though considerably older, were our best friends. A few streets away was another compound, including the tiny hospital and the home of the new missionaries, Dr. and Mrs. Walter Pott. Walter was China-born. Our relationship with these two families is one of the happiest memories of my life. We were one family in Christ; we all adored Mr. Wilson, as great a saint in the Lord as I ever knew; and we loved each other with a quiet, unpossessive love.

Whence came that emanation of love and power that was in the tall frame of Robert Wilson? The Chinese sensed it, and even when he became weakened with the lingering disease of sprue that finally carried him away, they came from miles around just to be in his presence. I remember a time when there had been a war of some sort, and the attacking soldiers or bandits had finally been bought off, but refused at the last minute to enter the boats drawn up at the canal bank to transport them elsewhere. Harried soldiers of the town came to Mr. Wilson and besought him to come to the canal bank and tell the soldiers to enter the boats. In vain did Mr. Wilson protest that he had no authority over the soldiers. Just come, said the townspeople. So he went with them, and the soldiers took one look at his great height and his gentle face and into the boats they went.

All of this puzzled me considerably, for from where came this man's real goodness and power? He did not run about saying, "Isn't Jesus wonderful?" nor talking about the Blood of the Lamb, nor did he even lace his words with quotations from the Bible. In fact, one thing that troubled my Presbyterian-trained mind a bit was that among these "churchmen," the Bible seemed to take second place to something else that I could not quite define. Even the Chinese preachers did not preach with the Bible open before them, thumping it vigorously from time to time—preferably with a fan—as Old Man Tai and others had done so effectively in Hsu-choufu. (In warm weather, Mr. Tai carried his fan in the collar of his Chinese robe, and on making a point would snatch it out, flip it open in a wide and thrilling gesture, flip it shut again, and thump the Bible with it. Having made the point, he would again flip the fan open and fan himself complacently for a moment while the congregation meditated upon his words from Holy Writ.)

I was not at all sure that the Episcopal church was sound. But then I had never been sure that the Presbyterian church was sufficient for life—for joy—for something that I could not express. It was all too much for me, and life had enough interest and zest without it.

I loved being a married woman. True, there were some matters of married life that seemed to me confusing, but my mother had told me that it would be so and that one must put up with these matters cheerfully. They were necessary, she explained, to the life of the male with his baser instincts, and eventually they would cause the birth of children. She had added that it gets better later on. Nevertheless, in spite of these perplexing male aspects of his nature, I adored my husband and I loved my home—the usual plain, square mission house with hallway, living room on one side, and on the other, a tiny square study. Behind the study was a little square dining room looking out on the compound where we could see the schoolboys passing to and fro.

It was easy for me to run this, my first home, for I understood the Chinese servants and could love them and see through their perfidies at the same time. This gave me a great advantage over Mrs. Wilson and Mrs. Pott, who were both American-born. I did not get excited and talk of dismissing servants merely because I caught them cheating. Actually, I did not consider as cheating the cut that they took on the purchase of certain articles. It was merely their lawful squeeze—merely the custom—and I knew and delighted in its intricacies because they were so funny. There was the normal 10 percent that the cook, the Dah S-fu or Great Administrator of the household, took as his due from all funds given him to shop with. And why wouldn't it be his due? He could talk price far better than I, and buy far more cheaply, and still take his cut. However, if it rose to 20 or 30 percent (and I knew this, though no American-born woman would know it, for as a child I had roamed the streets with cook or Chang Sao and seen the system at work), then I must bring it down to normal. This, however, must never be done in direct words, for the Oriental does not talk in direct words, and to force him to do so would cause him to lose face, and he would then leave. An Oriental would rather die than lose face. Therefore I would tell him solemnly that my husband could not afford the price of food and that his countenance was therefore sad and turned away from me, and that the cook would need to buy cheaper foodstuffs for a while. And the cook knew perfectly well what I meant, and I knew that he knew, and he knew that I knew that he knew, but the matter was presented to him in face-saving ways, and he would bring down his squeeze for a while.

One reason for my success as a housekeeper in China was a healthy appreciation for the importance of "saving face." Upon one occasion a goat managed to come in through the gatehouse, which was presided over by the gatekeeper, who lived with his family in a tiny house beside it. The animal happily lunched on Mrs. Wilson's Japanese lilies and wisteria vine and roamed nonchalantly about the compound searching for other delicacies. When the gatekeeper saw him, he pursued with roars of wrath and indignation, expressed in most graphic terms and including lurid descriptions of the goat's maternal ancestor. The goat was not at all affected by this, and whenever the gatekeeper would draw near him, he would kick up his rear end and caper away to other regions with the unhappy gatekeeper leaping after him. In a thoughtless moment, I made the mistake of mentioning this to Ted, just because I thought he would enjoy laughing over it. He did not.

"The gatekeeper should not permit goats on the compound," he said sternly. "I will speak to him about it."

"Oh no!" I cried, dismayed. "Oh no, don't do that. He wouldn't like it."

But Ted strode away to do his duty as manager of the compound, seeing no reason why he should not speak to the gatekeeper, as any American employer would unhesitatingly say to an employee, "Hey, better watch that gate!"

But the gatekeeper was not an American. He had lost face quite sufficiently through his necessary antics with the goat. In order to save his face, Ted should have pretended complete ignorance concerning this matter. For Ted to add rebuke to his already-accomplished loss of dignity so demeaned him that he resigned, having no other recourse according to Chinese kwei-ju (established custom, in so far as this can be translated).

"But there was no reason for him to quit!" said Ted, who was very tenderhearted and grieved over the little family bundling out to God-knows-where. "No American would have done that!"

But the gatekeeper was Chinese. The difference is utterly unshakable.

As I have said before, I know that I was set on earth to do pioneer work in healing. Why, I have often wondered, was I born in China? As I write this, I can see one reason which I never realized before: it is because, from infancy, I knew and accepted the fact that people, both individually and racially, are not identical but are delightfully different. They are not "equal," as we love to say, but vary tremendously in every way—by God's own decree and for His own purpose. Understanding this has made it possible for me to deal with all kinds of people and not to feel superior or judgmental. I understand that they have as much right to be themselves as I have to be myself, and I seek, therefore, not to conform them to me, but to help them to be themselves.

Many American do-gooders seem to think that if only everyone has an electric refrigerator everyone will be happy. Once in the Philippines, in a mountain college, the electricity failed and the Peace Corps personnel there were much agitated that no one did anything about it. But the Filipinos went to bed when the sun set and rose when it came up. The people worked by the light of day and carried their clothes down to the riverbank to pound them happily upon stones and rejoice in the rush of clear water and in the singing of birds and in the laughter of their fellowmen. They were not happy when the electricity once more shone and the washing machines ran again.

In certain places, the Army built houses for the villagers of South Vietnam whom they had bombed out: concrete boxes, each one lit with one electric light. The little people of Vietnam could not live in them. They sickened and died. Naturally! They could not live cut off from the warm earth and the whispering wind in the bamboos and the singing of cicadas in the dark trees at twilight—that was to be cut off from life.

So, to return to my Chinese servants, I could play the game with them because I understood and respected their differences. It was a great game, and I loved to play it. The servants loved it, too, and would look at me sometimes with a hidden smile behind their opaque eyes, even as the schoolboys used to do. Furthermore, they cherished me tenderly, and I knew that they would have risked their lives for Ted and me, which, later on, they did. If it started to rain while I was at Ted's school (the Proctor School) teaching English to his little boys, I would find Siao-loh at the door when I came out, holding raincoat, umbrella, and rubbers. If Ted and I went to the Potts' for dinner, walking the dark, slippery streets, we found the lantern lit on the hall floor and the correct wraps upon a chair. It was their joy thus to cherish us, and it was our joy to cherish them.

I may mention, lest some wonder about missionaries having servants instead of doing their own work, that it was a necessary part of Chinese economy. Obviously it would be quite impossible for us to carry water from the village well and chits to co-workers at school and to perform the intricate matter of marketing, with its necessities of talking price for everything. We had no conveniences of any sort: no electricity, running water, telephone—nothing.

But not only this, we would have been failing in our duty to Chinese society if we had done our own work and refused servants. In China there was no unemployment bureau and no social security and no pensions. There was no unemployment! Everyone was supposed to do his part toward the economy by hiring such labor as he could.

There were professional beggars, true, but that was considered an employment. In fact I once went to the Beggars' Guild in Soochow where those who were not working at the moment sat in the sun mending their rags and searching for livestock therein. And they had a water carrier bringing in their water. He was not a beggar. He was a water carrier. They were beggars, and it was not their place to carry water.

I did not sit idly by while my servants worked. I taught a full schedule in Ted's school. The students were younger boys, and the teaching was a bit frustrating at times, but still, it was the kind of work for which I had a gift, and I loved it.

"Is this a bench or a chair?" I would ask, articulating carefully. And the class of little boys would shout with delight, "Yess! Ziz iss a bench aw a shair!"

That first summer of our marriage we went with the Nortons, friends from Saint John's College, to spend a month in Peking. We had planned this venture, to my great delight, and then Ted had begun to have fears of the unrest of the country and had decided against going. I acquiesced. From the beginning of our marriage, I made the mistake of agreeing too easily to everything that he said, hiding my own feelings. We did not, as they would say nowadays, communicate very well. He would at times go into silence, and I would ask, "What is the matter?" and he would reply, "Nothing." I was too shy to persist in my inquiry, and therefore, if he did not want to speak of what was on his mind, neither would I speak of what was on my mind. Above all things, I desired a peaceful marriage with no nagging or irritation. But I went too far in retiring into myself. I should have learned from this Peking episode, after Ted chanced to see a letter that I was writing to a school friend in which I told of my great disappointment at not going to Peking.

"Oh, I didn't know that you felt like that about it!" said Ted. "Well, let's go then."

So we did, on the Blue Express from Nanking to Peking, passing right through the city of Hsuchoufu where I had traveled many a time by mule cart and slow boat.

Only one thing marred the trip a little bit. Ted had a strange habit of simply rising from his seat on the train and departing, I knew not whither. I still do not know. For I never said, "Where did you go?" being altogether too bent on preserving a polite peace at all costs.

The month at Peking was altogether delightful. Except for his way of wandering off somewhere, Ted was a wonderful companion, being so full of wit and humor that I must sternly deter myself or I could spend the rest of this book in recounting his funny remarks. However, I will merely say that we saw the Great Wall of China, the Temple of Heaven, the Summer Palace, and all the beautiful sights of that ancient city. As far as I recall, the sun shone every day, both on temple and courtyard, and on the charming half-Chinese house that we rented, together with the Nortons.

When we returned, we visited my parents in Kuling for a while, and then Ted went back to the station, leaving me to come later. There was peace and politeness between him and my parents, but he did not feel at home there—and that was quite natural.

After he left, it became obvious to me that I was going to have a baby, which fact I accepted complacently without any surprise. Of course I was going to have a baby. That was what marriage was all about. Ted, however, had somehow got the notion that I would not bear children. Nothing could have been more ridiculous, but I had told him of my repair job in the hospital and he had drawn from it dark prognostications as to my future barrenness. Therefore, when I met him in Chinkiang, where he had come to take me home, and told him of this perfectly natural development, he was so delighted and excited that he actually was sick in bed for one rather violent day!

The servants knew immediately, of course, that a "siao di-di" (small little brother) was expected, and their tender care of me was delightful. And I had husband, home, and school and would have been completely happy except for one small thing—abutting our compound was the tiny house of a Chinese doctor who took care of babies. He spent his time sticking needles into them to drive out the evil spirits, and they, poor things, spent their time in wailing. Ted had refused to buy this house for the compound because the doctor quite naturally put up the price. I begged him to buy it at any price in order that we might be rid of the heartbreaking torment of the babies crying. But probably in my campaign for peace I did not make quite enough fuss about it, and the crying continued. It was incomprehensible to me that Ted was insensitive to this when he was so very sensitive and, indeed, so fearful of many things that did not trouble me in the least. In fact, he let me know at about this time that he did not like Kuling and did not wish to go there again. Part of this was doubtless the quite natural desire to have me to himself and not to abide with his parents-in-law. But part of it, I know, was his fear. I had really frightened him by my showing off on mountain peaks. That nervousness seemed very strange in one who was otherwise a delightfully strong character.

Moreover, he was brave in his own way, or he would not have volunteered to go into the far north and do famine relief work all alone, building roads so that American produce could be brought to the starving. In fact, he would hardly have volunteered to teach mathematics and mechanical designing in Saint John's College in the first place if he had not had a spirit of adventure. The fears were hidden deep, but they were there.

I did not understand this at the time, and I am not sure that I understand it now, but I wonder. He told me once of spending the night in a Chinese temple during his famine-relief days; setting up his Army cot at the foot of a great Buddha. And he told of waking at night to find those eyes staring down at him and of being all of a sudden ridiculously full of fear. Was it ridiculous? If I had known then what I know now—if any one of us had known —could a spirit of fear have been rebuked and driven away from him? And if I had dared to believe in the healing through prayer that had taken place during my school days, and had been sufficiently filled with power to pray for Robert Wilson, could he have been healed of sprue? This I do not know. If *someone* had had this faith and power he could have been.

But God can redeem and use even the disappointments and the disillusionments of life. The spirit of adventure in me could nevermore find joyous release in exploring the wild places of Kuling and in climbing its dangerous heights. But it was and is still within me. And it has in many other ways climbed out on a limb, explored high places, and gone untrodden paths.

5

CARRYING a child in China was a glorious and triumphal thing. One walked the streets in stately dignity, and strangers smiled and asked when the little brother was to arrive. Ted was in a state of delight bordering on delirium and was tenderly indulgent over my times of morning discomfort and happy when I recovered and went back to my teaching. One of his first remarks on hearing of my condition was, "I'll have to get the carpenter Peu to build a fence around the canal outside the compound gate. That boy might run out there and fall into the water." At this I laughed loud and long, for save for the time in my seventh year when I feared for my father's health, I had hardly known fear since babyhood. Another of Ted's remarks when I made as though to slap him in a spirit of fun was, "Don't hit me, Agnes! Remember I'm going to be a father in the spring!"

The servants were almost as excited as Ted over this approaching event. My appetite was a bit erratic, and I craved red pepper, that my food might be more highly seasoned. Dah S-fu refused to buy it. He said that he could not find any, which was manifestly absurd, since the Chinese used it continually. He then said that it was not the season for red pepper. Also absurd, since red pepper is for always. Finally, when I refused to accept these subterfuges, he in desperation told me the truth. "I cannot buy the Missis red pepper! If the Missis eats red pepper now, when her son is born he will have pinkeye!" I did not get any red pepper during those nine months. And the cook must have been right, because when my son was born, he did not have pinkeye.

The cook knew perfectly well, of course, even before I forced him to the wall, that I did not believe any of his tales concerning babies born to mothers who ate red pepper, but it is not the custom in China to come right out with what one means. For instance, he would never ask for a day off, but when he desired one for some unmentioned purpose, he would come to me with tears in his eyes and tragically inform me that his old grandmother was dying and he had to go to her funeral and please would I give him gracious permission to do so, since he had hired a substitute to cook for me in his place. Occasionally he or some other servant would forget and announce the funeral of an old-old already buried some months before. But we ignored these trifling matters, and with due sympathy allowed him to go and do his duty to his family. Both of us knew that he had in mind other plans than attending a funeral. But this did not distress us, because we understood that it was the accepted way of asking, with social grace, for time off.

As the wang-mei time drew near, Ted and Walter Pott decided that I should go to Shanghai to have my baby. This I utterly refused to do. I could think of nothing more boring than sitting around visiting strangers while waiting to go to the hospital. Chinese women all had babies without recourse to either hospitals or doctors. There was nothing to it, I decided, even though Walter, having graduated to the mission from the Army, plaintively stated that he had delivered only three babies altogether in the course of his practice, and that he owned only one pair of forceps which he used for babies, teeth, and everything.

It was not quite as easy as I thought, that twenty-four hours of hard labor with Walter and Ted sitting by the bed. But how glad I was that Walter did not have to use forceps. The baby was perfect, without a mark or a scratch on him.

Another problem that Walter and Ted worried over was the question of whether or not I could nurse the baby and what to do if I could not, since milk is not attainable in China. They need not have worried. I could have supported twins. The only trouble was that nature's milk was apparently a bit too strong for the baby at first, and he therefore protested vigorously. The little house rang with his indignant howls for a couple of hours every night. Being left alone, however, this colic situation soon righted itself, and the baby Teddy became the most beautiful and charming and delightful infant ever to draw breath. This is not maternal prejudice. It is only the sober truth. Ask our Chinese friends—only, alas, they are long gone, long gone.

When our new amah carried the infant out of doors, he was immediately surrounded by a cloud of witnesses, to use biblical terms. In fact, when school classes were not in session, one could see no baby at all on looking out of the window, but only a crowd of blue-clad schoolboys. In the midst of this crowd would be the baby, thoroughly enjoying himself, as he still does on the grounds of his own school in the midst of a crowd of football players or horseback riders.

It was greatly to my glory that I had brought forth a son within a year and a month of our marriage. That he should have arrived on the first day of Ching Ming, the Chinese spring festival —this was a sign of the favor of heaven and earth.

Spring faded into hot summer, and for the sake of health we went away, not to Kuling with its shining mountaintops and its roaring waterfall, but to Mohkanshan, on little bamboo hills set in a steaming plain. Here Ted shortly became bored and went back to the station, leaving me and the baby and his amah with kindly strangers, Mr. and Mrs. Blain.

It was at this time that I felt the approaching footsteps of depression. I can remember looking out over the waves of hills and thinking, "Why can't I feel anything?" For all feeling seemed to have left me. It returned, however, as time went by, and the usual autumn war broke out in the plains, between one warlord and another. Indications were that the lines of communication would be cut for three months—until winter came and war became too inconvenient due to cold weather. Ted wired me to stay where I was on the other side of the battle lines and be safe. For the first time in my life, I disobeyed him, somewhat to the relief of the Blains, who certainly did not want to be left with me and the baby and the amah for three months. I therefore arose and, escorted by Mr. Blain, made my way by sedan chair to the railway station at Kashing, bound for Shanghai and thence out again to Changshu.

We found that we were not alone in our idea of fleeing the war. The station platform was a howling, surging mob of Chinese carrying bedding rolls and baskets of food and teapots and babies, all fighting for a place on that train. I have been in many a crowd, but never have I been frightened of one as I was that day.

Mr. Blain fought his way through the mob and secured a seat, and I passed the baby to him through the window. Then amah and I struggled over piles of bedding and human beings and somehow or other got ourselves in that train. Not even the conductor could get through the crowd that filled the aisles and even the baggage racks. He leaned into the windows when the train stopped and collected whatever money he could.

In Shanghai the platform was empty except for the insurging crowd. No one was leaving this Shanghai refuge for those fleeing war and destruction. Outside the station, however, was the usual line of waiting rickshas. We accepted the first that came and bowled along the familiar smelly streets of Tsaukato to Saint John's College and sanctuary.

The next day we took the train for Soochow, much to the consternation of our kind friends, for the war was due to begin at any moment and the first move in any war was to cut the railway track. There was no one on this train except the three of us and one Chinese gentleman who, after the fashion of the country, calmly removed his robe and sat in his underclothes, fanning himself contentedly. We arrived safely at Kunshan, the place where hostilities were to begin. There was not a villager in sight, only soldiers lolling about the station, their rifles stacked like stacks of corn. Every soldier had a fan, an umbrella, and a teapot, being thus prepared for any eventuality. Before the next train arrived, the soldiers cut the railroad track, but the amah and the baby and I arrived safely in Soochow and were welcomed somewhat uneasily by the Borrmans.

Travel into the interior was now impossible. The Chinese had hid their boats, lest the soldiers steal them. They would fill them with stones and sink them in small canals. Ted had been apprised of my arrival in Soochow, however, and somehow he had bribed a farmer to rent him a boat, hastily raised under cover of night from the muddy canal and carpeted with straw. Our own servants risked their lives to row that boat to Soochow, traveling by night lest they be caught. I awoke at midnight to loud banging on the front door and will never forget the joy of seeing Ted's face beaming at me.

Our journey home was delayed by the baby becoming ill from heat and exhaustion. However, with Dr. Wilkinson's treatment, he recovered speedily, and the next day we crept warily out of the city, through the water gate, and the cook and boy rowed the tiny sampan to Changshu.

(Where are they now, Kung-pao and Siao-loh? There is no word from behind the bamboo curtain—no word save word of the slaughter of all Christians.)

When we reached Changshu, we were cut off from communication for some three months, which did not trouble me in the least. I was at home, in the little house I loved, with my tiny garden and even the four rosebushes that had come first from Hsu-choufu. How they got to Changshu I do not remember, but I am sure that they were the same roses, now tall and strong and made stronger by reason of the fact that I sternly commanded the cook to pour upon them all of the water in which he washed the chickens. He much preferred to clean the chickens at the canal bank, where he could chat cozily with the water carriers filling their buckets and the women washing their garments and their chamber pots. It was proof of the cook's real love that he was persuaded to relinquish this joy in order that my roses should be properly nourished.

Ted at this time was still worried, quite unnecessarily, over what the baby's fate would be if nature's supply of milk should dwindle. (We did not know in those days that a baby could eat practically anything, though we should have known it, seeing the Chinese mothers chew their food and shove it into their babies' mouths.) The cook was therefore commanded to search for milk through the little city, which pursued the even tenor of its ways behind closed gates, while from time to time cannon thudded dully without, reminding the city fathers that the army was still awaiting their necessary bribe. The cook eventually found a few cans of Borden's condensed milk in the jewelry store, milk being considered a foreign gadget.

Some months later, we used it in making custard.

All this time, while the city fathers negotiated with the besieging army, I was well and happy, delighting in my fascinating little boy and caring little whether the cannon (carefully aimed at the sky) thudded without the city, or whether they did not. And when the trade guilds and the besieging army finally came to a financial decision and the siege was raised, I did not share Ted's feelings of relief, for I was still walking without fear. Indeed, Ted was really annoyed with me some time later, when he went to Shanghai by steam launch to attend a meeting of the bishop's, was delayed by bandits on the way back, and found me peacefully sleeping. I explained that I had sent Siao-loh to the canal bank to seek information concerning the Soochow launch. Siao-loh had returned and said that the bandits had held up the launch, shooting at it and killing one traveler, not a foreigner, and were now holding it till some dignitary should arrive and convene a court on the canal bank. Knowing Chinese ways, I realized that Ted's arrival would be delayed for some time and saw no reason why I should stay awake waiting for him. This seems inconceivable now; I am apt to swallow a lump in my throat when an automobile is late in delivering children and grandchildren to my door . . . but in those days I did not know fear.

When the baby was some seven months old, I began to experience various extremely uncomfortable sensations. I explained these to Mrs. Smith, wife of a newly arrived Methodist minister. We were walking together down a crowded street, and I suddenly noticed that she was grinning in a knowing manner.

"No!" I cried when she expressed to me her opinions upon the subject of my discomfort. I explained to her various reasons why I was sure that I was not pregnant again, but she still grinned.

"And anyway, I can't be, because I'm still nursing Teddy!" I cried. But I was.

I am ashamed to say that I rebelled strongly against my condition. Not that I did not desire babies. I wanted at least six. But we were planning to go "home" on furlough the next summer, and a more inconvenient time for childbearing could hardly be imagined. I did not know in those days that one's thoughts made any difference either to oneself or to an unborn child. (If only we could start life over again and know all from the beginning!) While I did not complain too vociferously, not wanting to be a poor sport, my inner resistance was great. It even seemed to go through me and affect Teddy's health, for he ran up a high fever and was very ill. Ted held him, to watch whether he was turning blue, while I searched *The Care and Feeding of Tropic Children* to try to diagnose his illness. Walter Pott and his family were on furlough, and we had no doctor, only a Chinese medical student left in charge of the dispensary. This young man looked at the baby in complete puzzlement, saying only, "Suppose give castor oil," which I had enough sense to do anyway, that being always the first step in the Orient. The next day the baby was well, but on the following day he again ran up a temperature of 105°. At this point I diagnosed the trouble as diurnal malaria and informed the Chinese student, who, with considerable relief, prescribed liquid quinine, to be administered every day.

Within weeks we began preparations for our furlough home to the United States, and before the month was over we had left Changshu for Shanghai. Missionaries and servants, baggage carriers, beggars, and dogs accompanied us to the slippery steps leading to the canal and stowed us on the barge behind the little steam launch. Many of us wept because it would, we thought, be months before we saw each other again. If I had known that never again would I see their faces, these friends who were closer than brothers, these servants who were our own family, part of my heart and of my home . . . I am glad I had no idea that I would never return to China, after we left in early 1925.

On the day that we reached Shanghai, Teddy had a temperature of 105°. But this was the last flare-up of malaria, and that was good, for we did not need malaria—we had enough difficulty as it was! On every other voyage of my life, I had been able to overcome seasickness. But in the middle of the third month of pregnancy, it was not so—but far otherwise. I lay upon the deck wrapped in a steamer rug and managed to contain myself. But if I tried to go down into the cabin and take care of my little boy . . . I will spare you the details. It could not be done. Ted therefore took sole charge of Teddy save when two angel-nuns would for a time take pity on him. I can see them now: the tiny little boy waddling along the deck holding by each hand one of these black-robed sisters, their veils fluttering in the wind.

Before leaving China, Teddy had begun to say a few words in Chinese, to the delight of the servants. But on this trip, hearing no Chinese at all, he ceased to communicate in words, and it was two months before he started again. By the time we arrived in America, the child was well. And just as it had never occurred to me to pray for God to heal him, so I did not think to give thanks for his recovery. God was very far away from me in those days, so far away that I did not even realize that He was gone.

We finished our trip by train, arriving finally in Media, Pennsylvania, where Ted's father and mother met us and took us to the big old rectory atop a rolling hill. This house was a refuge for any in the family who needed one. Two ancient aunts were there at the time and, indeed, until they died. I had dreaded meeting my parents-in-law for the first time with one baby toddling beside me and another within. But I need not have feared. I fell in love with them immediately, even though their Yankee speech was strange to my Southern ears. They were gentle, kind, completely secure in their love for each other and for their large family of children and grandchildren, and devoted to the little church on the hilltop where a few country people gathered on a Sunday. There was a feeling of peace in this church, or was it in my gentle old father-in-law who there ministered to his flock? I did not analyze it, but I felt something—a quietness, a misty otherworldliness. In fact, in the whole old house and even in the bit of garden and the chicken-yard behind it, there was a feeling of peace that I had not known before. I had been a bit tense about meeting Ted's sister and his four brothers and their families. I need not have worried. In all these years that I have known them, I have never heard an unkind word from any of them. I have, all told, seven sisters-in-law and have never exchanged a cross word with any of them!

It was a long time waiting for that baby to be born. I was clumsy with the weight of her, and what small chores I tried to do around the house were done slowly and poorly—but accepted with the most angelic patience by my mother-in-law. When I look back now, I blush to think of my inefficiency and, to be frank, laziness; and I smile to remember her unfailing gentleness. She reminded me of my grandmother, no longer upon this earth.

Ted was in Philadelphia by day, taking courses in education. Before leaving China, he had besought the bishop to give him a church. He loved school work, but he was, after all, a minister, having studied for orders and been ordained during his last furlough. But the bishop had told him, first, that he was needed at Changshu as business manager of the station and as school principal, and second, that his Chinese was so atrocious that he would

—— 75 ——

never be appointed as minister of a Chinese church. Ted, therefore, always a perfectionist, said that if education was to be his life work, he wanted to be completely qualified. And he asked permission for extension of his furlough so that he might get his M.A. degree. For the most part, I was alone on that hilltop, peeling apples on the front porch and watching down the long, curving drive for Ted's car to turn into it from the Baltimore Pike. The days seemed interminable. There has always been in me a driving restlessness so that I cannot be content with morning and evening and meals and dishes and nothing more.

On the first day of October, 1925, the baby decided to come. Furthermore, characteristically, she more or less took things into her own hands and reversed herself within me, so that she had to be brought by forceps. However, she arrived without spot or blemish, and she was as perfect a baby as one would ever see. I remember Mother Sanford sitting and holding her and saying over and over, "Why, she's a *beautiful* baby!" And so she was.

The only casualty connected with her birth was her father. The nurse had told him, "Sit here and I will call you when the baby is born." But she forgot to call him, for there was some little skirmish after her birth, a hemorrhage that was hard to stop. Doctors and their attendant nurses were sacrosanct in Ted's eyes, and he did not dare to move from the spot where they had placed him. So by the time someone noticed him and allowed him to emerge into the light of day, the poor man was convinced that both the baby and I had died and probably been buried. His enthusiasm about the cuddly baby was for a time dimmed by this circumstance. It took a month or so for him to fall in love with her, but he eventually did.

No one could help it; she was irresistible. Also, she was completely well-fed and satisfied. It proved impossible to wake her and nurse her at ten o'clock. The doctor had thought this advisable, but she thought otherwise and slept from six to six, a sleep from which no amount of shaking and bouncing could awaken her. And my weight, which must have been considerable, since I was, for a time, shaped like a dirigible, promptly went back to my usual one hundred and four pounds.

Now I realize that for a spiritual autobiography, this is extremely earthly. Well, so was I at this time. I was emotionally fulfilled with my adorable babies. I loved my husband and his parents and relatives. I looked forward with eager anticipation to going back to my own little home in China, to Dah S-fu and Siao-loh and amah, to my rosebushes and the fluted city wall beyond the compound and the templed hill in the distance, rosy at sunset time. I had no thought about God, except that one went to church on Sunday to worship Him, because it was the thing to do.

The only one in my own family to see my baby at this delightful cuddly stage of her development was my brother H.M. He was in his first year at Union Seminary in Richmond, Virginia, a fundamentalist school, impeccably "sound." Toward the end of the year, he had a nervous breakdown. My family were adept at them. We are of strong physical heritage, but we excel in having nervous breakdowns. When H.M. was able to leave the hospital, since he had no family in the United States except me, my wonderful parents-in-law invited him to come and live with them. He came and stayed for two months.

So far was God from all my awareness that it never occurred to me to wonder why H.M. had become so mentally disturbed that he was unable to read but had to do outdoor work of the simplest kind. He had found that he was not fitted for the ministry— that was the story we heard. But *why?* Later on, when he became an engineer, he did more ministry than most ordained clergymen. Many a "drunk" was healed by faith and love, as H.M. prayed for him and trusted him with a place in his business. Many a man was led to Christ. H.M. taught Bible classes and held prayer groups, together with his indefatigable wife, who still carries on this ministry, though H.M. has now departed to the other world where he, no doubt, ministers in ways we do not know.

Years later I talked to a small group of students at the seminary who became interested in the amazing fact that what Jesus said is true and that miracles can happen today through the prayer of faith. Then one of the professors wrote a book on Christian healing in which he neatly debunked the whole matter of miracles, not excluding those in the Bible. And the seminary could relax again, for a season. How many seasons God is going to allow to any seminary before He bursts upon them with His Holy Spirit and proclaims that He is alive and they are the ones who are dead, I do not know.

At any rate, H.M. was there with the Sanfords, who treated him as though he was their own son, while he looked for a job that he was able to do. The first work he found was unloading coal from freight cars down at the foot of the hill. Later Father Sanford and Ted between them found a surveyor in their little congregation who needed a rodman, and so my brother started in the surveying that was to become his life's work.

When green shoots began to appear through melting snow in the squashy backyard, and the pussywillow twigs grew rosy, and a thin green veil brooded over the trees below the hill, it occurred to me that I needed to be attired in something more springlike and more suitable to the United States than the garments made by a Chinese cloth-carpenter. I had crossed the ocean in them. But it was an hour's trip in to Philadelphia and another hour's trip getting home on the commuting train. How was I going to leave the baby for that length of time since she depended entirely on me for her sustenance? I borrowed a baby bottle from somewhere and left my brother to administer it at the correct time. When I returned two hours after Tookie's suppertime, the bottle was untouched, and H.M. was sitting beside the fussing baby holding a cup of warm milk and a spoon, with the sweat of extreme tension upon his brow.

"She won't take the bottle," he said. "She just won't. So whenever she opens her mouth to yell, I get in one drop—"

Some time after this, H.M. planned to return to the South, and I took my two babies and went with him as far as Richmond, to make my long-deferred visit to my Southern relatives and friends. We studied the timetable gravely and found that we had forty minutes' stop in Washington. Neither of us had ever seen the capital of the country, so we planned that I would take the first twenty minutes and view the city from the station, and he would take the second twenty minutes, after I returned to care for the babies. On arriving, I climbed the long flight of steps and emerged in the great station whence I looked with awe at the spectacle of wide streets and government buildings and the Washington Monument. Promptly twenty minutes later, I went serenely toward the gate and was met by, "Where you going, Lady?"

"I'm going to track twenty-two," I said innocently.

Whereupon the train man said, "Lady, that train's gone."

All hell broke loose. I tore down the stairs to see the last car trundling into the tunnel, and then and there, for the only time in my life, I threw a scene. I cried. I yelled. I demanded, "Stop that train!" until I blush to think of it.

"She can't stop now. It's too late," cried one man, holding a lantern aloft. But they signaled ahead for the train to stop.

"She's stopping, she's stopping!" yelled another, and on we went, for all the world like *The Perils of Pauline*. Three stalwart blue-coated men helped me down to the tracks. Two of them held my elbows, and they all uttered soothing remarks such as, "Now don't trip, Lady. Your babies will be all right."

The train stopped. There was my brother, leaning over the rail of the last car, his eyes popping out of his head with anxiety.

We returned to the babies, watched by kindly fellow travelers. But from then on people would wander through the car, look at me, and say, "Are you the lady who stopped the train in the tunnel?"

I remember little about that visit to Aunt Eliza, Aunt Willie, Aunt Junia, and various cousins and school friends. Time marches on, and the joys of visiting old school friends diminish sharply with each infant who arrives. I was more than glad to go back to the North, which had become my home, with Ted and his parents, his kindly brothers, and their energetic wives.

These sisters-in-law gave me furiously to think. Every one of them was briskly capable of cooking, washing, ironing, cleaning, and doing all such chores as in China were done by the servants and never in any land or clime had been done by me.

I had tried once, in China. It was on China New Year, and I commanded the cook and Siao-loh to depart and amuse themselves on the street for the day, which was only right and just. They were horrified.

"Who will cook the master's lunch?" asked Kung-pao, the cook.

"I will," I said grandly, for I had secured a cookbook, read several recipes, and determined to try them out.

Kung-pao's expression clearly indicated that he did not think

I was capable of doing so. He shook his head mournfully and said that he could not ascend the street and leave me alone in his kitchen.

"But it is American custom," I said grandly, "that every servant should have one day off a year, and this is the great feast day."

He finally departed, shaking his head dubiously.

I then gave the same command to Siao-loh and received the same answer: "Who will prepare the master's supper?"

This also I proclaimed myself able and ready to do, and Siao-loh departed, not without qualms. I entered the kitchen a suitable time before lunch, cookbook under my arm, only to find Kung-pao established there. He had been seized, he said, with a misery in his stomach and a dizziness in his head and therefore he had come home. And since he was here, he would now prepare the master's lunch.

I retreated in disorder and tried it again shortly before supper. There in the kitchen was Siao-loh looking as contented as a cat who has just eaten the canary.

"I went and played on the street as the Missis commanded," said he. "Then I spent all my money and I could play no more, so I came home. And since I am here, I will now prepare the master's supper."

These memories floated through my mind while I watched my sisters-in-law producing by a simple twist of the wrist a steaming-hot dinner. Oh well, I thought (for I was too shy and too much ashamed of my ignorance to offer to cook for this family), I did not really need to cook, for we would soon be going back to China. A warm flood of joy would sweep over me at the thought of the little mission house that we called our own and of Kung-pao and Siao-loh and amah beamingly awaiting us on the canal bank.

I did not know then that the bamboo curtain was about to fall, to separate all of us from those we loved the best. Rumors of Ted's school being set on fire and of riots in other schools and colleges perplexed me a bit, for hitherto wars and riots had been decently conducted by warlords in the prescribed manner. This new sporadic violence seemed to break the kwei-ju, the established custom. But that it broke it forever, I never dreamed.

Ted was more cognizant of the Chinese situation than I was, and far more worried. And one rainy spring Sunday an event occurred that was to change the flow of my life forever. It began most ordinarily.

Ted, supplying for his father who was away on a trip, went over to the little church, stoked the furnace and ran out in the rain to ring the bell, with a smudge on his face. Meanwhile, up the drive came a car of grave and reverend elegance. Ted washed away the smudge, put on his vestments, and took the service, preaching his usual brief, practical sermon. Three imposing men, who had gotten out of the car, listened from their seats on the back row.

"It was a visiting committee," said Ted, after they had shaken hands and departed.

"What does a visiting committee do?" I asked.

"They go big-game hunting," said Ted with a grin, "looking for a new minister. You can spot 'em every time."

"But you're going back to China," I said, laughing. "And how did they know about you, anyway?"

"Maybe from that woman in Media," he said. "Do you remember, where I substituted for Dad? She told me then that her church was empty, and she seemed to like me . . ."

And this, although I did not want to face it at the time, marked the end of an era.

6

"*Y*OU know I've always wanted my own church," said Ted. "And the bishop will never give it to me in China. I didn't get ordained just to be a schoolmaster all my life. It was a sort of a—a promise, you know."

I knew that he meant a promise to God. And I liked the fact that he did not too glibly talk of religious convictions.

"But you promised me that we would stay in China," I said, feeling my heart sink into my shoes at the desperate prospect of having to cook and clean and take care of babies and wash diapers and be a minister's wife as well. "I just can't do it," I muttered under my breath. "I just can't do it!"

The visiting committee came again and offered Ted a raise in salary, lifting it to the munificent sum of three thousand dollars a year. I looked at Ted's face and knew that I must go to Moorestown, New Jersey, wherever that might be.

"Things are changing in China," said Ted. "And the time is coming when all missionaries will have to leave."

I did not believe it. I simply could not believe it. But I remembered my father's prophecies and wondered . . .

"When do we go?" I asked, swallowing hard.

Ted breathed a great sigh of relief. "As soon as my school term is over," he said.

So we went to Moorestown, my heart sinking lower and lower at every mile. I did not like it. The flat land and the small square cottages and the highways full of hurtling traffic terrified me.

The vestry had agreed to renovate the old rectory, which was huge, dingy, and depressing. Therefore, we lived first in a rented house on a pleasant street with delightful neighbors, the Cadburys, of the English Cadbury Chocolate family, members of the Society of Friends and as gentle and gracious people as one could find. Teddy adored Mrs. Cadbury, whom he called simply, "Cadbury." My memories of life in that house are peaceful . . .

Eventually the rectory was finished, and we moved into it. This spacious dwelling-place was much like a mission house in China: four big square rooms downstairs and four upstairs, a capacious attic and a cellar. The floors were beautiful hardwood in contrast to our Chinese ningpo varnished planks. The windows were large and set opposite to each other to let in all available light and air, keeping the house cool and comfortable. If we could have stayed there, very likely I could have weathered the change and become as well-adjusted to American life as I had been to Chinese life. But then I might not have found the Lord, or rather, He might not have found me.

He intervened in our life at this time in a direct and utterly unexpected way. There arrived at the front door one day a stranger who introduced himself as an architect. He said to my amazed husband, "If someone offered you a new church, rectory, and parish house, would you accept it?"

"I'll bite," said Ted, grinning cheerfully. "What's the joke?"

But it was not a joke. Eldridge R. Johnson, of the Victor Company, whose home was in Moorestown, desired to give away some money and also to provide an opportunity for creative artistry for a nephew. The offer came from him and was bona fide. It was too bad that the newly done-over rectory would have to be abandoned in order that all three buildings should be welded together in the exquisite beauty of English Village Gothic architecture, but such was the case. And in answer to Ted's question, "How much money are you authorized to spend?" the architect said, "Oh, we may spend as much as we like." One could not refuse an offer such as this.

So we moved again, this time into a huge, old, dark house on Main Street, with traffic roaring by at all hours and dust falling from the ceilings. Darkness crept upon me in that house. Shadows fell and would not move. All my senses deadened under a weight that I could not understand. For did I not love my husband and children? And did anything matter as long as I had them to love?

Thus I would reason with myself, but reasoning did no good. I became utterly weighted down with dismal weariness. All of these years I have thought that it was simply this one more uprooting that upset me. But now I wonder.

I was not by nature a weakling. I had always kept within me a source of inward joy such that even the sunlight and the shadows of trees and little flowers in the grass could uplift my heart with delight. What had happened to these inner resources so that I was no longer able to see beauty even when it was there before my eyes? Could it have been the house itself? Some years ago I would have thought this utter foolishness, but now I am not so sure. For old houses do develop an atmosphere that can affect those who enter into them. Some people call such houses haunted, but I am sure that name would not have applied to the innocent old house on Main Street. But now, looking back, I can understand that house. It was filled with memories, many of them sorrowful ones: memories of frustration and discouragement and fear.

Thoughts as they enter the mind do not remain closed within it, but emanate the main essence of their feeling into the air. Thoughts continue beyond the thinker, and if a house or a place is sufficiently filled with them, their atmosphere remains until dispelled either consciously or unconsciously by a spiritual power. For instance, when Ted and I moved years later to Westboro, Massachusetts, we were surrounded by mental institutions—three of them and one reform school within a radius of a few miles. The atmosphere of that peaceful, pretty little town was heavy.

Some years later a friend wrote to me, saying, "You and Ted have done the most marvelous thing for this town. The whole atmosphere has changed and has become more warm and cheerful." There is nothing new about this knowledge. My Cistercian friends, the monks, tell me that it is on this principle that they work. They establish closed monasteries in strange far places where Christ is not known, and in their prayers day and night they believe that the atmosphere of His love penetrates the very air. Of this I am quite sure. Moreover, a heavy and "haunted" atmosphere can be dismissed from a house in one prayer by blessing the house in the name of Jesus Christ and commanding all dark or evil shadows to depart.

But I did not know these things at that time, and the darkness of the Moorestown house grew upon me. In such houses there develops sometimes a habit-pattern of accidents. I learned this years later from my brother H.M., then well and married, who wrote me that he had rented a house where the atmosphere was evil, and his children were continually hurting themselves, and I was to come down and pray for the house. On arriving, I found that someone who lived there long ago had committed suicide. No wonder it oppressed the soul with shades of darkness. We prayed for that house, opening every window and dismissing the dark thoughts, and blessing every room in the name of the Lord, and the atmosphere changed.

We could have done that in the old house on Main Street, but we did not know to do it. However, I can see that the Lord wonderfully protected us in spite of our ignorance, for we had two very narrow escapes. Once Teddy and I were walking down the sidewalk, and a lady hailed him from the other side of the street. He was the most friendly little boy that ever lived, and he promptly darted across the street and was knocked down by a car. The driver stopped and was terribly concerned, the child roared lustily, but I could see that it had been merely a light glancing blow and, except for a tiny bruise on his forehead, he was not hurt. I shudder when I think of what might have happened, had not the angel of the Lord stood round about him and protected him.

Then there was an evening when I had cooked a rather good dinner. I tottered with the garbage out through the kitchen, through the laundry, through the shed, and right off the end of the back porch. I had forgotten that the steps down to the brick walk were on the side of the porch and not the end. So there I landed on the tail end of my spine, garbage and all. For the only time in my life I saw stars—little explosions of green and red in the air, though why I should have done so when I fell not on my head but on my tail, I don't know. I sat there for a while and then crawled around and collected the garbage and put it in the garbage can and came into the house. I said nothing about this and did not seek medical help, though I could tell from the mirror that my whole posterior was as black as the kitchen stove with lightning streaks of red and green running through it. Perhaps I should have gone to a doctor, for he might have been able to straighten out the broken coccyx, which remained permanently twisted. But it did not occur to me to do so. Again, how wonderfully the Lord protected me, for I might have been paralyzed or in some other way seriously injured! I did not even know enough to thank Him then, so I thank Him now as I write.

One other incident comes to my mind with great vividness. Behind this house, the land sloped down into a swampy place where grew reeds and bulrushes, ironweed and wild sunflowers, and goldenrod. One day when the children were supposedly taking naps, I wandered a little way down into this delightful wilderness and picked wild flowers as I had done in Kuling years before. Just a tiny bit of that old feeling of release and utter delight in nature came into me, and probably I lost track of time, for Ted came and found me and was quite frightened. I dropped my wild flowers and returned home and wandered forth no more.

The months passed, and we finally moved into the new rectory, even while the lovely church was still being built and portions of saints and angels carved in stone lay among the fragments of rocks and bits of slate that littered the front lawn. The house was quaintly beautiful, as were the church and the parish house. The windows were small and deep-set, placed according to English Village Gothic style and not according to the demands of light and air. They really should be completely covered, I was told, with sheer glass curtains beneath the drapes, so that one could not see the outside world at all except through cloth. This I looked upon with horror and steadfastly refused to do, even though the kind donors offered the curtains as a gift. To be shut off completely, like an animal in a trap, not to be able to see even the pigeons mingling their pastel shades of grey and rose and blue with the lovely tiles of the church roof, not to see even the outward flame and gold of the maple trees on the other side of Main Street—this I would not endure! In the course of time I learned to like the new rectory, in spite of its overwhelming newness. After a while one's voice ceased to echo along the walls, and the starkness melted down into the warmth of the humanity that filled it.

The rectory was connected by exquisite cloisters with the church and also with the parish house and the chapel that was part of the parish house. When the time came that I learned to pray, that chapel became practically part of my house and my heart. Between the cloisters was a courtyard which Ted took as his own, making it beautiful with lilies and ferns and flowering shrubs. On the other side of the rectory, a driveway led back to parish house and garage, and beyond the turn in the drive was a bit of wasteland decorated with piles of old planks. These I promptly heaved over the hedge into the cemetery. I adopted the wasteland as my garden, and small though it was, it became a little paradise and a place of refuge from the bewildering world.

I found that the role of a minister's wife in an Episcopal church in the North did not in the least resemble the life I had known briefly in the South. Parishioners did not arrive to welcome me with flowers and cakes. Once when the senior warden was visiting Ted, his wife sat in the car in full view of my living-room windows and did not even ring the doorbell to say good morning.

In time, many of these people became my very good friends. I had not understood them at first, that was all. I had not comprehended the difference between a suburban society (for Moorestown was practically a suburb of Philadelphia) and the folks of a Southern community where everyone knew who everyone was and who their parents and their grandparents were even back to the Revolutionary War.

I was not the kind of minister's wife to sit in the front pew in all my glory and then stand on the steps with my husband and greet the congregation. And fortunately, he did not want me to do so. He told me most comfortingly that I was a member of the congregation like any other member of the congregation and should take a normal part in church activities but no more. My outward demeanor, therefore, suited him very well and was not unpleasing to the congregation, after they came to "understand" me. I was too small and shy and lacking in self-confidence, so they thought, to really take hold and act the part of a minister's wife, but for the rest, I minded my own business and took care of my children not too badly, and they smiled briefly at me when they met me, and let it go at that.

Once, at a Women's Auxiliary meeting, the wife of a vestryman said, "Mrs. Smith asked me whether you could come to Collingswood and talk about China, just informally, you know, to a small group, but I said oh no, you were too busy looking after your home and children, and anyway you were not the kind of person to do things like that." And I made no reply because I thought perhaps she was right. The kind of person that I used to be was dead. And the new person, whom I was now forced to be, had much trouble in living. This new one, for instance, had to cook three meals a day and knew absolutely nothing about cooking. It never occurred to me to let my family open the refrigerator and scramble for themselves. Nor did it occur to me that my husband should not be at home for lunch as well as for breakfast and dinner. It did cross my mind, as my children grew older, that they might occasionally have lunch at the high school one block away; but no, they preferred to come home, and home they came. Actually the family unity engendered by all of us sitting down to meals together has built a foundation of unity that still lasts.

My total ignorance of foodstuffs was gradually overcome. I remember pointing to a cut of meat in a grocery store and asking, "What is that?"

"Veal," said the clerk.

"But, what kind of an animal is a veal?" I asked.

"A calf, lady," he answered in disgust. "You've heard of a calf."

In China, one did not have veal or beef or lamb. In China, moreover, the cook attended to all shopping, marketing, and the exchanging of money from American to Chinese, the rate of which varied every day. I had never been in a bank, for even in college my relatives took charge of all money affairs. One day my husband did not have my housekeeping money at hand and instructed me to go to the bank and write a desk check for twenty dollars. This, to me, was wrapped in mystery as was all American life, but it was mine only to obey. So I went to a bank, wrote a desk check, and received twenty dollars. Later on, the bank, in which, as it happens, we did not have an account, called up my husband and said plaintively, "Your wife came in here and drew a check for twenty dollars."

"Well," said Ted, enjoying himself hugely, "you gave it to her, didn't you? Seems to me that's *your* worry." (He did, of course, give them back their money.)

My best friend in Moorestown was Elizabeth Kimbro, my lovely Negro helper. (In my inefficiency and clumsiness, my dreamy habit of mind, and my need of occasional solitude, I gave up everything else and economized furiously that I might squeeze out of the housekeeping allowance enough to pay for just a little help.) I know that nowadays one should speak of her as black, not Negro. But Elizabeth would not like this, and actually, she is not black but a very light brown. When her oldest daughter died, Elizabeth came straight to me from the hospital, before even going home, and we wept in each other's arms. I was the only white person at the child's funeral, and nobody thought it strange. I loved her and her gentle soft-spoken husband, Charles, and her smiling babies as they came, and her friends knew this. When another baby arrived, and she could not go out to work, I never had any trouble in getting help.

"How do you do it?" my acquaintances would ask me. "I can never get anyone to work for me!"

I loved Elizabeth and her friends and respected them, that was all. Coming from a really democratic country where the position of a servant was an honorable one—for all work was honorable—I did not embarrass them by familiarity, nor anger them by domination, but trusted them and set them free to do their work, as I was free to do mine.

My work was to care for husband, children, and house. That was made clear to me. Therefore I closed the doors of my mind to childish notions of writing or creating beauty in drama or paint, and set myself to do my whole duty as a wife and mother. I even made the children's clothes, an agonizing process, since I usually had to rip and re-sew. And I knit all their sweaters, unraveling them when they became too ragged, re-rolling the yarn and making a sweater for a smaller child. Fortunately, Teddy and "Tookie," as we called the little girl ("Little Two" in Chinese), were delightful children, so that there was much joy in taking care of them. When Tookie was one year old she put her little fat hand into a dish of prunes.

"No, no, baby," I said. "Don't do that."

Whereupon she replied in bright, intelligent tones, "It won't bite me!"

So I delighted in my little ones and longed for another. But underneath the domestic joys, there was always the feeling that the real me was dead.

When Tookie was four years old, the third baby arrived,

three weeks later than the doctor expected but otherwise being born much more easily than the other two. I do not remember my first glimpse of Teddy or Tookie, but I remember my introduction to Jack. He lay beside me on the bed, and I looked at him and said, "Hello." He gave me a wise and contemplative glance, as he still does, but did not reply!

For a while I was so delighted with this utterly charming little one that I did not miss the other self that I thought of as the real me. Like Tookie, the baby slept from six to six. Indeed, he was a miracle child! One could wake him in the middle of a nap, for instance, to show him off to visiting family or friends, and he would smile delightfully and go back to sleep.

Teddy and Tookie played with him in ways that were sometimes a bit alarming. When he was six months old, I heard him crying one day and ran upstairs to see what was the matter. Unless there was serious trouble, Jack never cried. Teddy and Tookie had stuffed him under the bureau.

"Why did you put him under the bureau?" I asked as I pulled him out.

"We had to," said Teddy airily.

"*Why* did you have to?"

"We were playing zoo, and he was the lion, and he had to get in the cage and roar."

I said, "Well, he's my baby, and you can't have him for a lion. Go get your teddy bear and put him under the bureau."

This suggestion satisfied them. Off they went to get the teddy bear, and the game of zoo went on constructively for quite some time, I myself being in turn the zoo-keeper and various visitors.

During this period when the darkness was deepening upon me, I played with my children. Indeed, during all of their childhood, whenever they said, "Mom, what can we do?" I took my hands out of the dishpan or wherever they might be, and helped them think of something. Many a play they acted upon my bed, with flowered hat or high-heeled shoes to point up the characters, and with me, of course, for the audience. My tiny bit of backyard, encircled by flower bed, was in turn a circus ground, a Tarzan jungle, or the frozen wastes of the Arctic Ocean. The living-room chairs spent much of their time upside down being tents and trains and steamers. But we had a deal: when I was using the living room and company was there, then they were not allowed to come in. It was my turn to play.

Because I loved them so much and enjoyed them so much, they did not, I think, sense too acutely the darkness that was creeping upon me. It was good that I thus delighted in them. On the other hand, I was not too strong on discipline, because I did not want them to be unhappy. Fortunately, Ted, while never harsh or rough, was a wonderful disciplinarian. He gave few orders, but those that he gave had to be obeyed. If he told a child to pick up his blocks, that child, even at the age of two, picked up his blocks. Ted simply put his own hand firmly over the little child's hand and gently steered it from block to block until all were put in place. If a child did not come when called, Ted went and got the child and put him in the corner for a season, that he might meditate upon his disobedience. But lest he become wearied, Ted always placed a chair in the corner, facing the wall.

Teddy said once when he was fourteen, "I see how you and Dad bring us up. When we were little you taught us what was right to do, so now that we are grown up, you let us make our own decisions." To a considerable extent that was true. And he added, "That works very well for me, but I doubt if it will for Tookie."

This, however, took place in the new era, after life began again for me.

By the time Jack was a year and a half old, I was very far under the darkness of depression. Nobody knew it; I was a good actress and had been brought up to contain and control myself. The congregation had made their own picture of me as a shy, stiff person with very little life of her own and were well content with that. Ted looked at me with worried eyes from time to time, but said nothing, for he did not know what to say. He was very kind to me, even permitting me at one time to go and visit my family, home on furlough, while he and Elizabeth and Miss Magee, our baby-sitter friend, took care of the children. I remember the four of them on the railroad platform when I returned, Ted holding the baby, and the little boy and girl standing on either side of him. It clutched at my heart, and I loved them and yearned over them more than ever, yet I grieved because I knew that the visit had accomplished nothing of healing. My wounds were too deep to be healed so easily.

And what were those wounds? If anyone had asked me at the time, I would have said, first of all, that the real part of me was simply not living, the creative one who longed, not only for children, but also for the children of the mind to be brought forth. I would have added that I wanted to be in China; that I was perfectly adapted for married life in China but not in Moorestown, New Jersey. This was true, and at the time I had much bitterness concerning it, and not a little resentment. For although one heard increasingly of riots and violence breaking out in the schools in China, exactly as they are now doing here, I still could not believe that missionary work in China was doomed and that God Himself had opened a door that we might escape before it was too late. At the same time, I might have remembered the dreadful smell of fertilized fields, I might have heard once more the wail of sick babies that arose day and night from the hut of the Chinese baby doctor, and I might have wondered whether, after all, I was not better off in Moorestown. Then, if I had permitted my mind to go back in time, shadows from the far past might have deepened over me: rams' horns blowing low over the city wall while my mother wept in the living room; horror pictures that would wake me at night in the cold sweat of a senseless fear, unreasonable—and I might have feared for the stability of my own mind.

But now, looking back, I can see that none of these things, not even the somewhat uneasy adjustment to married life, was the real cause.

The basic trouble was that I had forgotten whence I came, and I did not know the sealed orders with which I had been sent to this earth. I sensed my thwarted creativity. I wanted to be a writer, and I could not, for all of my time and thought and attention was upon being a wife and mother. But I had deliberately chosen the wife and mother role to that of the writer, so why should that alone cast me into the depths of despair?

At this time I came very near to the very deepest depths and could easily have drowned in them. I reached the place where sunlight was as the dark to me. I would go out to my garden and look upon the small, inquiring faces of pansies and up to the towering blue glory of delphiniums, and would feel nothing. I could no longer see beauty. And when one can no longer see beauty, one can no longer see God.

Long ago, in fact, I had forgotten God, though I did not know it, for how can one know the loss of something that has so entirely gone that even the memory has faded out? No longer did God speak to me through tiny blossoms opening upon a weed, or through wild violets upon a Chinese grave, or through pink sunlight on a far pagoda, or the shadow of curved roofs upon a moonlight night. God had departed from me and spoke to me no more, as King Saul said long ago—not through Urim, nor by dreams, nor by prophets, nor in any way at all. And if someone had not come to show me God, I would have left this world in the same way that King Saul left it—by my own hand. For many months I could not go near an upstairs window without wondering when I would throw myself out of it. I did not want to do it; I merely felt dully that some day I would. I seldom peeled vegetables without wondering whether the kitchen knife was sharp enough . . .

Someone *did* come; that is what this whole book is about. But I write these bits so that one in depression will know that I have been there too. I know what it is to wonder whether this life is real, or whether it is a dream from which one will awaken. I know what it is to be beset with fear day and night so that one does not know what one fears; one is just afraid. I even know the occasional moments when one's thoughts are like two piles of books that begin to slide into each other, so that one cannot quite catch them as they go.

How often have I said these things to someone in depression and watched his face light up with relief as he sees that I have been there too!

"Oh, you *understand!*" he will say.

"And the worst of it is," I will add, nodding agreement, "that other people *don't* understand and they always give you the wrong advice. 'You must make an effort,' they say. 'You must learn to stand upon your own feet. You must count your blessings.' " (I tried this once: "I have a wonderful husband and three lovely children and a nice house and enough to eat, so why *do* I feel this way? But I still do feel this way, so I must be going crazy!" That was the net result of my counting my blessings, and I never tried it again.)

My doctor said, after my amazing, instantaneous recovery from depression, that he had not thought I would last another year. Whether he expected a mental breakdown or suicide, I did not ask, for the question was no longer relevant.

Now as the reader perfectly well knows, God had not gone anywhere. He was right there. His presence was upon the altar every Sunday at the Communion service, but though I went to church faithfully, for I was born and brought up so to do, the windows of my own soul were closed, and I could not see Him. Christianity had become to me words—just words—only words. And the words did not mean anything because I could see no results following them.

At this point a question arises: did God permit Satan to send the depression in order to try me and test me and then to teach me how to help others?

I do not think so. I think, rather, that God tried to show me the sealed orders with which I had come into the world, and I could not accept what He was trying to tell me. True, I had talents of writing, painting, and drama, but I did not know that I also had a gift of healing. This gift is latent in everyone, but apparently in me it was a bit of a special gift, together with a special command, "This *do*." All unconsciously, I must have been obeying this command when I made the prayer-pact with God to pray for Oscar for seven years. But when Oscar was completely healed long before the seven years were finished, I doubted whether my prayers had anything to do with it!

If I had dared to give thanks for the answer to my prayers, I might have had the courage to pray in like fashion for the young woman in Kuling who was so grievously oppressed. Why had God shown it to me when no one else saw it, if He did not want me to pray the prayer of faith concerning it? But having once canceled out my bit of faith by failing to give thanks for its answer, it never occurred to me that one as young and worthless as I could pray for the missionary lady.

7.

*A*T the very time when my emotional disturbance brought me to the verge of despair, the Lord brought me a helper. No doubt He would have sent a minister to heal me long before, if only He could have found one who believed! I had reached bottom. I was no longer able to feel anything, except the ever-present fear that now extended to every detail of life, both rational and irrational. I knew intellectually that I loved my husband and children, but the only testimony to this in my emotions was intense fear for them whenever they were absent from me, and relief when they reappeared. The single exception to this was my youngest, my baby, for whom I still retained the love of a mother for an infant, in a "smothering" fashion. For the rest, I walked through life as through a dream, and indeed it often seemed to me a dream. Out of this dream I would suddenly awaken quite violently when something tore at my nerves. Then I would be apt to scream at some child or incontinently rush him into the closet. In other words, I was a complete failure as a mother and as a human being and most of all as a New England housewife.

The big house with its small casement windows was too much for me. Try as I would, I could not keep it clean and neat. The four bathrooms were tiled with diamond-shaped white tiles, and every footstep dirtied them; the kitchen was floored with a disconsolate brown linoleum that showed every spot.

Ted did not scold me for my ineptitude in housekeeping, but he found other ways of letting me see my inadequacy. Once he put up a mailbox inside the front door, because occasionally some child would pick up the mail that the postman dropped through the slot and would trot off to play post office with it. I realize now that I should have said, "*Take* that thing down!" Whereupon he should have uttered his disapproval of my carelessness with a loud voice, and we would have shouted it out and talked it over, and things would have been better. At least, so psychologists say. I am not sure. At any rate, neither of us was capable of this measure of self-expression. Ted, as a matter of fact, was very helpful to me as I tried to learn to cook. He always praised any dish that was good and never once fussed or refused to eat one that I knew was pretty awful. And the result was that I became quite a good cook. (He used to say later on that if all else failed I could make my fortune by writing the *Agnes Sanford Divine Cook Book*.)

No, it was not Ted who accused me of total inadequacy, it was myself. I had determined to make myself exactly like Ted's mother, whom I adored. I would then be, I felt, the kind of wife that he liked. Therefore, I completely denied my original nature and devoted every moment to fruitless endeavor.

And so I reached the depths because I was doing violence to my own soul.

My children, moreover, seemed to lose their natural healthiness and succumbed to various germs which they passed faithfully from one to another. Jack, when still a baby, had ear trouble, resulting, I am sure, from the time when he was one day old and the nurses left him uncovered except for his little shirt and diaper.

"He's cold," I would say. And the nurses would gaily reply, "Oh, it's a very warm day!" and go off about their own concerns.

Finally, when the baby was a year and a half old, he developed quite a serious ear infection and was ill with a high fever for six weeks. I prayed continually, but always with fear and not with faith.

"Oh, please make the baby well!" I would say, and then I would go and feel his forehead to see how much his temperature had risen.

And the Lord sent an angel, dressed in the conventional garb of an Episcopal minister. He was a young man of about my own age, extremely handsome and attractive, and it was only by the Lord's mercy that I did not fall violently in love with him. His church was in the next village, and I knew him and his wife. However, on this occasion, he had come on business to see Ted, and by the grace of God, Ted was not at home, so he chatted with me while awaiting his return.

"How are the children?" he asked.

"Oh, the baby's sick," I replied. "He's been sick for six weeks."

"Well," said he in his pleasant voice, quite casually, "I'll go up and say a little prayer for him."

This surprised me greatly. I believed in a vague, general way that God answered prayer for healing when He felt like it—unless for some reason He preferred for a person to remain ill. But why God would answer one person's prayer rather than another's, I could not imagine. I merely said, however, "Oh, the baby wouldn't understand. He's too little." I was gravely mistaken. The baby understood much better than I did, as events indicated.

At this point, with supreme wisdom, the minister, Hollis Colwell, simply went on about his ministry. He did not argue, preach, or in any way try to convince me of the reality of spiritual healing. If he had done so, I would have stiffened in my refusal, for I was not prepared to hear this iconoclastic "new thought." (It was as old as the hills, really, but I did not know it). He merely said, "That's all right. I'll just go up and say a little prayer for him." He was a minister. It was his business to minister God's healing power to the infant, and he simply went ahead and did it. Upstairs he strode, looking neither to the right nor to the left. And as I followed after him, I knew that he had some kind of power. I saw it in his very casualness, in his air of calm assurance, in his total lack of any desire to preach or to teach, but only to get the job done.

"Now, you shut your eyes and go to sleep," he said to the baby. "I'm going to ask God to come into your ears and make them well. And when you wake up, you'll be all right."

His prayer as I recall it was just as simple as were these opening remarks. He laid his hands upon the baby's ears and kept them there for several minutes. "Please, Lord Jesus," he said, "send your power right now into this baby's ears and take away all germs or infection and make them well. Thank You, Lord, for I believe that You are doing this, and I see these ears well as You made them to be."

The child shut his eyes, grew very pale as the fever died out of his face, and went to sleep. And when he woke up, his temperature was normal and his ears were well.

The strange thing is that this did not immediately show me a new world. Instead, it perplexed me greatly. Why did God answer the minister's prayers when He had not answered mine? I did not know that I myself blocked my own prayers, because of my lack of faith. Nor did I know that this prayer could not come through me because my mind was clogged with resentment and darkness and unhappiness, as a pipeline can be clogged with roots and dirt. This doubt and confusion remained in my mind, even though the child himself, whenever he subsequently had a bit of an earache, demanded that I pray for him. He would say, "Hurt. Pray," apparently understanding the matter sufficiently well, though I did not understand it at all. And I would put my hands on the ears as I had seen Hollis do and timidly pray. It must have been helpful to some extent, for the next time he had an earache the child said again, "Hurt. Pray."

In spite of this bit of light in the darkness, the darkness did not go away; in fact, it grew worse. Yet it never occurred to me to go to Hollis and ask him to pray for me. Or if it did flit through my mind, I shied away from the passing notion. One did not do things like that. It was not dignified. And besides, I did not know what queer business I might be getting into. How right I was!

Finally, however, God gave me the push that was needed to start me moving. It was at the altar rail on a Sunday morning.

All these years I had attended church regularly, from habit and from my lifelong training. (I have no criticism in my heart for those who go to church just from habit, for that habit saved my life.) Somehow God managed to get across His guidance as I knelt by the rail. Why the way was clear for it this particular morning, I do not know. Possibly there happened to be a group at the altar who had fulfilled the conditions: who were "in love and charity with their neighbors." Maybe someone there had made a special effort to forgive and thus prepare the soul for the receiving of the life of Christ through the Communion. He never knew the far-reaching results of that effort of devotion. At any rate, it seemed that the clouds in my mind parted just for a moment, and on that beam of light a voice said within me, "Go to Hollis Colwell and ask him to pray for you."

So I called and made an appointment to see him on Monday morning. On the way over to his parish, I must have sensed within me some sort of a breaking down of icy barriers, for I cried the whole way over, and I had not cried in years. (I still find it very hard to weep, the lifelong training in self-control being too strong.) Mr. Colwell took me to his study, leaving the door ajar: a wise move, for by this time I was terrified, and somehow the open door gave me a feeling that I could escape if I wanted to do so. He talked to me a little, but I have no idea what he said, for I was too confused to understand it. I thought only, "Oh, I wish he would stop talking and just pray." If he had not prayed at all but had merely tried counseling, whether directive or nondirective, I would not be here now. It is completely possible that I might not even have returned home. I am not imagining this. I know of four cases where it has happened: the minister has merely talked, or asked questions, and has not prayed, and the man has shot himself on the way home, or has run the car into a tree.

After a short time, the minister laid his hands on my head and prayed for the healing of my mental depression, quite as simply and naturally as he had prayed for the healing of Jack's ears. And it happened immediately! All heaven broke loose upon me and within me! Great waves of joy flooded my mind! I do not remember what I said or what Mr. Colwell said, but I sang and shouted at the top of my voice all the way home! Perhaps some of you are thinking, "That must have been the baptism in the Holy Spirit." No, it was not, as far as I know. I did not speak in tongues or any such thing, and neither did he, then or at any time. And I praise God for that, for if he had tried to lead me into a tremendous spiritual experience for which I was not in the least prepared, the excitement and confusion of it might have rocked me right off my base.

Other readers may wonder whether my real trouble may have been demon possession. It occurred to me long afterward that this may have been one of the troubling factors. I remembered the time when as a child I had worshiped the huge brass Buddha to see what would happen, thus opening my mind to a power that was not God, as one does when playing with a Ouija board or with automatic writing. Perhaps some Chinese "kwei" did take advantage of that crack in the armor of Jesus around me and slip into me. Some years after my visits with Hollis, a very sensitive man, Dr. Crump, visited me and said in departing, "Would it frighten you if I were to tell you that I saw a sort of Chinese demon behind you?"

"No," I said, having been brought up with the knowledge of Chinese demons. "But if it's there, you'd better tell it to go away."

"When they are seen, they always go away," said this remarkable medical doctor. And I knew that he had dismissed whatever shadow might have followed me from China.

What would have happened if at my first visit Hollis had said, "I see a devil in you," and had prayed an exorcism prayer? I would have been terrified, and even if the prayer had dislodged some old encrusted fear, it would have come back again, because the real problems of oncoming manic-depressive insanity and of my denial of my real personality would not have been healed.

I thank God for this man of God who prayed the simplest and most basic of all prayers: that Jesus would come into my mind and heal me.

"Come back and see me when you feel like it," he had said before I left his office. That was good, for after some days the waves of joy receded, and the darkness began to creep around the corners of my mind. So he prayed again, and once more I felt an inrush of God's light. But this time, Hollis knew that I was able to talk a bit, and so he asked me a few questions. Perhaps at this point some holy reader is pursing up the lips and saying, "Ah! He asked her what sins she was committing." No, he didn't. (And if you want to crush a newborn soul completely, just try asking that ill-considered question.)

Hollis said, "What do you like to do?"

And I replied, "I used to like to write, but I can't now because my mind is dead." (How often I had felt, as I grimly folded diapers, that I was sitting by the deathbed of my mind and watching the cells perish one by one.)

"Then you must write," said Hollis. "Take two hours every morning, and go over to the parish house by yourself and write."

"Oh, I can't!" I said, making loud outcry. "I have my children and—"

"You must," said Hollis. "Don't you see you have been trying to be a square peg in a round hole? To make yourself into something you are not?"

That was true. I was trying to be a perfect New England housewife and minister's wife and cook and laundress.

"But nobody will like me if I am myself!" I cried. "Not Ted nor his family nor the parish nor anybody!"

"They won't have you, unless you let yourself be yourself," said Hollis.

"But I'd have to get a baby-sitter, and that's expensive—"

"Not as expensive as a funeral," said Hollis inexorably. "You do it. Write two hours every day. Those are my orders."

It is possible that he explained these orders to Ted, for there was no objection from him. And I went over to the parish house every morning and wrote, leaving house and children in Elizabeth's capable hands. The plot that came to my mind was a strange one, it would seem, and yet it was divinely wise! I sat down and wrote a three-act blank-verse play in the classic tradition, called *The House of Saul.* This play, as first written, was a most bloodcurdling tragedy. It was taken directly from the Bible and ended with the death of Saul and Jonathan on the battlefield. It came to me, as I wrote, that Saul was a manic-depressive, as I had been, and until the scene in the witch's cave when he became entirely manic, every thought that Saul expressed, I had thought myself. And somehow, in writing all this out, I found healing and joy.

If Hollis Colwell, instead of ordering me to do the thing that was in tune with my nature, had spent an hour a week in counseling with me, how different my life would have been! I have known people who have been "in therapy" for four years and have not as yet attained the release that came to me very speedily through direct prayer, then through advice saying, "Do this," with the authority of a doctor saying, "Take this medicine."

"In the long run, you've got to learn to pray the prayer of faith yourself," said Hollis on my fourth or fifth visit. (I did not let myself become a burden to him, but I did see him once every four or six weeks.)

I looked at him noncommittally and thought, "I can never do that." But finally it came to me that since he was my mind-doctor and since he required it, I must try to pray as he suggested, making in my mind the picture of what I wanted and thanking God that it was becoming so—or better yet, that it *was* so, thinking in the ever-continuing present. So I would imagine my body strong and well, relieved of its accumulated pain and stress, and would say, "Thank You, God. Your power is working through me and I am doing this work in Your strength."

I did not in the beginning feel any immediate sense of relief. The unconscious mind is very obstinate and had become used to feeling the way of the flesh, the carnal rather than the spiritual way. But I prayed the prayer of thanksgiving just the same. And when the little voice within me would say, "Oh, yeah?" I would reply, "Shut up, you," and I would continue.

There was a Sunday morning when I awoke with the aches and chills that usually indicate the oncoming of flu, or as we called it in those days, grippe. Now I had the idea that whenever I met a germ, I would inevitably fall a victim of the same. So I cast back in my mind to remember when I had been with a sniffly friend, and of course, I could recall such a time. Therefore, I knew that I was getting sick with flu and went to the phone to call Elizabeth and see whether she could come and cook Sunday dinner for the family. She herself was sick and could not come and neither could any of my other helpers. So I said rather crossly, "Well, Lord, if You can't find me a helper, You'll just have to get me over this flu." Whereupon I went to church and sang in the choir as usual.

When church was over, I lay down on the sofa the better to have flu. And as I listened to my body, to my amazement I discovered that there was not an ache or a pain in it! I said, "Why, You really *did* heal me of this flu!" And from that time on it was easier to believe that He really wanted me to be well and that He could heal me.

The first point bothered me for quite a while because I had been brought up on the nauseating concept of the suffering saint. In fact, many points were perplexing to me as I tried to pursue the path of faith. So I decided to read what Jesus Himself said about faith and about the way of life, and to follow Him and nobody else. For the time being, I "laid on the table" all my preconceived ideas and paid no attention to what anyone said except Jesus—not the Bible nor St. Paul nor my husband nor anyone. I studied the four Gospels and did exactly what Our Lord commanded insofar as I was able to do so. And I found that He spoke the truth: His house of life was really built upon a rock.

I did not know that there were any other books upon the subject of the prayer of faith, except possibly *Science and Health*. I tried to read it, but to me it did not make sense. It did not speak to my condition. Not that I scorn Christian Scientists. I am grateful to them, for at a time when the Church had totally forgotten or denied healing, they dared to believe in it.

Then someone gave me a copy of Emmett Fox's *The Sermon on the Mount*, and although the language of this book was not that to which I was accustomed, speaking of "treating" and "demonstrating" when I would have said "praying" and "receiving answers to prayer," still it thrilled my soul because it made clear to me the reality of the spiritual body that interpenetrates the physical body, and of the spiritual world in which we really live. This book is based strongly and squarely on the words that Jesus actually said. It rounded out my two years' study of the Gospels, and I then undertook to trace through the whole Bible this thought of the spirit of man co-existing with the body of man.

At some point I had started a Bible class, which to me was the natural thing to do, as I had been brought up on the Bible. Seven women met in my living room during Sunday-school time on Sunday morning. Most of them were young mothers waiting to take their children home from Sunday school. We began at Genesis 1:1 and continued to Revelation 22:21. Someone asked me once how long that course in the Bible took us, and I said eighteen years, for so it was. And I found to my amazement that this idea of the spiritual body and the physical body, and of the Spirit of God permeating the spiritual body, is the very foundation stone of the whole Bible.

I would first read the next Sunday's chapter and study all the commentaries that I could find in my husband's study upon the passages. Then I would hold the chapter open and say, "Now Lord, I have done all I can with my conscious mind; show me what this passage really means," and illumination of a most wonderful kind would come into my mind. God showed me comfortingly that these ancient stories, beginning with Genesis, were not myths and fables, but statements of actual truth seen through the veil of time, for the most part with amazing accuracy. This degree of understanding released for me the power of the Bible to heal and to instruct. Understanding heals. Denying or misunderstanding God's power blocks healing. Needless to say, during all this time I not only studied, but also prayed for the gift of healing —the gift that is the natural expression of God's love.

As I have said in every one of my books, it is not enough to pray; one must also believe that the prayer is being answered. Being by nature cynical rather than gullible, this was very difficult for me. How could I believe, for instance, that my body was well and strong when the human part of me ached in every nerve? I searched the Scriptures for light on this subject and came gradually to realize that the very essence of Christianity—that which I had been taught from a child—was really true.

From infancy I had been told that I had a soul and that the soul would some day go to heaven. In heaven the soul (which would be myself) would meet and recognize loved ones. Then what would the soul look like? Obviously it would look like the human body in which it now abode. For my soul was not awaiting me in a heavenly bureau drawer, but was with me *now*, I thought, remembering the frightening parable of the man who had everything but lost his own soul (Luke 12:16–21). He had it or he could not have lost it.

The Bible also refers time and again to the spirit of man. "For what man knoweth the things of a man, save the spirit of man which is in him?" (I Cor. 2:11). Even the Old Testament is full of this concept. The difference between the soul and the spirit eluded me and still does. Possibly the spirit is the point of light that originally illumines the soul and that later, when filled with the Holy Spirit of Jesus, illumines the entire being. And this entire being, illumined with the saving love of Jesus Christ and with His Spirit, is I—the other one of me—the immortal one who will someday live in heaven. Then the tremendous truth dawned on me (and it is nothing new, but has been since the beginning) that this spiritual body is a part of me now, co-existing with the physical body.

Therefore when I prayed for healing, I could accept the

healing as already accomplished in the spiritual body, and so could know that it would be transferred to the physical body.

Many years later I was to know that this spirit or spiritual being within me could actually speak to God in a language that the conscious mind does not know. But long before I received the gift of tongues, I received the understanding that the healing power of God moves through the spiritual body of man into his physical body, and this understanding helped tremendously in my prayers for healing, either for myself or for others.

One time, for instance, I went forth from the dining room to the cloister in an agitated frame of mind, and banged the heavy door shut on my finger. Nearly all accidents can be traced to anger or an outward agitation. In anger, we would like to hurt someone, and since the subconscious cannot reach anyone but ourselves, the impulse to hurt rebounds on the one who is angry. My finger turned black immediately and the pain was excruciating.

I said, "I have a spiritual body, and in the spiritual body this finger is perfect." Immediately there appeared a tiny hole in the base of the fingernail and all the black blood oozed out, and from that time forth the finger did not hurt at all. Another day I spilled a kettle of boiling water over my foot, clad in shoe and stocking. I *immediately* claimed the power of the Spirit to heal the body (through Jesus Christ, of course, but one does not have time to think through the whole system of theology at a time like this), and stated by faith that the skin of my foot was not burned. And it was not! By the time I could remove the shoe and stocking, it was not even red.

At this point some people may be thinking, "But isn't this metaphysics? Isn't this the power of positive thinking?" Certainly! And I might point out that Jesus called it faith. I might also add that, when emergencies come upon those who have established firm habits of prayer and faith, whatever words directed toward wholeness and goodness come, they are actually prayers, and the Lord, knowing our hearts, graciously honors them as such.

Inevitably, somewhere along this search I became eager to pray a healing prayer for others.

There was a young man of eighteen, son of old friends from China. I knew him when he was a little boy; now he was in a mental institution. Ted and I went on a drive to New England and met him and his parents. I was heartbroken at seeing the fear and confusion and agony of this gentle and good young man, home for the weekend. I felt sure that he could be healed by prayer, as I had been healed. On returning home, I even asked poor Hollis Colwell, whom I had already inflicted with several depressed ones, whether he could go up to Vermont and pray for Rhett. He very wisely replied that he could not possibly take on everybody in the world and that if I was so concerned about others, I should learn to pray for them myself.

"How can I get this power?" I asked. For I recognized that he had a power. When he prayed, things happened. He told me one's power depended largely on eating the right foods: "What a man eats, that he is."

I looked at him gravely and considered this. He and his wife, I knew, were much interested in diet, buying everything from health-food stores. I had already, at Hollis's suggestion, modified my menus in ways that were sensible and comprehensible to me. I had studied *The Living Way*, by Dr. Robert Bell, who had been healed of crippling arthritis through a combination of prayer and diet. To this day I follow the diet system that I learned from him and his disciple, Hollis: I eat about four parts of fresh fruits and vegetables to one of meat and starches, having fresh fruits and vegetables at every meal—and I do mean fresh. I learned by experimenting that there is a quality of health and strength in fresh orange juice, squeezed by myself and drunk immediately, that is not in frozen or canned orange juice. And the same in somewhat lesser degree holds true for all canned and frozen foods, and for vitamins and pills made of grass, alfalfa, and so forth. Although no doubt excellent, they do not take the place of fresh foods. Nor does this seem at all strange to me. If I were canned or frozen or compressed into a pill, I would lack a certain vital quality that I now have.

However, good though a healthful diet may be, I could not believe that this alone could be the source of power. Moreover, I believed that if one had enough spiritual power, one could survive, for instance, on locusts and wild honey, a diet on which John the Baptist apparently thrived, but which I would find definitely distasteful. I did not argue the point with Hollis, for to argue with anyone is to put yourself at a disadvantage. But I went home and considered it, for one does not have to believe all that anyone says, whether parent or teacher or friend. We ourselves guard the doors of our own minds, and we have the right to choose what ideas shall enter there.

As regards Hollis, there were four possibilities: first that he did not mean what he said, with which method of circumlocution I was completely familiar due to my Chinese life.

Second, that he was lying.

Third, that he was mistaken in analyzing the source of power.

Fourth, that he was right.

I decided that he was simply mistaken—that aside from diet there were other ways of receiving and passing on God's power. So with the Bible as my textbook, I set myself to learn these ways. As a man "thinketh in his heart, so is. he" (Prov. 23:7). There were still currents of thought, despairing, and discouraged, and at times resentful, that ran through my heart or subconscious mind even while the conscious mind endeavored to pray. How could I train the unconscious flow of thoughts and pictures to dwell on God and not on man, on the spiritual kingdom and not on the temporal world? Books were not enough. For my subconscious had for so many years been steeped in destructive thinking that it needed strong measures to fix it on Christ and thus on pictures of His love and peace and joy.

So for a year, I prayed whenever my mind was not actively engaged on something demanding its full attention, "Lord Jesus Christ, Son of God, fill me with Thy life." Years afterward, when I mentioned this to my friend Abbot Lazarus of the Russian Orthodox Church, he exclaimed, "Why, that is the Jesus prayer!" So it was, almost to a word. This one-pointed concentration upon Jesus Christ had been practiced for generations, long before I ever thought of it.

All this does not mean that I immediately became a calm and happy person. Not at all! My vigorous self-training was, at times, like a drowning man clinging to a rope. I did not dare to abandon it, lest I perish. For the desire to die was still often with me, though not with its former urgency. Indeed there were times after I was healed of the depression when I actually *felt* worse than before. I understood this. I was now more conscious, more able to feel either good or bad. And the problems of life were far from solved. In my experience, I find that God will heal us up to the point of our being able to think and to pray and to reason, and from then on, while He still helps us, we must nevertheless fight the battles of life ourselves.

I was becoming a new person: the original person whom I was born to be. And this was the exact opposite of the person whom I had tried for some six years to make myself—a perfect minister's wife, mother of children, and cook, and laundress, and house-keeper. Before marriage, I had tried to tell my husband what kind of person I was, but he listened indulgently, thinking as any man thinks that as soon as he had me in his bed and kitchen I would become the kind of wife that his mother was, and that all his sisters were, and his aunts and cousins and ancestresses unto the third and fourth generation.

Frankly, he was not pleased to see me becoming interested in prayer and healing. And when I began, at the request of young mothers in my Bible class (now grown to some twenty women, and meeting in the chapel), to pray with the laying on of hands for their children, Ted was much disturbed, and I do not blame him. He looked down the years and saw me dashing here and there at the request of needy people and learning all sorts of revolutionary ideas. How right he was!

Indeed, I found it best not to talk about my experiments in prayer, and for some four or five years they were hardly mentioned. However, Ted would come into the dining room to find me talking with some depressed woman while ironing his shirts and would look at me gloomily and stalk out again—and I would know that I was out of his favor. Or the leading vestryman's wife would trip into the rectory and find a living-room chair upside down and some delightful baby face peeking out from under it with dancing eyes, being a polar bear, and Ted would not appreciate the necessity of the living room being used at this time as the Arctic Circle. Nor did he appreciate the necessity of the living room upon a rainy day being used as a barnyard. I entered it once and found it so, with some mysterious play being enacted in which Teddy was a cow, and a very stout visiting damsel was a fairy.

Poor Ted used to say in his lighter moments that I would let the children play with anything I had except the Bible and my wedding ring, and this may have been so, for I felt that children were more important than possessions and that they grew by inventive and creative playing. Let me say, however, that they did not have this freedom in any other aspect of their lives. They had to obey, they had to eat properly, and speak to guests nicely, and say, "thank you," and "please." And when the game was over, they had to help me straighten up the living room or hang up the clothes and restore the house to a house rather than a circus, a stage, or a zoo.

Ted, however, noted quite truly that my mind was not always on my housework, nor was my time continually occupied with it. I grieved over this delinquency on my part and developed a terrible sense of uneasiness and guilt, for indeed I was an unworthy and inadequate wife.

In China, the wife of the minister was also a missionary, due to necessity. The work was great and the laborers were few, and furthermore, it was not proper or decent for a man to call on a sick woman or help at a difficult childbirth or teach a women's Bible class. In America, therefore, I innocently expected that I could and should help Ted in his work. People would sometimes say, "Why don't you come with Mr. Sanford when he makes a call?" And because I delighted in people and fun and did not wish to spend my whole time talking baby talk, I longed to accompany him on some of his calls. But he said that if I did so, that would make it a social occasion rather than a parish call, and if people had a burden on their hearts, they would not be likely to tell it to the minister if his wife was sitting by. This is absolutely true, and I am immensely grateful that I was taught to be a member of the congregation, nothing more, and not a little Mrs. Minister.

But I was lonely. In the evenings when the children were in bed, I longed for some human companionship. This also was good—it was very good! For at times, this very loneliness drove me out to make a call on someone ill or in despair; and what a joy it was to see the light in their eyes and the joy upon their faces when I appeared at the front door! How wonderfully the Lord planned all these things. If I had given birth to some six or eight children as I had at one time planned—or if I had been completely satisfied with my home and family—then the work for which I was sent into the world would never have been done. The Lord even arranged a built-in baby-sitter, for I rented a third-floor room to a schoolteacher, and when the children were a bit older I had only to call up the stairs and say, "Is it all right with you if I go out a little while?" and know that she would be there in case of phone call or emergency.

All this time I had not forgotten the young man Rhett who was the prod that urged me on in trying to pray for others. We had seen him again, briefly, on another trip, and he tugged at my heartstrings even more strongly than he had on the former occasion. I had never heard of the phenomenon called "transference," well-known to counselors, and could not imagine why I loved him so much: his beautiful, lost face, his torn and afflicted mind, which was yet gracious and good in spite of all its burdens. I would gladly have died to see him well! I talked to him of my own healing, and, indeed, dared to pray for him as Hollis had prayed for me, but I knew that he was not yet healed.

It did not occur to me to pray for him from a distance. But for his sake, I plodded along, trying to learn this healing that is both an art and a science and also a work of God. For the most part, I did my little prayers in secret. But the time came when I felt strongly urged to march myself to a hospital and offer to pray for a child desperately ill with a streptococcus infection. This was in the days before the miracle drugs, and the child had the infection in the heart, the kidneys, and the bloodstream. His parents belonged to the parish but did not know that God could still heal today just as He has always done. (Later on, I would not have needed to go and pray for this child, because my husband would have done so himself. He became a wonderful man of prayer, and, indeed, the best pastor I have ever known.)

I was terrified. I would as soon have walked up to the mouth of a cannon, or so I thought. But the urge of compassion was strong, for I knew the child would die unless *something* intervened. So I drove to the hospital, having at last with a terrible struggle learned to drive, and walked in. I spoke to the mother, who promptly dissolved in tears and would have let me do anything I wanted to do. She took me to the room of the little three-year-old and there left me alone. Strange to say, as soon as I sat down beside the bed and began to talk to the child, I had no fear at all! The venture seemed as simple and as natural as if I had been doing it all my life.

"Larry, when you go to kindergarten they teach you about Jesus, don't they?"

The child nodded, his big blue eyes very solemn.

"Did they ever give you a picture of Jesus?"

He nodded again, his face brightening a bit. (Nowadays they would probably give the child a picture of a squirrel instead. It does not have the same effect.)

"Well, you remember, when people were sick, Jesus put His hand on them and prayed for them to get well, and they did, didn't they?"

This time Larry said, "Yes," in a small whisper.

"He told us we were to do the same thing," I said. "Now I'm not as big as Jesus, and I'm just starting to do this, but He *said* to; so shall we try? He said He'd be there to help us, you know, even though we don't see Him."

The child nodded, completely understanding. " 'Cause He's 'visible," he said, meaning "invisible."

I laid my hands on the region of the heart and simply asked Jesus to make him well, and then I thanked Jesus because I knew He was doing it. The next day the child's bloodstream and heart were free of infection. The kidneys took one more day. But in three days he was at home, completely recovered.

The parents never mentioned the matter to me. I was told by another that they were confused by the whole thing. They wondered whether this was quite "sound"; moreover, if it really were true, then what should one think about death? But at any rate, the child was well.

Surely, I thought, if God through my inadequate channel could do something as great as that—actually snatch a little child out of the jaws of death—surely He could heal a young man in mental distress. Therefore I planned my campaign with care, as we were again to journey to Vermont and I would thus have a chance to implement it. I had seen slight signs of enlivenment when I had talked to Rhett the previous summer—probably merely that he enjoyed my interest in him. Therefore, I concluded that more explanation of God's power and instruction in the prayer of faith, coupled with more hopeful living conditions and, of course, my own prayers for him would start the boy on the way to health.

Hitherto he had been intermittently with his parents and in the mental institution.

I even thought of his living in our rectory, but on that point Ted was quite firm. His home was sacrosanct. His children were his first responsibility, and the home must be kept free for their enjoyment and development. And he was quite right.

So with more zeal than discretion, I found through kind friends a good place for him to live and a bit of work that I thought would be perfect, tending flowers and plants in a friendly atmosphere. And Rhett came to Moorestown.

It did not work out. He became increasingly tense and at last went quite off his head and had to be taken back to the hospital.

Why?

One reason was that I chose too difficult a prayer objective. Yet I was so sure that God wanted me to do this! As a matter of fact, I was quite angry with God for some three months and would make no other attempt at praying the prayer of faith.

"You fooled me," I would mutter to the Almighty, who, fortunately, is big enough to take our occasional wrath at Him.

Finally, however, there came a day when hearing that a friend was suffering greatly with shingles, I thought, "Poor old Adele, I suppose I really ought to go and pray for her." And so I went, with no feeling of love and joy but impelled only by duty. In three days Adele was completely well.

Why did not my love for Rhett act as a healing agent? And I had no love really for Adele.

"Love heals," people say. I do not find that necessarily so. God's love heals, yes. But our own love, if too emotional, may even stand in the way of that great flow of God's love which is an energy rather than an emotion. What do we do then when one of our own is dangerously ill and we are torn apart with love and fear? We can, if possible, get someone else to help us pray for them—someone farther removed from their trouble. Or if that cannot be done, and it is an emergency situation, we can strive to rise high enough on faith to overcome the terrible fear that goes with human love. I remember saying to myself once in a time of dire family emergency, "I am not going to be a human mother at this time! I am going to pray only as a spiritual being!" And somehow, emotion got out of the way, and my child was healed immediately of a very high fever which could have been infantile paralysis, then epidemic near us.

Another lesson learned from this was the value of obedience. Some "psychologically oriented" people nowadays scorn the doing of something because one feels that one ought to do it. Well, praise God, I do not have to be psychologically oriented, but only Jesus oriented, and when He wants me to do something, I *want* to do it for His sake. I cannot think of anything more boring than to take what one considers the easy way, doing only what the human or physical part of us wants to do at all times.

But what then about Rhett? Gradually it came to me that I had not read God's first guidance quite clearly. He was saying, "See this boy Rhett. I want you to learn how to help people like him so that they will not have to go to mental institutions."

This I have done. Hundreds. Perhaps thousands.

A year or so later when we were in New England, I was in a mood of discouragement. "What am I doing, after all," I thought, "except the kind of thing a minister does (for Ted by this time was becoming quite strong in healing prayer), and a minister gets paid for it and I don't. And it takes so much time that I can't write anymore." And I was minded to stop.

One day Ted said, "Let's go to the hospital and see Rhett."

So I went in dread and the dread was well-founded. For there was Rhett, quiet and subdued but quite removed from reality. Moreover, there were others, scores of them—hundreds of them. So I made a final decision: "As long as there are people in the world in this darkness, this horror of great darkness, I *can't* stop."

8.

"BLESSED are they which are persecuted for righteousness' sake," Jesus said, "for theirs is the kingdom of heaven" (Matt. 5:10). That is, I take it, if they keep on seeking the kingdom and do not give up the fight. For there *is* a fight! The enemy attacks from within and from without. So it was in my case.

As I was beginning to recover from the shock of failure concerning Rhett, I failed again, and this also from my own lack of judgment. Lest the reader become discouraged, however, let me say now that with the single exception of Rhett, everyone for whom I prayed during the first three or four years of my healing adventure made a recovery.

The reason is that during these unknown years I was free to go where the Lord wanted me to go. He did not need to overwhelm me with too great a flow of love or, as psychologists call it, "transference" in order to direct me. Indeed, having been bitten once, I fought shy of too much emotional involvement. I learned to put Christ between me and the person for whom I was praying, to send my love to Christ and let Him do with it what He would. Thus people felt from me or through me, power rather than affection, and often they knew and said that it was the power of Christ's love. I myself was considered to be rather cold.

"If only Agnes had love," someone said, "she would be wonderful . . ." I can see, looking back, that my experience with Rhett saved me from worse trouble in the years to come, for I was in those days rather good-looking and exceedingly emotional by nature. If I had not learned to surround myself with a strong wall of protection, agapé might very easily have turned into eros. I might have felt that God guided me to leave my husband and children and canter off with somebody else, the better to have "freedom" to do God's work.

Not long after this, in spite of all careful "planning," I became pregnant, and it seemed to me that this happened too soon. I was afraid that the physical discomfort of pregnancy would cause me to lose my new life in the Spirit. How could I say, "I am God's child and therefore I walk in His strength and life and light," while I walked in misery from nausea? So I made up my mind that I would not have morning sickness or any kind of weakness, pregnant or not. I forced myself to take brisk walks and in every way to act alert and alive and would not let my body succumb to its usual ways of adjusting itself to the new life inside.

God forgive me, I did not realize what I was doing. Apparently nature knows what it is about in its purging and changing of the bodily energies, and when I refused these changes, something went wrong with the bodily energy and I became autointoxicated, self-poisoned. This showed itself in a bit of fever and general disease. But more important than this, it affected my mind and thinking and feeling. So it came to pass that I lost this baby about the middle of the third month because I had refused to let nature have its way with me.

At the time I thought little of this. I was relieved, when the pregnancy ceased, to be free again to feel and think like myself. But strangely, while the deep and bitter hurt of losing Rhett was in due time completely healed, so that now I only thank God for the lessons I learned in that misadventure, the sorrow of losing this child has never completely left me. I feel that I was meant to bring forth this child—that this one might have done more for God's kingdom than I have ever done—and that I lost this creative opportunity because I prayed in the wrong pattern. I should have blessed the tiny life, even in the beginning, and prayed for the coming infant, being completely willing to endure the discomforts of carrying it. I should have trusted God and nature to know the needs of the body and should not have dictated to nature that I would not feel this or that symptom. This was my second mistake in trying to walk the paths of faith.

Some of you may think, "But why didn't God just take care of the matter regardless of the way in which you prayed?" I don't know. Sometimes it seems that He does honor the basic intention of a prayer even when its definite petitions are not in line with His laws. But sometimes He does not, having given to us minds that we may use them and having entrusted us with the power of choice. Many of us wish that He had not given to us this terrible responsibility. But He has: we cannot help it. It is His intention that we shall become the sons of God, the children of God, the administrators upon earth of His heavenly power.

Therefore, we have to learn, as anyone who is going to help his father in managing a business has to learn, the laws of that business.

I learned to pray for my real desire: to fix my attention on the wholeness that I wanted for myself or for someone else, and not to refuse any temporary symptoms that God through nature might use in order to bring about that wholeness. I learned to say, "This pain (or that discomfort) is just God's power working in me to- ward health and life, and as soon as it has accomplished what the body is trying to do, it will go away." I learned also to pass on this attitude toward pain or discomfort to other people for whom I prayed. If someone would call me up and say, "Since you prayed for my knee it hurts more than ever! It's terrible!" I would reply, "Don't lose your nerve. This pain is only the body calling together all its energies in order to heal. Bless it and give thanks for it, and it will pass." And so it would. And if the person said, "Oh, do come again and pray for the pain to go away," I would reply, "Heavens no! That's the last thing you need at this moment! Give the body time to carry out the assignment God has given it, and do not disturb it until the effect of this prayer has worn off! Then, if needed, we will pray again."

But usually it was not needed.

The crisis of frustrated pregnancy passed, as all things do in time. Ted and I engaged our dear old friend Tacey Magee to stay with the children while we took rooms in a boardinghouse at Beach Haven, New Jersey, for a week, that I might recover my strength. Creativity, being balked in one area, flowed furiously in another. I wrote two stories and three poems in that week and I returned home a new woman, very grateful for Ted's kindness and thoughtfulness for me. Ted never really cared for the ocean, yet he himself planned this trip and carried it through with enthusiasm. There is no explaining the effect the ocean has always had upon my heart or unconscious self. Does my spirit remember? Was I really there in God when the seas separated themselves from the land and went into their own place according to the old story of Genesis, the most exciting passage of literature in the whole world? I do not know. But something deep within me awakes and comes to life when I wade into cold seas—something indescribable and unique, for I simply cannot stir up that evanescent whirl of new life except by going down again to the lonely sea.

In fact, unless I submerge myself from time to time in nature, the sea first of all, but also the mountains soaring up inscrutable, unchangeable yet ever-changing, or even the dirt, full of life, mothering green plants of every sort—unless I have this refreshment, this recharging with life—the current of life flowing through spirit and mind wrings me dry, and the heart is starved, and the body falters. And as I see others who pray and strive but who do not see God's face in sun and wind and sea and dirt, I perceive in them a withering process.

I returned home recharged with life and poured it out more and more to people in distress. Some of them forgot my injunction to silence and told of it, even to Ted. And he began to believe. The first I knew of this was his words to another, quoted to me with some laughter: "I don't know what this is my wife does, but you'd better go to her." We never worked together for the same person, and it was good that we did not, for first, we were too different in nature and thinking, and second, we were able to help twice as many people by working alone. As time went on, Ted became more and more effective in counseling and prayer for his own people, and the time came when I never worked with his parishioners unless he sent them to me.

"She's begun calling me her Rock of Gibraltar," he panted one day, rushing over to the house from an interview with a woman parishioner, his eyes starting from his head. "You'd better take over."

Many wonderful healings took place during this time. Those that delighted me most were healings through the prayers of my Bible-class members. I have believed from the beginning that all healing comes from God and that anyone who is willing to be a channel and tries to fulfill the conditions, hungering and thirsting for righteousness even though not always attaining it, can pray the prayer of faith and see miracles of healing. A young mother called one day and asked me to come and pray for Jimmie, quite sick with pneumonia.

"Why don't *you* do it, Peggy?" I replied. "Just put your hands on his chest and ask the power of God through Jesus Christ to come in and heal him; I'll pray with you from a distance." She did so, and the little boy was quite well in the morning. Several days later he pointed out a lifelong condition to his mother and said, "Let's ask Jesus to make that well, too." So they did, mother and child together, and that also was healed.

On the other hand, there were some mothers who leaned on me at all times and called me continually. This was terrible, because in order to save money, Ted and I had the same telephone; and while listening to their tale of woe, I could hear his office phone clicking on and off and could feel his rising tide of irritation. Moreover, another real trouble emerged and that was that neither these inveterate demanders nor any others who called upon me saw any necessity of helping me out financially. I really needed money. For I simply could not adequately take care of home and family and also be called hither and yon. There was an emotional need, also, for the flow of God's power demands a return of gratitude, and when that does not come, the effort of pouring out love becomes very wearing.

I remember the first time I realized this. I had been working in prayer for many months for a woman depressed as I had been, and the improvement was very slow. Finally I asked God *why?* And the answer that came to me was that His healing love is a *flow*, and she was blocking the flow because she never felt or showed any gratitude.

I still do not know the answer to this problem. Some said to me, "Why don't you go professional? You know, have a card printed calling yourself a counselor or a therapist or something and charge for these visits?" That I could not do, for then I would run into the danger of helping people in hopes of recompense. Moreover, my greatest joy was to help those who could not afford to help me—just as my greatest temptation to wrath was in helping those who could have eased my way and never thought of it.

In those days my Bible class had a lending library. One wealthy woman owed a fine of a dime and gave me a quarter, telling me graciously to keep the change. Another wealthy woman called on me, not only to pray for her family at various times, but also to arrange the flowers for her son's wedding, saying that she knew I liked to do such things. It saved her considerable money. She gave me, it being during wartime when sugar was scarce, three tablespoons of sugar in an envelope.

While I was struggling with this problem and was strongly tempted to give up the whole idea of healing, my brother H.M. dropped in to visit on his travels for the national Coast and Geodetic Survey, and I talked to him about my financial problems.

"Why don't you ask God for the money you need?" he said.

Now I had been brought up with the idea that money is filthy lucre and that to pray for money would be worshiping mammon. In fact, I had a poverty complex, and this very thing could have been one reason for the lack of any material flow of gratitude toward me. Seeing my total lack of faith at the idea of praying for money, my brother instructed me upon the subject.

Within three weeks, my feeling about money had entirely changed. Nothing had happened on the outside, but within me I *knew* that the cash I needed to set me more free to do God's work was coming to me. It began to come, not in any miraculous way, but simply through the inner change. Once the literature department of the Woman's Club called up and asked me to give a talk on the English poets of the nineteenth century. And I found myself saying without any premeditation, "No, I cannot give free talks anymore. I find that my time is too much in demand for that."

"Oh, but we will be glad to pay you!" the lady cried, and forthwith did so, as they would have expected to pay any other lecturer. And to my great surprise, I found that this change of attitude on my part caused people to like and respect me *more*, not less. My husband's salary meanwhile remained what it had been when he was called to Moorestown: $3,000 a year, in addition to rectory and car.

Shortly after this, the Lord opened another way for the flow of His supply. I was invited to teach a course in healing at an adult education program at the Friends' School. This greatly delighted me, for I loved teaching. The bell would ring and I would go into my classroom just as in the days of old. Someone told a publisher about these lectures, and Eugene Exman of Harpers wrote to me and asked me to write a book for his publishing company. Thus I came to produce *The Healing Light,* and quite a job it was, for my gift of writing had been largely starved out of me by the too-demanding work of healing. It is a natural law that a talent neglected tends to die. "Every branch in me that beareth not fruit, he taketh away . . ." (John 15:2).

I owe much gratitude to a friend, Agnes Budd, a member of the Society of Friends and one excelling in the art of criticism. Once a week I would engage my friend Elizabeth to take care of the family, and I would go to the house of the other Agnes and write and rewrite in the light of her literary criticism. At length the book was ready, and I sent it off, only to have it return again like a homing pigeon. It was too forthright, said Harpers. What if people tried those ways of prayer and they did not work?

"They will work," I replied, being less cognizant then than now of the lions in the path that occasionally prevent God's will from being done.

"Why not write something simply *inspirational?*" they asked. No, I would not, having no interest whatsoever in merely inspirational writing. "If this thing is true, it's *got* to work," I said grimly.

Other publishers, however, tended to agree with Harpers, and after a number of rejections, the manuscript sat dismally in my bureau drawer for two years. And I thought sadly that it evidently was the Lord's will that I give up forever my lifelong dream of being a writer, and that I spend my time running around praying for those who would not or could not pray for themselves. But this was not the Lord's will. The failure of a cherished dream is not always the Lord's will—in fact, I may say that it never is, provided the dream came from Him! It is the failure of people to see His will and to do it!

God found a way to bring His will to pass by sending Dr. John Gaynor Banks to lecture in Moorestown and to stay with me. We talked until far into the night, and finally he said, "You should write these ideas into a book."

"I have," I replied, "but no one will publish it."

"Give it to me," he said. "I will print some excerpts from it in my magazine (*Sharing*), and that may open the way for its being published."

And I did, and it did, for Dr. Glenn Clark read the excerpts and sent for the manuscript. Upon reading it he remarked, "This is the best book on healing ever written. It is much better than any of mine, and I am going to see to it that it is published even if I have to publish it myself." He wrote a foreword for the book and sent it again to his own publisher, Harpers, hoping that his name on it would give it the needed push. But it did not, and so, true to his word, he published it himself. The Macalester Park Publishing Company had never brought forth a book before, only Dr. Clark's pamphlets and literature regarding his Camps Farthest Out. The book was, therefore, never publicized in the usual way, for its publisher is not on the jobbers' lists. It sold slowly at first, but it has sold unwaveringly for over twenty-five years, and has certainly become a best seller.

This book, I thought rather sadly, would mark the beginning and the end of my writing for publication. But for me to be really myself—my complete self—every capacity in me had to be used. Every flow of creativity that God had given me must find its channel.

I am not a single-tracker. This has at times disturbed me, but I have had to accept the fact that my nature is diversified. It can be unified only by giving all its parts to God, that He may work through them according to His own design for me, but it cannot be unified by lopping off every other talent and interest except that of prayer. I have tried it, and it does not work. I become dull, dried up, and my prayer power diminishes.

How many of me are there? First, the one who prays. Second, the writer. Third, the actress. Fourth, the painter. And all of these abide in and work through a human wife and mother whose dominant concern is her husband and children.

Let's face it. God has given me a number of talents. Why? I don't know. Ask Him! He does what He pleases, serenely undisturbed by human prattle about equality. Jesus said this specifically and definitely: "And unto one he gave five talents, to another two, and to another one; to every man according to his several ability" (Matt. 25:15).

"But that is not fair!" some people say. God is apparently

blandly unconcerned about being fair. Nor is He interested in making everybody after such a fashion that all they want to do is pray. In fact, as someone said, "God is not primarily interested in religion. He is primarily interested in creation." Study that with the help of the Bible and of the dictionary and you will see that it is true.

I have found it impractical to fuse the one who teaches and practices healing, the one who creates books, the one who creates plays, and the one who creates pictures into one person and to do all four things at the same time. These four parts of my complex personality have to take turns living. The two dominant ones are the teacher-healer and the teacher-writer. When I am writing a book, whether fiction or nonfiction (in other words, whether I am teaching through exposition or through parable), I must live in that book. Work with my hands is helpful, for while I am pulling up weeds or washing dishes, my subconscious is free to brood upon the book. But the intense activity of holding a teaching-healing mission or throwing my whole soul into a painting or into a play does not work well with writing. I cannot do lecturing or writing unless every energy of mind and spirit is involved in it. Therefore I try to keep about six months a year free from missions in order to write.

As for the painter and the actress, these are nonprofessional activities that pop into my life from time to time and give me great joy and release. They are for fun. I cannot relax and enjoy myself by merely being inactive. I am too easily bored. I can take only a very small amount of simply chattering or lounging. To chat is hard work, to listen to chatter is harder, and to lounge on sand or in sun is insupportable! So apparently I need for refreshment and recreation a fun-activity, and how wonderful the Lord is that He provides this also! Indeed, if we will take note of our own natures and honor them, not being afraid to have hobbies, even golf or fishing, wood carving or flower arranging, we will see that He takes care of *all* our needs.

In Moorestown, He took care of a very special need in a somewhat peculiar manner, as He so often does.

My parents had come "home" on furlough and to spend some time with me, my father happily typing away at the vast and fascinating correspondence with which he felt the pulse of the world, my mother enjoying the family and earnestly endeavoring to lead them into the paths of truth. ("Grandmother's been telling me about gambling," said Tookie delightedly one day, "so I'm going to take my marbles down to the school and *gamble*.") With them came my brother Hugh, now high-school age. It seemed expedient to all of us that he should live with me and attend the Moorestown high school, a very fine school directed by Miss Mary Roberts, a wonderful Quaker lady or "Friend." Indeed, she was a friend to my son and to uncounted numbers of children.

I remember with tenderness and a bit of amusement this visit of my parents. Having finally learned to drive that violent American fire-carriage, the automobile, I once drove my father and mother to 30th Street station in Philadelphia, where Dada was to take a train. The station was not quite completed at that time, and the entrance and exit amid mountains of concrete were particularly confusing. I entered an exit. Up roared a policeman, a vast red-faced man. In the style of the City of Brotherly Love in those days he opened his mouth and began a furious tirade. My mother was a tiny lady, weighing possibly ninety pounds wringing wet. She held up one hand in a gesture of queenly dignity.

"My good man," said she, quietly but firmly, "my daughter is *here*. How she got here, I do not know, but she is here. Now if you have any intelligence whatsoever, you will simply tell her quietly and calmly how to get out."

The policeman gasped, gulped, and told me. Thus she routed the Philadelphia police. Whereupon Mother folded her gloved hands upon her black silk lap and serenely enjoyed the scenery, though not without an occasional caustic comment upon the same. Her chief complaint about the United States was that it was too quiet. There was no talking in the streets, no laughter, no cheerful tramp-tramp of human footsteps, only useless mechanical noise.

My parents returned to China. I saw them off at the station, looking wistfully after the departing train and not knowing that I would never see my father again.

Hugh remained and took his gentle place in the family as though he were an older son. (One day Elizabeth saw me and

Mother descend from the Philadelphia bus at the corner by the church. "Mr. Hugh," she said, "your mother and grandmother's coming back.")

My brother Hugh is a very unusual person. He is in the world —vaguely—but not of it, his mind being always preoccupied with music (at which he was a near genius), with ships (which he adores), and with the mystical aspects of religion. He was at that time caught and bound in the forms of religion, yet feeling after it in his spirit with a desperate longing. He went through high school with no difficulty, yet seemed hardly aware of it, most of his consciousness being elsewhere. Being totally uninterested in sports or in any standard type of amusement or fun, he made only one friend. This was a tall and excitable youth by the name of Clyde, rejoicing in a nature a shade more eccentric than my brother's. He affected a vast square of purple velvet, which he wore as a cape, and in this he would come bounding down Main Street, explode into the rectory, and do interpretative dances over the furniture while Hugh laughingly improvised upon the piano.

Clyde was a dramatic near genius as Hugh was a musical one. In spite of all their foolishness, these two youths set a match to my own smoldering bit of dramatic flair. Up to this time it had faltered pedestrianly along in the wake of a very tame dramatic society which put on about one play a year in the community house. I attended tryouts, but as I had not fully emerged from my stultifying attempt at being an American (even a Yankee, forsooth), an Episcopalian, and a minister's wife, I did not shine in these readings. If I was given a part in a play, my lines consisted mainly of such terse remarks as, "Dinner is served, madam."

Apparently it took something as crazy as Hugh and Clyde to shake me loose from this. Between us, we got up the most ridiculous stunts and parodies, two of which, mock grand operas entitled *Letherwriggle* and *Lohegrins*, were put on in the parish house to the somewhat stunned delight of congregation and friends. Hugh sat at the piano beaming with mirth and cheerfully transposing songs from various operas into the same key, and as he played, my actors and choruses gave tongue in imitation foreign languages, uttering whatever sounds came to their minds. The audience chortled with mirth, as a boat made of a clothes basket went down in a sea of small boys lying under an old green stage curtain, moving arms and legs to simulate waves.

Ted, meanwhile, sat with a somewhat unwilling grin on his handsome face, for all this was quite out of character for the woman whom he conceived his wife to be. Ted himself was extremely witty, but my somewhat raucous wit did not please him. Usually, therefore, I tried to maintain the serene dignity of his mother, who laughed dutifully at the jokes of her husband and her five tall sons but never told jokes herself, although from the knowing twinkle in her eyes, I think that she could have told them if she had so desired.

So all the foolishness with Hugh and Clyde released in me a pent-up dramatic urge. However, learning stagecraft from Clyde, I was asked to direct plays more often than to act in them, and all this was a peripheral activity that took up only a small portion of my time. But what a tremendously exciting and deeply gratifying portion!

The plays in which I took part were, for the most part, innocent comedies or melodrama. Once the Woman's Club asked me to produce a Christmas play for their December meeting. So I wrote *Mary of Nazareth*, a play taking about fifty minutes and fitting into no standard category. It is a blank-verse, realistic study of the time before the birth of Christ: of Mary's wonderings and misgivings and obedience, and of the doubts and questions of her young husband. The theme being of a delicate nature, the play was acted in a very stylized manner, purposely underacted rather than overacted, by four women and a company of angels appearing dimly at times through a gauze curtain. They stood on a tier of steps against the bare wall of the gymnasium, with arms upraised, their cheesecloth draperies falling back from them. On either side of this tableau were thousand-watt floodlights set upon the floor, covered with midnight blue gelatin sheets and controlled by a rheostat. These cast the angels' shadows back upon the wall where they interlaced, growing dimmer and dimmer until it seemed that the whole sky was filled with angels. When the play was over, the audience sat in absolute silence for five minutes before beginning to clap—the only time I have seen an audience so overwhelmed.

Out of this stage work grew the Christmas midnight service,

held for fifteen years at Trinity Church in Moorestown. It grew gradually. At first Ted suggested that I train three of his men singers as the Three Wise Men, coming up the aisle and offering gifts at the manger of the Christ Child. Bit by bit, we added to this service, until at last it took fifty minutes and involved some seventy singers. Before many Christmases, the church became so crowded that Ted put on a carol service for the pageant only, followed an hour later by the Midnight Eucharist in which the carol service was used as the introit. Ted was a perfectionist, and every service was done with a dignity and beauty that comes not only from inspiration but from careful planning.

Preparations for the service began, more or less, at seven-thirty on Christmas Eve though a few participants would probably arrive sooner and join the family in a supper at the rectory. Before finishing our meal, we would see the makeup men from Van Horn's Theatrical Company in Philadelphia walk past our dining-room windows, makeup kits in their hands. I would dash over to the parish house where my own makeup was already spread out on a table, and the three of us would begin. We did not do a regular theatrical makeup; nothing, in fact, except the darkening of the skin, and the affixing of beards and moustaches. These were fashioned of crêpe hair, fastened to the face by spirit gum and trimmed afterward as a barber would trim them.

Then we costumed these ordinary businessmen, transforming them into shepherds and kings of the Orient. We had made the shepherds' costumes of old curtains and dyed sheets, and the headdresses of bits of striped material. The shepherds' costumes were in the earth colors: shades of brown and tan, dull green and faded maroon. The kings were gorgeously appareled in crimson and purple and gold, real costumes from the East. Joseph, also, was in earth colors and Mary in blue and white.

There were angels appearing from behind the huge cedar trees that decorated the chancel, the light dimmed upon them gradually so that they appeared to materialize—to float rather than to walk—toward the altar rail and up upon pedestals that lifted them above it. I designed their robes from Fra Angelico angels and bought the material at a silk store that was selling out: metal cloth of blue and purple, lavender and green, shot through with gold or silver. The wings were made at Van Horn's, tall wings, stretching from knee to a foot above the head. These wings came to me as bare frames of cloth and heavy wiring, and I covered them with stiff shining silk in shades of blue and purple, lavender and green. The colors were graduated and interwoven. The angel in blue, for instance, had wings that began with green and went through every shade of blue to purple. The whole effect was iridescent, unreal, and heavenly! If this play were put on today, I would have had young men for angels but in those days men did not wear long hair, so I compromised with tall young women with hair of golden tints.

Toward the end of our stay in Moorestown we added to this cast a few bedraggled captive Israelites who trudged down the church aisle roped together, led by Babylonian soldiers, singing a mournful dirge. This was followed by Isaiah's prophecy from the *Messiah*, sung offstage. The captives then lifted up their heads and walked away into the chancel. On the singing of "The First Noel" by the choir (seated in the back of the church) and the congregation, the shepherds seeing the star called by gestures to other shepherds who ran up to the chancel and took their places on platforms below the pulpit.

Then came "While Shepherds Watched Their Flocks by Night," sung by choir and congregation, during which the angels appeared, miraculously floating down from heaven, as some thought, mounted the steps, and raised their golden trumpets, made of pasteboard and gilt paper. Every position that the angels took was carefully trained: trumpets up, trumpets down, standing, kneeling; as indeed every position taken by kings or shepherds was rehearsed and carefully balanced as in a painting.

Stylized as all this was, it looked alive and real, and the reason was that every rehearsal was begun with prayer and conducted as a service of devotion. The singers were given a prayer-program as well as a program of singing and procession. At every point in the service, they were instructed in what to pray for: the coming of the Savior, the awakening of the church, the ending of war, the establishment of the Kingdom, and so forth. It is not only the voice that projects. The mind also projects. The whole church was filled with an emanation, a radiation, of a spiritual power. No wonder people were moved to tears. No wonder people were touched and healed and even converted in and through this service! It spoke

not to the conscious mind alone, but also to the deep unconscious.

The shepherds then went down the side aisle singing, led by a
wonderful tenor whom I would not have known except for my lit-
tle-theater work. During a blackout, the screen was removed from
the platform below the reading desk and there stood Joseph, with
Mary seated beside him, looking into the manger: and from the
manger a light shining—the only light in the church. On their
knees in the dark, the people sang "Away in a Manger" and other
Christmas lullabies until the light dimmed on again and the shepherds walked down the center aisle singing, "Oh Come All Ye
Faithful," bowed before the manger, and grouped themselves
again upon the platform.

There entered then the three kings, magnificent, joyous, and
triumphant. All of the kings had glorious voices, and each processed alone up the aisle, singing a different verse of "We Three
Kings of Orient Are," as the congregation joined in the chorus
and in the last verse. The kings left their gifts before the manger
and stood on the chancel steps while everyone together sang with
great vigor, "Shout the Glad Tidings."

At this point the angels joined in the singing: not the four visible angels standing on their pedestals and looking up as did shepherds and kings, but unseen angels (or so the congregation
thought) heard from the heavens. This effect was produced by a
Victrola in the sacristy where a devoted vestryman played Gou-
nod's *Sanctus*, beginning very softly with "Holy, Holy, Lord God
Almighty," working up to a tremendous crescendo and fading
away again, so that no one could tell of a certainty when the faraway music began and when it ended. During this, many of the
shepherds and kings dropped on their knees and so did the congregation, quite spontaneously. Finally the shepherds bowed at the
manger one by one and went out on "Shepherds in the Fields
Abiding." The kings departed on the verse, "Sages Leave Your
Contemplation." Finally, as the congregation sang, "Angels from
the Realms of Glory," the four angels came down from their pedestals and grouped themselves about the manger. All the lights
were dimmed down until there remained only the glow from
within the manger lighting Mary's gentle face and Joseph's wistfulness and the shining angels, their robes glimmering in the half-

light. The congregation then sang "Silent Night" upon their knees. At the amen, the manger light was dimmed off, and in complete blackness Mary and Joseph descended, the angels slipped out behind them, and four of Ted's young men whisked away the pedestals and the steps leading to them.

On came the lights again. At the nine-thirty service Ted and the choir processed, singing, into the chancel, and the service was concluded with prayer. At the eleven-thirty service, this being in the place of the Gospel, the Communion service went upon its stately way.

Between the two services, the seventy or so singers repaired to the parish house where a group of women served sandwiches and cocoa and I darted about with the bottle of spirit gum, straightening moustaches and reinforcing sagging beards. The men from Van Horn's could have taken their checks and gone home long ago. But they stayed through both services and went forth at last with the light of another world upon their faces, as did many another person coming to this service from near and far.

The service ended at about one o'clock, and a group of men cleared the church for the eight o'clock Communion service on Christmas morning.

Meanwhile, parish house and even rectory were invaded by kings and shepherds removing beards and moustaches, and wiping away the greasepaint and powder that had darkened their faces as they would have been darkened under the Eastern sun in faraway Palestine. Even if I wended my way to the rectory at 2:00 A.M. with some vague thought of going to bed, I would as likely as not find a Wise Man from the East emerging from my bathroom. (How I loved having a rectory that was part of the church complex, so that Ted's life and mine and even those of the children were closely interwoven with the life of the church.)

None of us slept till Christmas morning. The young people were apt to wander down the street singing Christmas carols, being too full of joy to go to bed. Ted had to rise for early church, and I would have breakfast ready when he returned. Then I would prepare Christmas dinner and go to the eleven o'clock church for my own Communion, being somewhat too involved and too covered with greasepaint and hair to attend at midnight. On returning, I dished up dinner, sometimes, praise God, with my beaming

Elizabeth to help. Then I took a much-needed nap while the children put up and trimmed the tree. Finally, just as daylight was dimming, and the inner lights of the house and of the heart were lit again, we had our family Christmas.

I am writing this on the day after Christmas. Yesterday my daughter asked me, "Mother, did we mind having our own Christmas in the late afternoon? We loved it, didn't we?"

"Yes, you loved it," I said, for they did.

"Other kids don't know what to do Christmas afternoon," my children said. "And we're just beginning to open our presents. It's great!"

"There is only one trouble about that Moorestown Christmas," my children still say wistfully from time to time. "We will never have that kind of a Christmas again."

But, please God, as the light of the Holy Spirit brightens upon the horizon of mankind and of the church, they will yet see Christmases more glorious than those. Maybe the angels will really sing from the high heavens and be heard again by faithful men.

Maybe they will.

9.

$\mathcal{S}$UMMERS were a problem during the first years in Moorestown. The weather was hot and humid, and toward August the stone house had become saturated with heat, which it retained day and night. The children did not want to go to summer camps even if we could have afforded to send them. They preferred the unorganized creativity of the games and projects that they themselves devised at home.

"Did you tell those children they could take off all their clothes," demanded dark Ellen one day during an interregnum of Elizabeth, "and tie bathtowels around their middles and stick kitchen knives in them and swing offen that there tree?"

"Well, no," I said feebly, "not exactly . . ." For while failing to foresee the substitution of loincloths for shorts, I had offered no opposition to the fascinating game of Tarzan, and all summer long the small backyard echoed to the hoarse bellowing of Johnny Weissmuller.

On one occasion I did suffer a slight shock on beholding a very plump little girl, apparently quite naked, tied to a tree, while Teddy and Tookie leaped in war dance about her, being cannibals preparing for lunch. The accusation of indecent exposure, however, was indignantly denied, and it was demonstrated that the damsel was duly clad in shorts invisible beneath four coils of rope.

On sunny days when the parish car was available, I would fill it with children and drive to a nearby swimming hole, or even down to the Atlantic Ocean at Beach Haven, accompanied to the great delight of everyone by "Aunt Sara." My unmarried sister Sara was a schoolteacher and she spent her vacations with us until she entered nurse's training at the age of twenty-nine. (This work had always been her heart's desire, but it was frowned upon by the family.) She became night supervisor in the University of Pennsylvania hospital, and then Directress of Nurses' Education, which position she held until her marriage.

Three summers during this fourteen-year period, Ted exchanged pulpits for a month with a minister of a seaside resort church, and so the whole family spent a blissful month on the Jersey coast.

To this day the rolling breakers of the great sea exhilarate me in a way beyond any describing, touching apparently a deep area in the soul that nothing else can reach. But Ted longed for his own lost hills of New England, and the ocean spoke to him not at all.

We could not afford a vacation in New England. One summer, however, a parishioner told us of some small and very rough cabins on a lake in Maine, available for fifty dollars a month. Ted at that time needed a vacation very badly, being worn down by the continually increasing burdens of a congregation that turned to him for help in every crisis. Remembering my brother's instructions concerning prayer for money, I prayed for fifty dollars. (In spite of all that H.M. said, I still would not have considered it right to pray for more than an absolute need.) In two days I received an offer to set up and conduct a daily vacation Bible school under the Council of Churches for a period of three weeks—for the total sum of fifty dollars. My impulse was to decline this, feeling that such a venture was beyond my abilities. My heart quailed at the thought of managing a crowd of unruly children.

"You'd better not do it," said Ted. "That's not your line at all."

"I know," I replied. "But I asked for fifty dollars, and here's a chance to earn it. And I can do anything I really want to do. ("God helping me," I thought, but did not say it aloud. In those days one did not lightly give tongue to the name of God.)

"I reckon you can, at that," said Ted, looking at me with a kind of quizzical respect.

So I did, engaging a red-haired teacher with a commanding mien to be my assistant. We planned to keep the children so interested that they would not have time to get into mischief. My assistant was in charge of all manner of work projects and recreation, and I taught the laws of prayer and faith, as later written down in *Let's Believe.* The school was a roaring success, and the children's varied prayer projects must have moved the angels to laughter and to tears. My own son Jack's first project was a financial one. He and a young friend, Ike, had become overstimulated by the spectacle of an abandoned greenhouse, with the result that they mowed lawns all summer in order to pay for the broken panes of glass.

Jack went home from Bible school one day, and his father took some change from his pocket and said sternly, "Jack, you have paid back all that money except twenty-eight cents. Now I will give you this last twenty-eight cents, and don't let me hear of you ever doing such a thing as that again."

"Hot dog," remarked Jack succinctly. "I prayed for that!"

The Bible school ended with a triumphant parents' day, marred only slightly by one small incident.

"Jimmy fell in the goldfish pond!" cried Betty, every red hair standing on end.

"Good!" I exclaimed, being somewhat weary by that time of over-ambitious Jimmy.

The school being finished, we packed the car, took our fifty dollars and hied us to Maine. There was a tiny cabin, a boat, a cold lake, loons wailing over it at night and the wind in the pine trees by day. Ted settled down into the bliss of his childhood when he had roamed over the little hills of Vermont, and he devised a game: "Let's look for a summer cottage of our own."

The next fall, when the children went to school, we engaged Tacey Magee as housekeeper and went up to New England for a week's vacation, visiting relatives and old haunts of Ted's childhood. (My own childhood was gone—long gone and forgotten. There was only an occasional wistful moment of loneliness. Ted could see again the places he loved as a child. I could not—never again.)

Ted's father had been rector for twenty-nine years at Immanuel Church, Bellows Falls, Vermont. We drove there and visited the beautiful old church on a hill, and the rectory beside it that had once overflowed with Ted's family. His grandmother had written there a story of the rectory children, called "The Little Brown

House." We saw the fireplace in the study where Ted's wonderful father had carved in Latin, "Oh ye fire and heat, praise ye the Lord."

Moved with nostalgia for his childhood, Ted said, "Let's drive up to Warren's Pond where we used to go on Sunday-school picnics."

So we did, and there it was, just the same—the dirt road around the lake with its lilies and reeds and its flaming maples leaning over and touching the still blue waters; the few old cottages half-hid in trees beside it; the gentle hills holding it up, as one might hold a cup up to the sky. We both loved it so much that in a wild venture of faith we rented an old white house beside it for two weeks the next fall. (We could not have afforded this for the summer months, but in the fall the rent was very small, this being the time of the depression.)

Ted took that time to outline his Sunday-school course for the year. He was still a missionary at heart, or rather, I might say, he was a real minister. He wanted to teach his children the Word of God. He wanted to acquaint them with Jesus. He was not interested in teaching them to understand themselves, or to become acquainted with the church's work, good though that might be. Therefore he wrote his own lesson helps, to be adapted by the Sunday-school teachers (all professionals at every age level).

While Ted was doing this work and study in the blessed peace of the old house at Alstead, with nothing to hear except the lapping of little waves upon the pebbly beach, I would take the flat-bottomed rowboat and explore the lakeshore, among the drifting red and yellow of fallen leaves and the low song of the wind in the pine trees. Once I pulled the boat up on crunching pebbles and climbed over rocks to the top of a little knoll covered with whispering pine trees and with maples thinned by autumn winds. There I lay flat upon the leafy ground, my costume closely resembling that of the captive maid threatened by cannibals.

Only I was not threatened by anybody. Noonday sun shining through thin trees and reflected from the dancing waters of the lake protected me from any chill. October winds seemed to have driven insects away, for no crawling creature disturbed my deep meditation.

There beside the dancing waters of the lake I prayed that

God's life would enter into me through the sunlight. Full upon me it shone, red through my eyelids, closed lest I look full into that blinding source of light.

It happened. In a time that was not time, for I was beyond time—in a time that might have been a split second or might have been eternity, for indeed I entered into eternity—I was filled with such unbearable bliss that I thought, "If this doesn't stop, I'll die. But I don't want it to stop, I don't want it to stop!"

It did. But I have known the joy of heaven, unendurable surely to one who has not at least tried to live in God. Now I understand a bit of the Bible's strange words about heaven and hell. The same radiation of God's life could be either heaven or hell. If a soul be able to endure it, that quivering, utterly indescribable bliss could be heaven. If one knew not God, then surely the soul would shrivel and die like a moth in a candle flame, or else wander lost in the darkness trying to escape that unbearable intensity of light.

It passed. I was myself again, yet never again quite the same. From this time forth I knew God. "I have heard of thee by the hearing of the ear: but now mine eye seeth thee" (Job 42:5).

For many years I told this to no one. The after-effects of it were puzzling to me and a bit frightening. There was an intense burning within the head, as though a hot coal of fire abode therein. And around the head was a tightness like a tight band. Indeed, I wondered uneasily during the two weeks before it gradually faded away whether I might be developing a brain tumor. If so, I thought, that split second of living in God was worth it.

I have tried often since to reproduce the exact circumstances of the spiritual experience that came to me upon that day, but am usually frustrated by ants crawling upon my person. Perhaps spiritual experiences cannot be reproduced. Certainly this particular one has never come to me again.

During that vacation, Ted and I again played our game of looking for a summer cottage. To me this was only a game. We could not possibly afford a summer cottage. True, I spent bits of money here and there for Elizabeth or some substitute to help me so that my soul could breathe in aloneness and could free itself in writing. Later on, my teaching and lecturing began to provide for this one need of my soul, paramount to all others: time. But until then, I economized in ways hardly possible save to one born and brought up with only the stark necessities of life. I weighed, still, my usual 104 pounds, and joyfully wore the congregation's cast-offs, which could always be taken in a bit if necessary. Only once was I slightly embarrassed by this. A faithful church woman met me in the cloister en route to a parish dinner.

"Oh, Agnes," she cried, "that has been a very handsome dress."

As for children's jackets, boots, and suits, this same faithful soul told me with earnest helpfulness of the pawnshops on South Street, Philadelphia, and thither I went, feeling perfectly at home among dark faces and little stalls set up on the sidewalk.

A *summer home?* Surely Ted was only dreaming! Moreover, in point of fact, I did not really want the responsibility of another house. However, one singing fall morning Ted said to me, "When you go for the milk, ask Mrs. Craig if there is any house around here for sale."

So I trudged down the dirt road by the lake, red leaves trembling down to the shining waters beside me, and entered the shed door of the old farmhouse. (Front doors in these areas are hardly used at all.)

"Yes," said she to my question. "The little white house up the hill is for sale."

I left my milk bottles among forget-me-nots and ferns where an even smaller dirt road turned off the lake road, and up the hill I went, through overshadowing woods, beside shining meadows, under an old apple tree where an even tinier road rambled rockily up the hill. There was a bit of lawn swung like a hammock between house and barn, and beyond it a low stone wall from which one looked out over meadows and trees down to the shining lake, cradled like a cup in a circle of gentle hills.

I looked and loved it, and knew that it belonged to me.

"Oh, it *can't* be!" I whispered aloud and went through tall grass to the little house resting low upon the ground, its windows almost flush with the uncut grass. Rather ragged shades were pulled partway down. I stooped and peered beneath them.

It *was.* It was mine. I loved it as I loved the fields and the stone wall and the far hills dreaming in the pale gold sunlight of fall. The plaster on the daffodil-yellow walls was cracked and crumbly, the green-painted floor sloped a bit, for the foundations were sagging. But there it was, three rooms put together to make one, seven windows, a huge brick fireplace, little crooked stairs leading up to a second story under the steep roof—it was mine. I felt as though my soul had lived there long before.

I went down the road on the wings of the wind, found Ted, and told him of the little house dreaming alone upon the hilltop. When he saw it, his brown eyes sparkled with delight. Neither one of us ever had a doubt about it.

But how to buy it? I do not remember considering time payments or mortgages, for I did not know that there were such things. In China, the method was very simple: if you had the money, you bought the desire of your heart; and if you did not have the money, you did not. (I have never learned to live otherwise, and am perhaps the only person in the Greater Los Angeles area who has no charge account or credit card.)

It is amazing the way the Lord works! The old lady who owned the house was eager to get rid of it before it should slide down the hill, as it was preparing to do. No one knows how old the house is, but the original Boston Post Road, Montreal to Boston, made of split logs laid through the wilderness, went right past its front door, and just beyond the barn are the overgrown foundations of the original tiny schoolhouse.

Prices of abandoned New England farmsteads were absurdly low in this depression time of 1930. With $2,000 we could buy the house and have it jacked up and the foundations rebuilt, which was an immediate necessity. The Lord must have foreseen this long since, for Ted as a very young man had taken out a $2,000 endowment policy to while away the time, waiting for a train. And it was due in four years. He was able to get a loan on it, and after much correspondence, bought the house the next winter and engaged our wonderful neighbor, Heman Chase, to jack it up and rebuild the old stone foundations. As soon as the policy came due, the loan was repaid in full, and the house was ours.

We could have bought the furniture as well for another $800, but that we did not have. So we arranged to use the former owner's furniture that first summer while we bought our own.

Our method of buying our own furniture was great fun. Teddy was away that summer earning his money for college by surveying, and Sara was with me. Sara and Tookie and I drove through hills and dales to every country auction and sat on the grass outside old barns, listened to the delightful patter of the auctioneer, and indulged in the fascinating game of buying with great rapidity a number of necessary articles. We would drive home with the car hung over with chairs and tables and bedsteads, tied on by grinning country youths.

"You couldn't get out until I untied you," said Ted in horror on one occasion when the demands of the furniture eliminated the possibility of opening the car door. "What would happen if the car caught on fire?"

"But it didn't catch on fire!" I cried indisputably, and dragged out peach-baskets full of china which I had bought sight unseen for forty cents a basket. Ted, meanwhile, spread upon the lawn a double bedstead purchased for twenty-five cents and poured kerosene into its cracks in case of bedbugs. But there were no bedbugs, and the bed still abides in the little house.

The old house had no kitchen or bathroom. A very long woodshed led to the two-holer familiar to every New Englander. There was, of course, no plumbing in the house, and no electricity. Since I was brought up with oil lamps and an outhouse, this did not trouble me at all, and we enjoyed it thus for fifteen years. Every morning after breakfast I would clean and fill the oil lamps, Ted would draw water from the old well, and the children would bring it in buckets and fill the large tin tub in the woodshed. Meat and butter were kept down the well in another bucket, and vegetables reposed in a screened-in closet down in the crunchy, pebble-floored cellar.

Ted, however, felt that the oil stove in the woodshed was a bit of a hazard, and promptly set about building kitchen and pantry in one end of the shed. He loved creating with wood and nails and paint as I love creating with dirt and trowel and flower seeds. It was a bit hectic that first summer, as I had to cook while stepping over planks and listening to hammer blows. Occasionally I wondered whether we had made a mistake in our guidance in buying this house alone upon a hilltop, with only one other house, half-hidden in trees, visible some half-mile away.

We had not made a mistake. God knew that we needed this home for our souls and this refuge from the world.

10.

*L*IVING at Alstead, however, occupied only one month during the year, just as my theatrical work and other bits of amusement took up only a small portion of my time during the other eleven months. Most of it was taken up with cooking (no dishwashing, for Ted made a rule that the children wash the dishes) and housekeeping, at which I remained hopelessly inept. Once in exasperation I said, "Lord, You help me with everything else. Why won't You help me to clean house?" And the answer which I heard as distinctly as a voice in my ears said, "Because that is not the kind of work I want you to do." So to this day, except for the daily bedmaking and occasional dusting, I do not clean house. All life is an attempt at learning balance. And this amount of housework proved good for me, including as it did an attempt at neatness, for I had learned that a disorderly house tends to create a disorderly mind.

There was also gardening, which is still my joy and delight, for one feels the life of the earth through the hands, and the benediction of God's love through the sunshine, and the pure joy of the Kingdom through the color and fragrance of flowers. Moreover, while the mind and body are so occupied and comforted, the subconscious broods happily on the subject of one's book or lectures, and when it is time to write, the thoughts are there, ready to flow. But I am looking too far into the future, for at that time I did not write: this one channel of creativity seemed blocked and crowded out by too many demands for prayer and healing.

Some of these demands came from my ever-increasing Bible class which now filled the chapel and included men as well as women. However, I sternly and continually taught them that they could themselves learn to be channels of God's healing power. And except in very serious matters, I did not go to their homes, but prayed for them themselves to be the channels for healing. Other calls to pray for people came simply from compassion.

Jack used to play with a small friend whose older sister lay in bed with a very serious heart condition. One day as I drove Jack to the home (this was in the era when every mother was primarily a chauffeur), I spoke to the child's mother. It is so very simple to speak in a case like this. Any mother would snatch at any straw that might lead to a lifesaving rope—or at least so I found it. On the sketchiest suggestion that my prayer might help, the mother escorted me to the child's room and left me there. One never has any trouble praying for children, because the things that seem to us grown people so perplexing are usually simple to them. They have not quite forgotten God from whom they came. I knelt by the bed and laid my hands above and below the heart and prayed for it to be healed, every valve opening and closing perfectly, the blood flowing in and out without difficulty of any kind. And I felt the power entering in a flow that caused my hands to quiver or vibrate in a way that I could not quite control, though I tried my best to quiet them.

The child was perfectly well, able to walk downstairs, the next day.

One time, whether in this era or later (I have never kept a diary), Elizabeth's son came to tell me that his "Ma" was dying of cancer and wanted me to come to see her. This, of course, was in one of the intervals when she was not working for me. There were times when she had another baby; there were times when I could not afford to pay her; there were times when she got a better job. I was rather put out that she had not notified me when she first became ill, but anyway, I climbed into the car with the dark brother and was driven out to the country to the little house I knew so well. There she lay in a rather large bedroom, not well-lighted; I remember the white teeth and white eyeballs shining out from the gloom around the walls, for all her relatives had come to the deathbed. But there was great love between us and great faith, and I prayed for healing. She made a complete recovery almost immediately, a matter that did not particularly surprise either of us. She is still living and doing well.

Calls to pray came to me not only from Moorestown and the surrounding area, but also from distant places. The first such call that I ever had was from Miss Lelia Robertson of Norfolk, still one of my very best friends. She stopped at my house on her way back from Atlantic City and urged me to drive down to Norfolk with her and pray for a man dying of a heart attack. This opportunity pleased me greatly. To hear the soft Southern accent—for remember, I am Virginian by ancestry, and my parents and all my friends in the Southern Presbyterian Mission spoke with a Southern accent—to feel the balmy rain blowing across the crepe myrtles, to see the beaming, black faces of Lelia's Negro friends and helpers—it was like coming home! It was like going to heaven!

The man for whom I was first asked to pray did not make a recovery. But various others did receive help in this informal, friendly visit. There was no lecture this time, only friends one by one or in small groups.

Thus my work spread, little by little. At first my meetings were just here and there in someone's home. Later on, it was in a parish house or guild room at the instigation of the women, for ministers looked on me with suspicion. Then gradually, churches opened their doors to me and we worked out the system of holding missions: not exactly healing missions but teaching-healing missions.

The Healing Light started this nationwide and indeed, almost worldwide lecturing. Soon after the book was published, Glenn Clark invited me to a small conference of potential leaders of his Camps Farthest Out, and until a feeling of fellowship grew in the little camp in the Minnesota woods, I disliked the thing intensely. Roland and Marcia Brown were at this first small conference, and Rebecca and Wally Beard and others, many of whom have since become well-known.

Then I was asked to be a leader in a CFO at Lake Winnipesaukee in New Hampshire. This was an eye-opener to me, for people loved me! They would give me a rose or a handkerchief or even a small check in an envelope. They would even put their arms around me and be as affectionate as I would permit them to be. (I have always avoided any holy hugging or pious petting by those of the opposite sex . . . until now, that is, when having reached the age of discretion I find the dangers are, shall we say, slight.)

"You need release in love," a handsome and attractive man once said to me at this camp. "And I could hold you in my arms and love you in a way that would help you greatly." I pondered the matter, but replied the next day, "No, because my husband would take a dim view of you hugging and releasing me in love behind a bush. And anything that my husband could not see, I won't do."

Nevertheless, the awareness of being loved and appreciated was most comforting to me. People at large in Moorestown referred to me usually as "that woman" now that they were beginning to be advised of my activities. It was not the thing to consort with me.

My husband, being a good man and a faithful priest, let me go on these occasional missions or trips, feeling no doubt that it was his duty and mine. But he did not like it. And as I had told Hollis Colwell long before would be the case, he was disappointed that I was not at all the woman he thought he had married. In fact, now that I was no longer in depression, he came near to being in that state himself. And I knew that it was my fault. I should have been waiting at the door with my little apron on every time he entered.

But the larger call drove me on, prodded me on, forced me on. For Christian people must know that Jesus lives and heals today—they must! So for many years, whether at home or at a conference, I bore a burden of guilt. Therefore, I still retreated within myself, not daring to let myself really care for anyone lest I be rejected. This was aggravated by the fact that my best friend in Moorestown, Marion Otter, one whom I had really dared to love, fell ill of a lingering blood disease and died. I dared to love my children and they loved me. For years I never sat down that someone did not climb into my lap. This was a great comfort. But beyond that, I did not dare to venture forth in love, but more and more tended to retreat behind barriers of reserve.

But at the Camp Farthest Out, this barrier began to melt. These camps were started by Dr. Clark as ventures in creative living and have a wonderfully balanced program of meditation, recreation, creative painting or writing or singing, lectures on spiritual truth, and always, prayer. They are very loosely held together and vary according to the leadership. I found it difficult at first to enter into some of the more childish frisking about with singing and calisthenics. But my walls of reserve began there to melt down.

Two women from Ottawa were at the first CFO I attended. They invited me to lecture in that beautiful city. My first visit there was very informal. I spent a night or so in the home of the doctor and his wife who had invited me and talked to a small group in the Sunday-school room of some church.

I prayed for many people, and apparently they were healed or helped, for in a year or so a larger meeting was arranged. The churches still looked askance at me since I proclaimed the heretical news that Jesus lives and heals today. Therefore, the doctor's wife and her trained-nurse friend stepped forth boldly on faith and rented the ballroom of the Chateau Laurier for the lectures, and two bedrooms, one for rest and one for my work of prayer with individuals. The ballroom was filled each night, and the offerings took care of expenses. Whatever was left over (if there was any—I do not remember) was given to me for an honorarium.

During this visit, there was much concern for Bishop Jefferson, an elderly and much-beloved bishop who was reported to be dying. After long consultation, it was finally decided that I might be allowed to go to the hospital to see him. There he lay on his bed, a small and utterly charming person, completely dignified, dying or no. He asked me various searching questions, including "Do you have a fee for these services?" (He was the first person who had ever even considered the possibility that I might have.) Being satisfied with my replies, he folded his hands on his breast, closed his eyes and said, "Very well. Then you may pray for me." This I did, and with great confidence, for it was only a matter of a spreading infection, a type of trouble that God's power usually heals rather rapidly.

No one told me that he had recovered, but I knew that he must have done so. Two years later, after Ted had begun going with me on an occasional mission, we received an engraved invitation from Bishop's Court in Ottawa to come to that city, hold a mission in the Cathedral and stay with Bishop and Mrs. Jefferson in Bishop's Court. So we did, to our great joy, the bishop and his wife being utterly delightful people. He was Irish by ancestry. He would read us Irish fairy tales in the evening after the lecture and would say, "There *are* little people, you know." Ted thought he was jesting, but I am not sure.

Things are done in a formal manner in the Anglican Church. At the morning service preceding the mission, the dean presented us to the bishop and said, "Reverend Father in God, I present to you these persons to be commissioned as missioners in your city." Whereupon the bishop intoned, "Lord have mercy upon us, Christ have mercy upon us, Lord have mercy upon us," and nobody thought it was funny except me.

Ted preached at morning meetings and I at evening services, and the mission overflowed into chapel and parish hall, both of which were wired for the occasion. There was also an afternoon meeting for children. Mothers brought their little ones, and I talked with my props: an apple and a potato, a pitcher of water and two glasses, an electric fan—just as I have recounted in *Let's Believe*. In came a young red-haired woman followed by sixty-seven children, filling up some four long pews.

"Who in the world is that?" I asked after the meeting.

"Oh, don't you remember?" was the reply. "You prayed for her last time you were here. She was supposed to be dying."

"But all those children?"

"Oh, that's her Bible class. One afternoon a week she gathers all these children from the street and teaches them that Jesus lives and heals today. That's her thank-offering."

Now I have gone far into the future in this account of how, over the years, one little talk grew into a mission in a cathedral. Let me go back and catch up the threads of the story, and as I do so, let me rejoice, for it is marvelous how God uses even our difficulties and mistakes in building the pattern for our lives and for the kingdom of heaven on earth.

My greatest difficulty in carrying on the work of missions was the burden that it placed upon Ted. At times, indeed, I decided to stop my work altogether. Once I returned from some trip on Saturday and, as usual on such occasions, found myself very much out of favor in the home. Elizabeth had failed to come, young

Ted had rebelled against washing the dishes, the bottom had burned out of the Pyrex coffeepot, father Ted could not find a clean shirt with buttons, and someone had stopped up the toilet. On Sunday morning I went to early church, got the children off to Sunday school, put the dinner in the oven, taught the Bible class and went to the eleven o'clock service. I rushed back from church and endeavored to get dinner on the table while members of the congregation came in the front door and in the side door to see me. Finally I got them away, and we sat down to dinner. The phone rang.

"Would you come to my city and do a mission?" asked a masculine voice, mentioning his name.

"No!" I snapped, for as they say nowadays, I had had it. "I'll *never do another mission.*" And I hung up the phone.

"Who was that you were talking to?" asked Ted.

"Oh, I don't know," I said, flouncing down in my chair. "I think he said his name was Austin Pardue."

"Bishop Pardue!" Ted exclaimed. "Don't you know who he is?"

There was nothing to do except drown myself, and to that I felt disinclined. I could not call him up and say, "I'm sorry, I didn't know you were a bishop . . ."

Three years later I did go to Pittsburgh, to lecture in a Congregational church, and then I did call him.

"Ever since I yelled at you on the phone," I said, "I decided that I would take the first chance that came to make a trip to Pittsburgh and try to curry favor with you."

The bishop, God bless him, laughed.

"I gather," he said, "that I just called at the wrong time."

We had lunch together, and with much merriment, made friends.

If I wanted to tack a moral to this, I would say, "Listen my children, always bridle your tongue"—which advice, indeed, I do find in the Bible—just as I said to them, "Always make your bed before you go out in the morning." (One time only I failed to do this of a Sunday morning, and that day a maiden lady of uncertain years fainted in church, and the wardens and vestry carried her out and laid her on *my* unmade bed.)

About this time, Ted and I both decided to take courses at

the University of Pennsylvania to modernize our knowledge of psychology. We thought that if we were to help people in prayer, it would be of use to us to know as much as we possibly could about the minds of men and how they worked. I am afraid it did not occur to either of us to pray for guidance about this. We took for granted that the matter could be decided by common sense, as of course some things can be. But God raised His hand and prevented this move. I am loath to think that God ever sends illness on purpose, but this time it does seem possible that He did. Ted suddenly got a very serious eye infection, was rushed to the hospital, and forbidden to use his eyes for some three or four months. I spent much of my time reading to him in a darkened room, and thus my own eyes were so strained that for years I could use them only sparingly.

So we could not take courses in psychology. There was no decision to be made. God had made it.

When I first became interested in healing, I thought to study books on physiology, the study of the human body. But it came to me that this would not necessarily help me in healing, for my attention would be too closely riveted to the human workings of the body. This might make it more difficult for me to grasp the reality of God's power that can superimpose a higher spiritual law upon a lower physical law and bring forth miracles of healing and even of resurrection. I see now that the same thing can apply to the study of the laws of the human brain and personality. While with some people it might be helpful, to others a study of psychology would not be helpful, for it could slow them up in their grasp and comprehension and acceptance of the spiritual mind and personality.

For instance, I once had dinner with the rector of a church, his assistant rector also being present. During the meal, the phone rang, and the rector spoke for quite some time to the person calling him and then returned to the table with a gesture of exasperation.

"It's that woman again," he said to his assistant.

"Oh no! Not again!" lamented the young man.

"She has the most terrible guilt complex," the rector explained to me. "Both of us have been working with her for two years."

Whereupon, with somewhat less than my usual tact, I exclaimed, "What on earth have you birds been *doing* for two years? Why don't you simply lead her to make a confession, and then pray the prayer of absolution with real faith and set her *free* from her guilt complex?"

They gave me no answer. Either they had not thought of confession and forgiveness as the answer to the woman's guilt complex, or they did not believe in the power of Jesus Christ to forgive sins.

11.

ALKING the way of the Spirit is like walking a tight-rope. One must use every effort to avoid toppling over on one side or on the other. I tried constantly to keep in balance by judging everything according to the yardstick of the Ten Commandments and the measure of Jesus Christ. Adventures of faith that claimed Buddha or Mohammed or the Masters of the Far East as their inspiration, I set to one side in the beginning. But even with these safeguards, I made mistakes. The easiest way to avoid these mistakes, I know, is to cling to what one has been taught in one's own church and to believe that all others are in danger of hellfire. It was more or less in this ethos that I had been brought up—and the result was that I myself was in danger because I was beset by evil and depressive thinking, and there was no one at that time in the church of my childhood to rebuke the spirit of darkness and to set me free from it.

During these first years, I was feeling my way. Hollis Colwell had moved to the West Coast, and at any rate, though I made great use all my life of the healing that came through him, there was not much that he could teach me about how to pray for others. I was now feeling the sweep of the power through me more and more when I laid hands on someone to pray, but in praying from a distance, nothing happened. There was some key that I was not turning.

Someone told me of a group that met once a week in a "Chapel of Truth" in Philadelphia, and there I went in 1930, to learn what I could. It was a tiny place in an office building, and the leader of the group was a sweet-faced woman no longer young.

Much of what she said, I had already picked up in bits of reading or had figured out for myself. But one thing I had not. So I asked her one day, "Why is it that when you pray for people at a distance you report the next week that they are well, or better, and when I pray thus nothing happens at all?"

"Oh, my dear," said she, "that is because you are seeing them sick."

"But they *are* sick," I replied. "That's why I am praying for them."

"Yes, but unless you can learn to see them well, you only fasten the sickness upon them," she said.

This good lady was completely a Christian. She had been a faithful member of a Baptist church and had taught a Bible class there. Then she was struck with a deadly illness. Someone came to the hospital and prayed for her, and she was healed. She went back to the church and told this to her Bible class with innocent joy and thanksgiving. The story spread, and she was soon called to the minister's office and informed that if she intended to spread such stories she must give up her Bible class. In fact, it was intimated that her absence could be endured if she were to leave the church.

"But I *was* healed!" she cried, as did the blind man who said simply, "Whereas I was blind, now I see" (John 9:25).

The minister looked pained and replied severely that such miracles did not happen today; this was a new dispensation and Jesus said, "Blessed are they that have not seen, and yet have believed" (John 20:29).

My friend might have quoted other remarks of Jesus about obeying Him and doing the works that He did. But all she could say was, "But it happened! I *was* healed!"

So she perforce left the church. "But people *must* know that Jesus heals today!" she said in her gentle way. "I must tell them! So, I rented this little place and teach about Him here since I cannot do it in the church. And I pray for the whole body of ordained clergy every day. And you know," she added, beaming, "they're getting nicer all the time!"

The art of intercession that I learned from this really Christian lady did me great good. But one notion of hers proved harmful, and of that I speak, so as to warn others. She taught that anyone who really desired to be a channel for God's healing should pray to be set free from the desires of the flesh so that all that person's energies might go into healing. The thought filled me with great sadness. Nevertheless, if this was the way to power, I thought, one must go this way. One must really be willing to give up all, for Him. Therefore, when she prayed after that pattern, I accepted her prayer. But its results were quite devastating, and it was some time before it became possible again to live anything approaching a normal married life.

I know that there have been great saints who were celibates, and I can see the value of this dedication. But one must make a decision like that before one takes marriage vows, or else one must never make it. Observation has shown me that those who are inflated with a swelling (and spurious) desire for holiness, so that though remaining married they deny themselves to their mate, are thereby breaking their marriage vows.

Nor do I believe in breaking up a marriage and marrying a more "spiritual" person so that one can be more free to serve God. I cannot see that one can best serve God by breaking one's solemn promise to love and cherish one's mate, and by deserting one's children, and the Bible, of course, expressly forbids it. Nevertheless, I have known it to be done by "Spirit-filled" Christians.

On another occasion, also, I took a step in a direction that proved to be the wrong one. An eminent Quaker gentleman came to see me and urged me to go with him to a different kind of prayer group wherein one communicated directly with the departed. No, he said, it was not exactly a séance—not a commercial one, at any rate. The family who held this little meeting in their home was a real Christian family, and every meeting began with prayer and was carried on in the name of Christ.

So we went together, this Quaker gentleman and I, on the Philadelphia subway, far out into the northeast section of the town—a trip that later became quite familiar to me, for Tookie and I frequented Shibe Park to yell vociferously for the Philadelphia Phillies—and, note, they did at one time win the pennant.

We entered a small, middle-class home and met the family: father and mother quite ordinary and indistinguishable from anybody else, and a pasty-faced youth introduced as Sylvester, the medium. Then we retired to a dark upstairs room, and the father duly opened the meeting with prayer in the name of Jesus Christ. (The mere uttering of His name, I have found, is not necessarily a shield against all evil.) Sylvester promptly went into a trance. It was rather revolting, for he moaned and groaned at a great rate and then began to speak in a voice not his own. The words that he uttered were quite shockingly banal.

"Oh dearie me, my father cut off my head when I was six years old," said the voice. "Yes he did, my dears . . ."

"That's his guide speaking," said the mother hoarsely.

It is unnecessary for me to bore my readers by repeating the utterances of this "guide" or of other voices entering into the room through it—or him—or her. The voices varied in tone but not at all in mental quality, being all on a subnormal or moronic level. During this rather tedious affair, moreover, "trumpets" touched one here and there, and later on ectoplasm appeared like a thin blue rope swung out into the air from the region of Sylvester's navel.

The séance ended, and we went home strangely unaffected either for good or for ill, and completely unenlightened.

I wanted to find out what this was all about, but I came to no conclusion of any kind. Therefore, I went once more, carefully keeping an open mind, for I sincerely desired to understand this matter and to rid myself from any prejudice concerning it. This time I was asked to pray for the medium's mother, who had a slight heart ailment. I did this with the laying on of hands and with no feeling of anything except that she would speedily recover, as people practically always did under such conditions. When we went into the séance, the voices kept saying, "Mrs. (I forget her name) is not feeling well tonight, so we are using the young lady."

"Do you feel all right?" some voice from midair would ask me while Sylvester half-sat, half-lay, breathing heavily and moaning from time to time.

I would reply that I was all right, for indeed I felt nothing.

After the séance, Sylvester was to ride on the subway to the midnight shift of the factory where he worked. I traveled toward home on the same subway, so we had quite a talk, he having by this time awakened from his uneasy trance.

If I had desired to learn, I did so.

"They bother me all the time," he complained. "I tell them to go away, see, and they won't. Gee! I can see them crawling up my drinking-water glass and . . ." The poor young man also complained that he always suffered a horrible headache after a séance, and the odor upon his breath was intolerable.

The next day I felt terrible. I was so drained of life that I could hardly move. I was in deep depression, and, most frightening of all, I could taste in my own mouth that odor that had been on Sylvester's breath.

"Oh Lord," I said out loud, "if You will get me out of this, I promise You I will never go near a séance again."

I have kept this promise, somewhat to the irritation of some of my friends, who consider me narrow-minded. And so I am. "Strait is the gate, and narrow is the way, which leadeth unto life . . ." (Matt. 7:14).

Shortly after this, I prayed with the laying on of hands for a friend who attended séances regularly. She was not healed of her affliction, whatever it was. The next day her son had his jugular vein cut in an automobile accident and was only narrowly saved from death by constant prayer.

Two months later the Quaker gentleman reported to me that Sylvester's mother had died of her heart condition, a fact that surprised me greatly.

Some months afterward I prayed with a lady involved in automatic writing and slightly connected with some spiritualistic group, and her husband, who had been perfectly well, died within twenty hours of a brain hemorrhage.

I began to be extremely nervous about joining in prayer with anyone involved in spiritualism, and yet it became increasingly difficult not to do so. For instance, a dear old friend in Washington began writing me about the wonderful things that happened when she and two other ladies with whom she lived would join in prayer. One of these ladies, it seemed, had gifts as a medium. And I would be surprised, they told me, at the people who came into their group to communicate in some way: Woodrow Wilson, and the Japanese emperor on a white horse, and I forget who else. Now these three ladies were highly educated and most honorable. Before retiring, two had been ministers of Congregational churches, and one had been a school principal. They were not at all like poor Sylvester, and I was greatly perplexed as to what to do.

"At least come and have lunch with us the next time you speak in Washington," they wrote. (At that time I had a monthly class in that city.) "It really hurts my feelings that you won't come near me," wrote my friend, "after all that we have done together . . ." She had been to see me more than once, and we had indeed worked together in some very productive prayer sessions.

So I thought, "Well, it won't hurt just to have lunch together, and she promised there would be no séances." And off to Washington I went.

After lunch my friend said, "Now we must just have a prayer together before we go," and as my mother had taught me to be polite and courteous when a guest at meals, I could not refuse, and we sat down in a circle to pray. Almost immediately the lady with the gift of mediumship went into a trance—at least I suppose it was such a condition, though it was with complete dignity and composure, with none of the accompaniments of ectoplasm and trumpets. According to her and her friends, various visitors arrived to consort with us in prayer. I was not aware of any of these, and this prayer meeting was conducted in full daylight and seemed no different from any other group, except for these rather boring interpolations from whoever the unseen visitors might be.

While I was on my way home on the train, my friend had a stroke and died.

Four times in a row! That was enough for me. Whatever the explanation of this phenomenon might be, I was evidently not a good person to pray with or for anyone involved in spiritualism. This troubled me greatly, for there were times when with all my determination I could not help it. I might find myself involved with a group and find out later that there was a spiritualist among us. The results were not so drastic in a group, the mind of the group overshadowing and to some extent protecting the participants. But even when thus shielded, I have known undesirable aftereffects of praying in such a group, and as far as I know, no healings have resulted. That is why, in the questionnaire concerning admittance to the School of Pastoral Care that Ted and I later founded, the question is asked concerning the person's participation in spiritualism. Those who have been involved are not accepted. This is for their protection and the protection of the group.

The reader may bring forth all kinds of reasons as to why this ought not to be. But, praise God, this book is not a series of lectures, but is merely an autobiography, and I do not have to argue about the reasons! I am merely stating facts.

However, I myself greatly desired to understand and, if possible, to be set free from this hampering restriction concerning those for whom I might pray. Therefore, when a chance came to me, I consulted a woman whom I consider a final authority upon all matters of the occult; her innate wisdom and acquired knowledge are great and so is her real devotion to Jesus Christ.

"What can I do to prevent these things from happening?" I asked her.

She replied, "You can do nothing except to abstain. You may meet socially with people interested in spiritualism, but you must not pray for them. This is for their own protection."

"Why?"

"Because they do actually conduct a current of supernatural power from the lower regions, and you happen to conduct a particularly pure current of supernatural power directly from heaven. Now these two currents are inimical. They cannot mix together, as direct current electricity cannot mix with alternating current. One must choose one or the other. When you do mix the two, there comes an explosion of a destructive nature. You are surrounded with protection, and it cannot touch you, so it rebounds upon the other person." This gives me furiously to think, as the French say. But I am not going to do your thinking for you, my friends and readers. Do it yourself, not forgetting to check with the Bible! And I will give you this clue: look up the word "abomination" in the concordance, and proceed from there.

"But many good people are involved in spiritualism!" you may cry.

Yes. It horrifies me to go to Christian conferences and see books about Edgar Cayce, and other spiritualistic literature, for sale along with my books. They do not belong together. This confusion between the power of the Holy Spirit and the danger of spiritualism is the greatest menace to the Christian church today. It is our duty to combat it however we can.

Let us first be quite clear as to what spiritualism is. Many years ago I heard in a prayer group a woman speak in tongues, and I was scared to death, as were many others in that group. I was sure that she must be possessed by the devil, or something of that kind. But I was mistaken, of course. Speaking in tongues is not spiritualism, as is made abundantly clear throughout my teaching.

One of the first things I learned was to "see the Christ" in everybody. I was perfectly able to translate that into more ordinarily accepted terms, such as to see the highest potential of good in everyone. This is an absolute essential for healing, for by seeing the good in another person, one is able to bring it out.

This learned capacity, together with a modicum of psychology, helped me to avoid the dreadful mistake of "seeing the devil" in people here and there, and rushing upon them to cast it out. I see that in ninety-nine out of a hundred cases it is not the devil that makes a person angry or terrified, but something in himself that needs resolving and healing through the love of Christ. It is "the Christ in him," or the buried impulse toward good in him, that brings the anger or fear up to utterance, so that someone looking upon him with the love of Christ can heal him by Christ's love and forgiveness.

However, when the trouble really is possession—when the person tells me himself that he is possessed and cannot control the possessing thing—then I have learned that I have God's power and His permission to cast it out.

Some people tell me glibly that every "born-again Christian" (their term) has the power to cast out devils. If so, what are they doing with it, I'd like to know? Why don't they go into mental institutions (for that is where most of the tormented ones are found) and set the prisoners free?

Please God, one day we *will* be strong enough in the Lord to do so, and then the kingdom of heaven can come upon this earth. The power does potentially belong to all Christians, but its understanding and its use still have to be learned. For most Christians this would include seeing the highest potential good in every person, and feeling for him enough compassion to release that good and set him free to be a child of God.

When I encounter someone who is really possessed, and I command the possessing spirit to leave the person, it leaves. My knowledge of this kind of authority began dimly in childhood. My father learned through an old Chinese minister trained by Dada himself that the name of Jesus strikes terror to the hearts of the possessed nowadays, just as it did in Bible times. Demons cannot stand before it. The old man would order the demon, in the name of Jesus Christ, to leave the person, and with true Chinese fervor would yell at it until it did. The possessed person would then come back to his real self, smooth back his hair, straighten out his clothes, and speak normally.

Knowing this in childhood, however, it did not at first occur to me that it might in any way refer to me or to civilized Americans, among whom, so I thought, there were none demon-possessed. I have found out differently. There are, in fact, many who are tormented, disturbed, oppressed by an evil being or evil power. So great is the danger of this that I will not have anywhere around me any object, idol, or fetish that even remotely suggests a power not of God. As I have said, a command given in the name of Jesus can dismiss the enemy and set free the one held prisoner by the devil. But the person giving the command must be completely filled with the power and the love of Christ, able to see beyond the possessing evil to the potential good in the person, and able to call forth that goodness.

I once met with a prayer group that had become obsessed with seeing the devil in people, and they did nothing but cast out "demons" from this person and that person, and finally from each other. They were speaking the words of exorcism without having the power to recreate a person by seeing and calling forth the potential Christ-power in him. The result was that they themselves were attacked by the enemy, as were the seven sons of Sceva by the possessed man who said, "Jesus I know, and Paul I know; but who are ye?" (Acts 19:15).*

Looking back, I find it hard to remember when I first dared to pray a prayer of exorcism. I remember two women who once arrived at a conference complaining that they had been to a séance and had there become possessed. (This often happens; and being

---

* For a further discussion of this matter, read *The Challenging Counterfeit* published by Logos International.

filled with the Spirit does not necessarily put the person in less danger, but is actually apt to make his position more dangerous.) One of them was released immediately when I commanded in the name of Jesus Christ that the evil thing, whatever it might be, should leave her; and when I said to our Lord, "Now I put this departing thing into Your hands, Lord Jesus. You will know what to do with it. I do not know. But I ask You to see to it that it never again enters into or comes near this woman or her house or her church or indeed this earth-plane." I then prayed for the love of Christ to come into the woman and fill up all the empty places that had been filled with evil, and finally, that she be surrounded with protection. And so it was.

But the other woman had been so mentally disturbed by this spiritualistic encounter, and was, I imagine, such an unstable person anyway, that although the evil spirit departed immediately, it took days of prayer before she was restored to God's peace.

A young man in New Zealand claimed that he had become possessed while in a concentration camp, and that there were three demons in him. He was completely set free in one prayer, and then I noticed that he had bright blue eyes! So great was his darkness before the prayer, that they had looked quite black.

I remember another incident in New Zealand when a young lady told me that *something* had come into her while she was playing with the Ouija board (a highly dangerous pastime, especially for a Christian), and that it was taking over her whole personality. She said, "I don't feel that it is a demon exactly; it doesn't seem to be particularly evil; but it has pushed my real self to the wall so that I simply cannot be myself anymore."

In requesting this interfering personality to leave her, therefore, I spoke with courtesy, simply saying, "This is not your home, and you cannot stay here. Leave this woman, therefore, and turn about and go in the opposite direction. Look for the light of Christ, and I will ask Him to send an angel and lead you whither you should go. But go away from this earth, for you cannot fulfill your life here."

The woman sighed deeply—persons often do when set free— and said contentedly, "It spoke before it left. It said, 'I'm sorry! Good-bye.'"

Long ago Old Man Tai said to my father, who asked him how

he did this work of exorcism, "Why, just as Jesus does! Is there any other way?"

In seeking light upon this subject, I look to see how Jesus did it. I find that He never used the prayer of exorcism unless the person was definitely mentally upset. He did not pray for the healing of an illness by casting out the devil. Truly the devil has much to do with the whole problem of illness. However, Jesus overcame the work of the devil by healing the disease, thus setting people free from the bonds of the Evil One (Luke 13:16).

On one occasion, the person was so overcome by the power of the Spirit that upon being set free he fell upon the ground as dead (Mark 9:26), but Jesus did not require any dramatic manifestation upon setting a person free. In my experience, save for one or two who have made some outcry, the person gives no sign at all of being freed, or else simply sighs deeply as in profound relaxation and perhaps says, "It's gone."

On the other hand, occasionally the person does not even know that the evil thing has gone until several days later. I prayed once for the wife of a psychiatrist during the course of a conference. Her husband had brought her to me after she had spent four years in a mental institution. He wanted me to pray this prayer for her. She, however, was terrified of it.

"Don't pray for exorcism!" she commanded me. "A minister once prayed for exorcism, and it didn't happen. And I couldn't stand another disappointment like that." (The minister must have said the prayer at her request and must have been afraid as he did so. Of course, if one is afraid of the demon, it will not leave.)

This made things a bit difficult. I knew that the exorcism prayer was necessary, for both the lady and her husband had told me that ever since the age of thirteen something that she called "the beast" had possessed or troubled her. It had from time to time tried to push her under a train or over a cliff or into deep water. I also knew that, in her disturbed condition, any argument might throw her completely off the deep end. (The doctors had given her many shock treatments and had told her husband that he might as well put her in the hospital for life and forget her, and bring up his four children as best he might.) So I said that I would now lay hands on her and pray for an eczema condition and other physical difficulties. I prayed this and then said quietly, "Now I'll just pray in silence for a few minutes," which I did, addressing "the beast" very forcibly, but with no sound.

She told me later that she did not know at first that anything had happened. She sat on a rock above the lake. Three days later it occurred to her that this was the first time since girlhood that she had sat near to deep water without feeling the old horrible impulse to throw herself into it!

This woman became so perfectly well that some years later she and her husband, ex-missionaries to China, went to India and worked for some years in the Lucknow Medical Center. She is a trained nurse, her husband is a medical doctor and a psychiatrist, and both of them do counseling and prayer through the power of the Holy Spirit of Jesus Christ. In going to the mission field when no longer young, they had to pass the extensive physical and mental tests given to all missionaries. They recounted their whole experience, and passed with flying colors!

12.

*L*ET me now go back to the story of our life in Moorestown. The era of Hugh and Clyde, my theatrical chums, had passed away. With it somehow the old world began to disintegrate and a new world to emerge—and not a better one.

Hugh graduated from the Philadelphia Conservatory and took a position as organist and choir and glee-club director at Hampden-Sydney College. Clyde disappeared to realms unknown, and the last I knew he was putting on festival pageants somewhere in the islands of Greece.

There were thunderclouds in the air, and one did not know then that they were the clouds of far-off war. In China, the Japanese were marching steadily southward, occupying village after village almost without opposition. Who could oppose the Japanese? Around the cities, however, there were skirmishes and even wars of the advanced modern kind, using airplanes and tanks instead of old cannon firing round black balls that seldom hit anything. My parents with their faithful servants were at Kuling, waiting for life to quiet down so that they could go home again. But they never went home except to that continuing city that was their real home.

After a year at Hampden-Sydney, Hugh received two rather interesting offers, but threw away all three openings and went to China where he had no job at all. I was furious. Looking back now, I can see that it was guidance, but Hugh was too naïve to recognize it as such, and would not have known how to tell me if he had recognized it. Two days before his ship was to anchor in the muddy waters of the Whangpoo off Shanghai, the Japanese began an intensive bombing of that city.

No mail came through. I did not hear from Hugh for three months. Finally a letter came. He described with enthusiasm the length, structure, and tonnage of the ship on which he had traveled. Finally he said, "And while in Shanghai, I found it very interesting to listen to the bombs as they fell. They exploded in four distinct musical tones, just right for the third movement of the symphony I am composing."

He had been helped out of Shanghai for the purpose of smuggling money to stranded missionaries. He carried some thousands of dollars strapped around his waist beneath his clothes. Meanwhile, he had lost his passport. But so innocent and guileless did he look, that he simply followed humbly in the wake of some large, important-looking personage, and on the assumption, presumably, that he belonged to this man's party, he was not questioned and finally arrived in Kuling.

It would take a whole book to write of Hugh's wanderings and adventures in China, and someday maybe I will write that book. He secured a position as music teacher in a college in Nanking. Meanwhile, war broke out between the two places, and all communications were cut. Nevertheless he arrived, having walked two hundred miles across the steaming plains, full of their usual cholera and dysentery.

That college was eventually destroyed, and Hugh made his way by truck and on foot to Kwei-lin and thence, when it was destroyed by bombs and fire, to Kunming, where the remnant of the college carried on in a Buddhist temple. There Hugh taught music without a piano and without any textbooks. When this college went to pieces, Hugh was way out on the Burma Road without work, money, or friends. How by God's mercy he secured funds and finally found his way by sea and land back to Kuling is a miracle beyond any believing. But he did.

Kuling had been bombed in desultory and halfhearted fashion, and was lonely and almost abandoned. Mother had become rather vague and forgetful, and welcomed Hugh with joy but without any particular surprise. Dada was laboring on with his writing and correspondence, under a strain that no one realized until the day when he finished typing, cleaned his typewriter, covered it, and fell over dead.

I was lecturing somewhere when I received the cable. But for twenty-four hours, ever since his actual death, I had seen his face in my mind: a young, beaming Dada as he had looked at the age of about thirty-three when he returned well from Johns Hopkins Hospital.

We have a spiritual eye that sees farther than the physical eyes. My spiritual being must have known that he was dead. Why then would I "see" not the worn and aging man I had last remembered, but the man he had been in the very prime of life? Was I discerning his ever-living being in the heavens? And can it be that when we go to this continuing city we there appear as we were at our very most beautiful and wholesome? I wonder. I saw, you understand, no visible form with my eyes. This was not a ghost nor a vision, so far as I know what a vision is. It was only an inner knowing.

I gave my talk that evening over a deep sadness, as I have had to do so many times, so very many times. It is amazing how one can live and function on two levels at once—the inner one grieving and deeply preoccupied, the surface one sounding off with quite the usual force and vivacity.

"I will not leave you comfortless," Jesus said to His disciples. "I will come to you." (John 14:18). So He has come in His Holy Spirit, and even now before the completion of His coming He does not leave us comfortless. Throughout the bourn of time and space He had led Hugh to be with my parents at this time. (True, Junia had married a Presbyterian missionary and they were at this moment in Harbin, Manchuria. But that was almost as far away as the United States, and fully as difficult of access.)

Hugh took charge of the funeral, and my father was buried on the top of the last lonely hill in the Kuling Valley in a cemetery now abandoned, as all of Kuling is abandoned and in the hands of the Communists. Everything that we had is gone.

Hugh brought Mother home to me. I remember meeting them at the train: Hugh and a skinny little old lady in the same black coat in which she had left America, and with the same air of authority in her sparkling eyes and in her whole small person.

I thought, "She cannot go to church tomorrow in that awful coat with the ratty little fur collar!" So that evening I took off the molted collar and sponged and pressed the ancient coat, vowing to buy her another one next week.

We went to Strawbridge-Clothier, and against her protests, I bought her a beautiful and most suitable coat, black but with a certain new elegance. She would never wear it. Not once. She would hide it. On one occasion I found it sewed up into an old sheet and hidden in the top of the linen closet. Throughout the two years that she lived at the rectory, she wore that old coat.

The rectory was hardly the place for her. Poor dear, she would leap eagerly to the phone whenever it rang, would answer with her usual air of authority, and then would forget the entire thing. The undertaker would call up later in the week: "Where is Mr. Sanford? We are waiting for him at the funeral parlor." Or she would march out to the sidewalk, collar any passing man and order him to come in and fix the light switch. And he would enter, looking utterly perplexed but not daring to disobey the little old lady who spoke with the authority of a queen.

She became more and more divorced from reality, and her struggles to cope with a household that she vaguely felt was hers to command were pathetic. It was for me a good lesson in patience, never my outstanding virtue. It was also good for the children to have contact with an old person who needed forbearance and love. But the time came when we had to find for her another abiding-place. By God's grace we found one, after one or two false tries. She was established in a private home in the next town where a wise and authoritative woman made a living by taking care of four old ladies. Mother was relieved there from the burden of responsibility and at first was actually happier there than she had been in Moorestown.

I went to see her every other day, taking my teen-age son with me—in fact, letting Jack drive the car! He had broken his pelvic bone playing football and was commanded to walk on crutches for a month, and I did not want to leave him alone in the house. (The doctor had said that he would never walk without a limp, and he not only does so but won his gold shoe in track while at college.) Mother could not remember which one of her daughters I was, and assumed that she still lived with me.

"I haven't seen you all day," she would say. She enjoyed driving with us and going to a drugstore and having a sundae. But she became more and more senile. I tried praying for the healing of this mental condition and had no success whatsoever, though I could pray for a cold or poison ivy and she would be perfectly well the next day. So I asked for guidance: "Lord, may I pray for her to be healed of senility?"

The answer was, "No. Life has been too hard for her, and she is gradually retreating from it. This forgetfulness is her protection. Pray therefore that she remember the happy things, and find more and more enjoyment in them, and continue to forget all that troubles her."

The answer to this prayer was wonderful. Mother took more and more delight in those beauties of nature that had always been her greatest joy. She was allowed to wander on the large lawn, the lady of the house keeping watch from the window. There she would pick dandelions and gather fall leaves, rejoicing in shades of color that to me were quite invisible. Even when the leaves were completely brown, she would see in them flaming ruby and shining gold. Furthermore, she would collect them and hide them here and there, under her mattress and behind her bureau drawers —a harmless and comforting amusement which was permitted without any fuss or scolding. She stayed in this home till shortly before the end when Junia, now returned from China, took care of her for a short time. Finally the Lord received her into His continuing city where I know that she sees beauties far beyond my ken, even as she saw them in the dead leaves here below.

While Mother was with me, I kept on with my missions, with Tacey Magee and Elizabeth to keep house during the four or five days when I was away. Mother being there was no drawback during those times. It was good for the children to come home from high school and find not only Elizabeth making cookies in the kitchen but also Grandmother sitting in the living room knitting and looking over her glasses to smile at them. And there was in me a driving compulsion: *I had to go forth and tell people that Jesus heals!*

"Go ye into all the world, and preach the gospel to every creature," Jesus commanded His disciples (Mark 16:15). As another zealous woman said to me, I had a bad case of the go-yes. Here were churches full of "Christian" people and they did not know that Jesus is alive today and can work miracles through His people, even as He did through His disciples while He walked the earth. Those who called themselves Christians seemed to me blind and deaf, and there was no one to tell them the truth: that Jesus is alive and that He heals today.

For indeed, in the beginning years of my work, there was no one. Dr. Worcester of the Emmanuel Movement in Boston had kindled a small flame, but he had died, and the flame had gone out. On the West Coast, Dr. Robert Bell and Dr. John Gaynor Banks did the healing works of Jesus, but on the East, where I lived, the works of these apostles of a new day were not known. Moreover, at the time when I was beginning my work, they were drawing near to the end of theirs. So I carried on, although the strain was great. In fact, once during this interval, a very perceptive friend with whom I worked rather closely at the time told me that if I kept up this pace I would not last another year. I believed my friend, Ray Bendell, for up until then every word of knowledge that the Lord had given him had been true. But I thought, "If I haul down my flag now, that will be the end of all I have tried to teach. And if I have only one year left, it may be that during that time I will reach someone else who will pick up the flag and carry it on."

So on I went. The South was the most open field for me, and that was a bit surprising, for the reaction of some Southern churches to *The Healing Light* was one of unmitigated horror. This was the comment of one rather conservative church magazine: "We can only say that we rejoice that Mrs. Sanford's sainted parents went to their reward before this book was published." (Their timing was not quite accurate, for the book had been published several years before they became aware of it.)

As before recounted, at first I walked softly, speaking only to small groups in homes or parish halls—lest I be burned at the stake, which I literally would have been a few hundred years sooner. But more and more churches opened to me, and great were the rewards of joy that recompensed for many sorrows.

North Carolina, where I had gone to college, became one of my spiritual homes: Raleigh, Charlotte, Fayetteville, Wilmington, Greensboro, Asheville, where I went again and again, meetings being instigated by the untiring efforts of a lady older than myself, Mrs. Mary Avery.

I met there a medical doctor, Dr. Curtis Crump, with whom I worked rather closely. Once he asked me to go with him to an

Army tuberculosis hospital, and there we went from bed to bed and prayed together with the laying on of hands for thirty men. On my next trip to Asheville a month later, we searched for these men and could not find them. Every one had either gone home well or had been sent to the recuperation hospital. On my third visit to Asheville, we were not permitted to visit that hospital. So it is. Next only to clergy, doctors have been those most opposed to this healing that takes cognizance of the spirit as well as the body —of the unconscious as well as the conscious mind. Thank God, this is now changing, as doctors recognize more and more that many diseases are psychosomatic and require the healing of the psyche or soul as well as that of the soma or body.

"Then what are we going to do this afternoon?" I asked rather disconsolately, for I loved working with Curtis.

"We're going down to darky-town," he said, in words no longer fashionable and with a love also no longer fashionable. "I have lots of patients down there, and they can't afford hospitals. We've got to get them well."

(It would be ridiculous to refer to this little section of small, simple homes as a "ghetto." Here in Los Angeles we have a China-town and a Japanese town, and no one calls them by that absurd name. It is quite natural for those of a like race to feel at home to-gether.)

So all afternoon we went from house to house and were greeted everywhere with great joy, natural to the people at seeing their beloved physician. With a simple willingness they entered with us into the world of prayer. I remember a young woman re-covering from tuberculosis. Dr. Crump told me that she had come into his office in the last stages of this disease and had nearly died of a hemorrhage right there on his office floor. She would have died except that he lifted her in his arms and put her on the sofa, then laid his hands on her chest and prayed for healing. She re-sponded and was nearly well. But she was overjoyed to see us and to have another prayer for the completion of her healing. She lay upon the bed, and the two of us knelt on either side of her, laid hands on her chest and prayed for healing. As we said "Amen," she opened her mouth and with grave dignity led us in the Lord's Prayer. It was so natural and so beautiful that I have tears in my eyes at this moment as I write of it.

When I had returned home, a minister from Asheville called

me and asked me to pray for the daughter of a doctor, nearly dead of spinal meningitis. He said that her parents were praying for her to die, because her father knew that if she lived she would be completely paralyzed and an idiot. This was a difficult assignment! I said, "Wait until I get guidance," which one has to get rather rapidly when talking over the long-distance telephone. I lifted the situation up before the Lord and waited for Him to say no, but He did not. What I "heard" was, "Tell him to ask Dr. Crump to pray for the girl with the laying on of hands and to tell you the hour when he will be with her; then pray at that time for both the doctor and the patient." I reported this to the minister, who called me later to inform me that Dr. Crump would be with the girl at nine o'clock. Therefore, at that time I went into the chapel (which was rapidly becoming my spiritual home) and so prayed.

The next day the minister called me and said that the girl was entirely well except for one arm, and that the doctor would see her again and pray for that arm. So he did, whether more than once I do not know. But on my next visit to Asheville, the mother brought the girl to meet me on her way to dancing class, and I beheld a pretty, happy child, entirely well.

Some months later, a boy in the same town became ill with the same disease, and Dr. Crump asked permission of the healed girl's father, who happened to be a physician in the children's hospital, to come to pray for him.

The girl's father refused.

Another one of my favorite towns during this period was Louisville, Kentucky. My own cousin, William Campbell, the senior warden at the Church of the Good Shepherd, arranged for my coming to Louisville and entertained me in his home. The mission went so well that I was eagerly invited again, more than once. On the second mission, my daughter Virginia, then a college girl, accompanied me to talk to the young people and help me with prayer appointments. Both of us had these prayer sessions all day long in the church. One of the persons brought to Virginia was a young Negro girl, daughter of the headwaiter at the country club. The girl was carried in, being paralyzed with polio. A year later, when again both of us came to Louisville, she was reported to be walking and nearly well. Her father, however, desired us to see her again, and for some reason the best time was on a certain evening when other cousins, Dr. and Mrs. James Bruce, were having a dinner party for us. The dinner was half-an-hour late because all of us desired to put it off so that Clint and his daughter could come. This time she walked into the room with the help of only a small cane and sat down and played the piano for us, to the delight of the whole company.

Before we left that city, Clint made a request of my cousin, Bill.

"I want you to have a party at the country club for Mrs. Sanford and her daughter," he said, "because I crave the honor of serving them." His word was law among these people who loved him so much. They put on a luncheon party for ministers and doctors at the Country Club, and Clint presided, beaming.

On my last visit there (for I never continue indefinitely going back to the same place, feeling that eventually they should learn what I have to teach and should practice it), another cousin gave a dinner party in his home, engaging outside help for it. Among these was William, a most accomplished butler, although of a rather peculiar cast of countenance. It embarrasses me to this day to remember that I committed the gaucherie of commenting on this.

My hostess drew herself up proudly and looked down her nose at me. "William," she said coldly, "is a *very fine gentleman.*"

I have never forgotten that rebuke. Among the gentlefolk of the South there seems to be an unwritten code of which one of the tenets is that one never comments upon the appearance of someone of another race.

All this time, my tension increased: there was the constant conflict between taking care of my husband and family, and taking care of God's lost children in a world and a church that had forgotten His reality even while accepting Him as Savior. I could not look ahead and see the working out of this. I could only go from day to day and from month to month doing the best I could to balance one duty against another duty. One thing, however, made the balancing a bit easier, and that was that Ted more and more appreciated the fact that these missions were not totally without financial recompense, as was the work that I did constantly in Moorestown. He saw that I did greatly ease his financial burden—and in our circumstances this was most important, for Ted's salary was still $3,000.

Then, in another way, God came to the rescue of this difficult situation. Ted and I began to do missions together. The idea of this may have come first from me, but it developed that all such invitations were to him and me, and not to me alone, and all decisions concerning them were in his hands. He arranged with his vestry to be away three or four weeks a year (usually between Sundays), and we traveled together by train—for he would never set foot on an airplane—to Ottawa, as previously mentioned, and to Birmingham, Atlanta, Fort Lauderdale, and West Palm Beach, to Cincinnati, and various other places. Ted greatly enjoyed this, especially the missions in mild climates in the middle of a Northern winter! He would take the morning talks and I the evening ones and we would both have healing appointments hour after hour. Until they came to know Ted, people usually wanted to talk to me. He faced this philosophically and overcame it with his usual wit and charm. Once in Birmingham a lady burst in upon him, furiously proclaiming, "I *wanted* an appointment with your *wife*."

"I don't blame you," said Ted. "I've been trying to get an appointment with her myself for two weeks."

The lady collapsed into laughter, was healed and released in a wonderful way by his counseling and prayer, and from that time on adored him. I have met her from time to time over the years, and she is still the new woman who was born that day.

It took a great man to be able to sit in the pew and listen to his wife talk from the pulpit—and Ted was a great man. My talking puzzled and delighted him. Of course, I never had lectured in his church or in his town.

"How do you do it?" he said one time. "You aren't lecturing or teaching, you're just talking—as though you were talking to your friends."

"Well, I am," I said. But it was more than that. Let me try to explain it. First of all, I do not like to see women leading a church service or preaching in one, and I will never talk at a regular worship service. My talks are preceded, however, with shortened evening prayer because I need that time of worship to enter into the presence of the Lord. I sit in the front pew with my eyes upon the cross and pray for the Holy Spirit to fill me and fill the church. When the time for the talk comes, I go into the pulpit in order to be better seen and heard. My talk has been carefully prepared, though not written down, for that would impede the flow of the Spirit. I have memorized my outline and have chosen the illustrations that I shall use but have not memorized the text.

As I begin to speak, I listen for the words, and they come to me out of the air, as it were. I hear them in my mind before I speak them, and while speaking one sentence, I hear the key words of the next. Also, I sense and feel the thoughts of the congregation, for I project my spirit into the whole church and try to make a rapport between me and all who are there. I never cast my eyes down to a manuscript (which, of course, I do not have; I take nothing at all into the pulpit with me) or even to the Bible. When I desire to quote a Bible passage, I memorize it beforehand and am infinitely grateful for the practice of memorizing Scriptures taught me by my Presbyterian parents.

Thus, there is a surge of feeling and a rush of power between me and the people, and more and more it comes to pass that healings take place then and there, though in all quietness and secrecy. I am not merely speaking words. I am being a channel for the flow of God's power to all the people, so that He (not I) can heal and inspire, convict and comfort. Sometimes the words that I hear in my mind are not those included in my prepared outline. If so, I follow them without fear, for I know that God is speaking through me to the need of someone there.

"How did you know to say that?" people often ask me. "I was just wishing you would explain that point."

Or, again and again, "How did you know that that was my need right at that moment?"

I did not know it. God knew it, and such was the rapport between us that He was able to convey it.

At the end of the talk, I close with a prayer. That, however, does not end the service, for I do not consider that I have the authority either to open or to close a worship time in a church. I go back to my seat in the congregation, and the minister of the church closes the service with hymn and prayer and benediction. Thus I speak always simply as a member of the congregation and not as a member of the clerical staff.

Ted, on the other hand, would speak quite naturally and simply from the standpoint of the clergy, the established order of the church, which he was and represented with such dignity and beauty that I never dreamed of trying to make him someone other than himself.

"Why don't you pray for Mr. Sanford to come to a CFO with you?" some bright-faced lady asked me once.

And I replied with horror, "Oh no! He's not that kind of person at all!"

Ted was a great comfort to the more conventional of his people and indeed to everybody, for all that he said in his simple, straightforward way was understandable and practical.

"You and Mr. Sanford make such a wonderful team," people often told me. "You're so different, yet you both believe and teach the same things."

God has His own ways of getting His work done in the world. And while a marriage of those completely compatible and content with sex and children is no doubt the foundation of society, sometimes He brings together those who are utterly different so that by this very difference, even friction, they will ignite a spark of energy that will light a fire and bring forth a light to enlighten all of life around them. Those who rush to the divorce court at the first sign of incompatibility might do well to consider this and to ask God, "*Why?* For what purpose did You bring us together?"

According to what people have told me, Ted was the most wonderful confessor ever known. (Strangely, he never made a confession himself, nor was he ever willing that anyone should pray for him.) A woman flew all the way across the continent one time to ask him to hear her confession, and through that one interview she was completely transformed and has so remained. Therefore his taking half the load of personal appointments was a wonderful help, for the demand for prayers for healing of soul and body was overwhelming. Naturally! For this "cure of souls," for which the priests of the church are duly appointed has become almost obsolete. Ministers become more and more preoccupied with trying to change society without changing the individual—whereas Jesus sought to change individuals, knowing that only through transformed and born-again people can society be changed.

We always ended a mission with a service of healing with the laying on of hands, in which we and the rector and often other ministers assisted. But I do not share the enthusiasm of many "healers" for this type of service, because too many people who go to the altar are not healed. Many of them need more time and more understanding of themselves and of the nature of their problem or illness that they may really be healed in the inner being. Nevertheless, there is a demand for such healing services, and many people are helped by them, although I myself find them exhausting and am always uneasily aware of those who do not receive healing. We prepare them for this possibility. We never tell them that it is God's will for them to be sick, for this we do not believe. If this were true, one would not dare to pray at all, nor indeed to go to a doctor. But we do let them know that there are sometimes obstacles to healing, so that if healing does not come at that moment, they will not despair, but will continue in faith both to pray and to live the life of power as outlined in the Sermon on the Mount. It is good to do what one can with a healing service, but I know of no work more difficult.

The time came when I was so drained of strength by this work that I contemplated giving up missions altogether. Ted advised me to go ahead but to keep the afternoons free for rest and preparation, and so I did.

Now I know that some people say that there should be no effort concerning this matter—that one simply lets go and lets God. People are different, and if you can do that, my friend, and see the signs following—miracles taking place—then thank the Lord. But with me it is not so. If I do not make the tremendous effort of synchronizing all I have in spirit, mind, and body and hurling it into the work, nothing happens either in the pulpit or out of it. The time for me to let go and let God is when the work is finished, and even that has not always been easy.

Today there are classes in listening and in becoming sensitive. If one is doing God's work of healing and prayer, one has to listen not only to the words of the one for whom one prays, but also to the thoughts behind the words, and even to the unknown feelings from which those thoughts spring. And this makes one as sensitive as most people can bear to be.

13.

*T*HERE was a time when I made a trip alone to a church in the South and stopped afterward to visit my brother H.M., then surveying in Augusta, Georgia.

"Would you mind going with us to visit an old man in Macon?" asked H.M.

"What kind of an old man?"

"Well, I don't know. People say he's a very holy man, sort of a prophet. So we have asked him to come with us and have a picnic lunch somewhere."

H.M. and Anne and the three children and I drove to Macon. We found Brother Rufus Moseley, took him into the car among children and lunch baskets, and looked for a picnic place. The old man with the keen eyes and the wizened face of an Old Testament prophet suggested the public park, not knowing that a fair had ended there the day before—and not caring. We wended our way through torn newspapers and empty cardboard boxes and sat down on some wooden benches. We unpacked the lunch and chose sandwiches. Brother Rufus began to talk. Three hours later I came back to earth to find myself still sitting there with my sandwich in my hand, listening to such as I had never heard before. For this old man had truly seen Jesus and had been filled with His Spirit.

Time would not avail me to tell all that he told us. Indeed, he has told it himself in his books, *Manifest Victory* (recently reissued as a Logos classic) and *Perfect Everything*.

But here was a person who had *seen*—here was a man who had experienced in some measure that which the disciples experienced on the Day of Pentecost, and whose face shone with the joy of it, so that when he talked of the Lord, years fell away from him, and he was no longer an old man, but a youth, flaming with joy and love.

I cannot remember just what he said. But the man himself I will never forget.

Brother Rufus owned a pecan grove and wrote columns for newspapers. But he worked less and less at these things and darted about to any kind of religious meeting, talking often to small groups of Pentecostal friends. Some of his remarks have become classics.

"What have you to say about our financial problem, Brother Rufus?" the chairman of a church board once asked of his elderly visitor, probably in the bantering tones that one is apt to take toward small children.

"Well, it's like this," replied Brother Rufus in his Southern drawl. "You can feed a cow so good and milk her so easy that she positively enjoys it. Or you can feed her so poorly and milk her so hard that she sets up a regular resentment against it."

Another story about this remarkable old man is that he was once asked to conduct a funeral for some people in the mountains who had no minister. Brother Rufus said that when he was asked to do something he didn't know how to do, he always went to the Bible to see how Jesus did it. "And I found," said he, "that Jesus didn't conduct any funerals. He only conducted resurrections."

There came a time when Brother Rufus was in Philadelphia, and I invited him to come to Moorestown and talk to my Bible class, now grown quite large. I was delighted, for whenever I was with Brother Rufus, the light of the Spirit shone through him into me in such a way that I almost floated on waves of joy. Indeed, I would come down the staircase with my hand on the banister and my feet touching only about every fourth step, so light my body seemed.

It was the seventh of December.

During the course of Mr. Moseley's talk on the love of Jesus and the joy of the Holy Spirit, I was called to the telephone, and there I heard the astounding news that the Japanese had attacked Pearl Harbor. For two years the clouds of war had been darkening the horizon. Indeed, I had felt its shadow for three weeks before war was declared. (I have since learned that when one feels an unaccountable depression, one should pray that whatever be the unknown cause of it may be healed, or at least minimized. If enough of us had felt the shadow of coming events and had prayed, would it have stopped the assassination at Sarajevo that first plunged us into a world war? I do not know . . .)

Pearl Harbor. Unbelievable. Incomprehensible. But we were in it. Hugh, who had until this moment been a pacifist, left his choir-directing and volunteered for the Army. Here he was a puzzle to the whole armed forces until they finally made him chaplain's assistant and started him playing the piano. Ted, who had been attending the University of the South in Sewanee, Tennessee, joined the V-12 unit and at the end of his sophomore year, left the college to serve as an officer in the Navy.

And in my Bible class a group of dismayed mothers set ourselves to study a way to pray for our sons in service.

We could not pray for God to protect our sons and help them to kill other mothers' sons. So we prayed not only that God would surround our sons with a circle of light that nothing could get through to hurt them, but also that He would as much as possible protect them from having to kill others. We did not, of course, demand that our sons be pacifists, seeing all too well the two sides of this perplexing question and respecting their right to make their own decision. But we did pray fervently that the armed forces would find for them other kinds of service than killing, and in many cases they were appointed to be pharmacists' assistants, ground-crew mechanics, and the like.

I was somewhat dismayed when Ted volunteered for Scouts and Raiders. This was the most dangerous type of service, particularly when he later on specialized in underwater demolition. But it did not require killing! Therefore, I accepted it with thanksgiving. Some of our sons, however, were in the very thick of the action, and yet were protected. Not so much as a hair of the head of any one of them was injured. One of them was going through the jungle with three other soldiers when he heard a voice say, "Jump." He jumped and was saved. A bomb fell where he had stood, and all the others were killed. The reader will now think, "Why didn't God tell the other three to jump?"

He did. I am sure He did. But the others did not hear Him.

They had not been taught to listen to Him, and they were not surrounded by prayer.

All of our young men from the parish (and we expanded our group to pray for the whole 130 of them) had been taught to listen and to trust. My husband taught them. Every man, before leaving for Europe, came to Ted for prayer. Ted gave each of them a small New Testament to put in his pocket and prayed for them and blessed a cross for them to wear. It was never announced that they should come to see their rector before leaving. They just did, because they loved and trusted him. Every one of them was on his acolyte list, and with every one of them he had always communicated personally, giving them their times for serving. Moreover, he had always held a monthly class for his servers, teaching them the mysteries of the Cross so that they could the better serve before the Lord's altar. Ted cared little for youth groups, treating his youth always as people, just as he treated everyone else in the congregation. His young men were trained to believe that they were his assistants in filling the house of the Lord with beauty and with dignity and with power. They prayed together with him before every service, and not only then but during the service itself. No youth group or group of any kind ever took place during a worship service in the church, for that was the most important thing of all, the most life-giving and joy-creating, and nothing was allowed to stand in the way of it.

Our prayer group found, moreover, that we could not pray for victory, but only for peace and for the family of nations. We prayed, therefore, that the war would end in whatever way and at whatever time was best for all mothers' sons and for the establishment of the kingdom of God. We also found, as we became more and more involved in prayer, that in order to conserve our power upon this plane, we were required to abstain completely from any war activity, even to buying war savings stamps or taking our leftover grease to the grocery stores to be collected for making gunpowder or something. We did not argue with others about this, for nothing dissipates prayer-power so quickly as argument. We simply did it.

One of our young men was in the forefront of all four of the invasions. A friend of his wrote to his mother: "What is this with George? I've seen him wading out of a landing barge with his gun held over his head and men falling on every side of him and nothing can touch him! I swear the bullets are deflected!"

What would happen if all mothers knew how so to pray? The answer is obvious: we would no longer have wars. And the time must come when that is so.

One of the mothers in our prayer group had been given a gift of discernment. We found that if she and I went together into the chapel and prayed for a young man missing in action, she would see in her mind a picture of him and would thus be able to reassure his parents.

"I see him sitting on a wooden box in the corner of a barbed-wire fence," she said once. "He looks thin and tired, but he is not sick. He has on shorts and a T-shirt, so it must be in a tropical country." And so he was, as we learned afterward. Once she had an impression of a young man in a dark tunnel, and the interpretation of that is obvious. He was no longer in this world. I did not have this gift, nor could Jeannie bring it forth alone. But when the two of us were together in prayer, the perception came to her, even as it came to many a person in the Bible.

This chapter began with the story of Rufus Moseley and the strange joy that he brought into my life, a joy connected, however, always with Pearl Harbor and the war. And it comes to me on writing this that God brought the modern-day prophet into my life at this very moment on purpose to give me the strength to carry on my prayers through this difficult time. Brother Rufus often came to my house in passing by, even as the prophet Elisha often came to the Shunammite woman's house. And joy came with him. Yet I knew this joy only through him and did not know how to enter into it myself. It was the light of the Holy Spirit of Jesus, but he had received this light alone, in a vision of Christ entering into him, and he was not able to tell another how to have this vision. It never occurred to me then that it was possible for one person to lay hands on another as in the Book of Acts and pray for that person to receive the Holy Spirit. And Brother Rufus made no offer to do so. The light, therefore, was evanescent, filling one with glory in the presence of this old man but fading into a wistfulness of forgotten joy in his absence. I did not know then that I was to receive this light into myself not many years hence.

Although the Lord upheld me, yet the way was desperately difficult, for at this time of life the fears that had always been my haunting shadow became intensified almost beyond endurance. It may have been partly middle age which I was rapidly approaching. But I decided that I was not going to sit in a doctor's office for ten years "having a needle," and I did not. It must have been not only the change of life but also the reverberation of the fears of many people whose sons were far away in the war . . . for thoughts do not fall to the ground, but set up a vibration in the air, fainter than the vibration of speech but equally real. And the more I took upon me the burden of prayer for the 130 young men in the congregation and for all the other men facing death and worse than death, the more the wild currents of fear swept through my mind.

I told no one of this, for I was the one to whom all the others came for comfort and support. One woman, however, knew it. She was a simple, uneducated woman who lived on the street back of me and whose grandson played with Jack. We had become acquainted through the little boys, and I had prayed for healing for her husband when he was dying of a heart attack—and he had been healed. So we talked about the Lord many a time. She would come into the kitchen door, usually with her hair straggling over her neck and a petticoat showing, and would say with conviction, "Satan's bothering you again."

I did not know about this Satan business, my ideas about his activities being rather vague. But fears were unquestionably bothering me, and I would admit it, and she would immediately go into battle with Satan, and in loud tones, while I sat meekly on the kitchen stool beside the sink, she would command him to go away and "not bother Mrs. Sanford anymore." And I would feel better! This, I thought, was no doubt merely symbolic, but it was a comfort just the same.

About this time I felt that although the Lord did not allow me to take any part in destroying life, I might help to save it. Therefore I volunteered as a Grey Lady in the Red Cross, working in Tilton Army Hospital. Once a week the rattly Red Cross station wagon would pick me up along with four or five other volunteers and drive us to Fort Dix. We would walk up the long ramp to the hospital, spread out like chicken coops as are all Army hospitals, and would there be instructed in our duties by the Red Cross ladies.

Each one of us was given a two-level cart filled with cigarettes, comic books and adventure magazines, candy, cookies, and sometimes flowers or fruit. Pushing this before us, we were to cover a certain section of wards, greeting each soldier with a cheery word and offering him his choice from our wagon. We were not to touch the men, for obvious reasons, and for reasons a bit less obvious, we were forbidden to talk to them of God. I had every intention of following these rules and did so for about two months. But then as I stood beside a soldier who resembled my older son, big brown eyes and short, boyish nose, I could not stand to see him lie there "rotting" (to use their own words) with an infected bone that would not heal. It was an agonizing choice: whether to obey the rules of the Army and the Red Cross or whether to obey the voice of God.

"I know a power that could make you well," I said.

"Oh, yeah?" remarked the youth with something less than full enthusiasm.

"Yeah," I replied, for I find that without any intention of doing so, I fall into the manner of speech of the one with whom I talk. "I don't guarantee anything, but it once got me out of a pretty bad jam, and it has helped a lot of other people. Want me to tell you about it?"

"Okay, shoot."

"If I do, you've got to promise to keep it a secret," I said. "Because I'm not supposed to talk like this."

"Okay," remarked the boy again with a shade of relief on his face. He did not want to be the object of comment any more than I did.

"Well, it's like this: there's a power in the air, sort of like electricity, and I've learned how to let it come through me into a person—and it does help him to get well. You know—sort of like X ray."

The boy shrugged. "May as well try it," he muttered.

"It's God's power. So I have to talk to God. Okay?"

He nodded with a resigned and somewhat furtive look about him.

"Don't worry! Nobody'll know I'm talking to God. And look, we want the power to come right into that leg, so it will be better if I slide my hands under these comics and things. It's all right, I won't let anybody see me. You'll be able to feel the power come in."

I "talked to God," with my eyes open, glancing at the boy in a friendly sort of way so as not to be seen of men to pray.

"Feels hot," he said.

"Sure," I said, "it's like electricity."

I left him, and the next week the leg was much better. Within a month, during which we prayed each week, the leg was healed.

Some of my readers may wonder why I did not first ask him whether he believed in Jesus Christ. The answer is that he would then have set me down as a professional soul-saver and would have shut up like a clam. The next question is, "Is it right to pray for healing for one who is not a Christian?"

This question troubled me for some time at an earlier stage in my life. The Lord Himself answered it for me. He put me in a position where I had to pray for a non-Christian. I made a date to pray for a man who would not give me his name. On the way home, I suddenly remembered his face and knew that he was Jewish.

"Lord, how come You do me this way?" said I, as my Negro friend Alice Smothers remarks in moments of perplexity.

The answer was: "Blind Bartimaeus was a Jew. The ten lepers were Jews. They did not know that I was the Messiah, but I prayed for them just the same." And I knew that I was simply to follow Jesus and do as He did, whether it fitted in with my theology or not.

C. S. Lewis once said, "God is always saving people in ways that I don't like."

And very often God does save them through healing.

From this time on, I prayed for healing as I went about the wards, and only two of the hundreds for whom I prayed failed to receive a healing. It was a greater measure of success than I ever knew at any other time or situation. Possibly this was partly because they owed me nothing and I owed them nothing. Or possibly it was because they were not suffering as a result of their own sins but from the sins of the nation: *our* sins. Another factor was that their healing must be kept secret. Thus they did not waste energy in words, and I was free to follow God's guidance.

Before entering any ward, I would pray, "Lord, show me to whom I should speak." And I would then follow my "hunch," speaking to the one among the thirty-six to whom my compassion flowed the most freely.

There was once a soldier, recuperating rapidly but still bedfast, who said to me, "You don't remember me, do you?"

"No, I don't," I replied.

"I was in Ward 16," he said. "And you came along and prayed for me. My leg was all full of osteo, see, and now it's well."

Praise the Lord! One prayer—no follow-up—the man forgotten. Yet he was healed!

Very soon I began to teach these men the prayer of faith. Strangely, the ones most hesitant about learning this positive approach to prayer were the good Christians. I remember a Mennonite youth lying for months with a third-degree burn showing the anklebone. It simply would not heal. He was bitterly unhappy, not so much about his ankle as about his soul, for the rough and evil talk that he heard in the ward wounded him deeply. (I never heard it. I do not remember a single blasphemous or dirty word being spoken in my presence.) He brought forth all the usual objections to healing: Was it God's will? Did Jesus heal today? Finally I persuaded him to try it, assuring him that if it was not God's will, it would not happen.

The next week the ankle was completely healed. The most joyful part of the venture was that the young man glowed like a light.

"I didn't know Christianity was like this," he said. "It's true—it's true."

I hope that when he went back to his Mennonite church he found others who knew that Jesus is true.

There was one Christian boy, a Roman Catholic, whom I could not reach at all—though nowadays I find, praise God, Roman Catholics are more open than average Protestants to the power of God.

"But only saints can do miracles," he objected, when I suggested praying for him.

"Well, what makes a saint?" I inquired, remembering Saint Paul's customary salutation, for instance, "To the saints which are at Ephesus" (Eph. 1:1).

"You can't be a saint until you're dead," explained the boy, and that seemed to put the matter beyond the bounds of possibility.

Later on, however, I did find a way to approach a Roman Catholic soldier. I went to the convent in our town, adjoining the parochial school, and introduced myself to Mother Saint Eugene, explaining my problem with the soldiers.

"We will pray for them!" said she joyously, and no one could have been more completely friendly and faithful. "And we'll pray for the Protestant boys, too. Give us a list of those you see." So I gave them a list, and every morning at their Mass all the nuns prayed for them joyously at the top of their lungs.

I then tried to find more prayer help by writing to the Poor Clares and the Holy Cross Fathers. But I soon gathered that they were interested in the state of the souls of the suffering ones, but were extremely dubious about God's will to heal the bodies, not knowing that Jesus is alive today and walks the streets of New Jersey just as He walked the streets of Palestine, longing to heal wherever He finds a human body through whom to work.

Mother Saint Eugene was a tremendous help with this work. After meeting her, if I found a Roman Catholic man unwilling for me to pray for him, I would just give him my suggestions about the prayer of faith and then say, "Would you like me to ask Mother Saint Eugene and the sisters to pray for you?" and, thank God, his face would light up immediately.

In another book I have told the story of Abie, a Jewish man who learned the prayer of faith, though in other than religious words. He had told me that he did not believe that there was any God.

"Well, then," I replied, "what would you call the power that makes the birds sing and the flowers bloom?"

"Nature," said he.

"All right," I replied, for in healing a person one must always first come down to his level so that one can later lift him to God's level. "Call it Nature. So ask this Nature to come into you and help your leg to get well. Then imagine the leg well and say 'thanks a lot' to whatever power is coming in from outside to get it well."

This he said he would do, though he would not let me pray for him.

"I'd rather do it myself," he said.

"Fine," I replied, for I always accepted whatever suggestion came from the individual, knowing that it was for him to choose and not for me to argue.

"Red Cross," said he as I was leaving, "see those two men down at the end of the ward? Better not talk to them that way. They won't believe you. They're Christians."

I thanked him for this advice and followed it. "You're a Roman Catholic, aren't you?" I said to the first one, seeing a holy medal on his chest.

"Yes ma'am."

"Fine! So you have hold of something that can help you get well, don't you?"

"Huh?"

"Don't the priests teach you that when you receive the Mass you are receiving the Body and Blood of Christ?"

"Oh, yes ma'am!"

"Well, then, doesn't His body include His bones?"

"Huh?"

"And can't you say, after the priest brings you the Mass, 'Thank You, Lord, because Your body and blood that I have received is helping my bones to get well'?"

"I never thought of that!"

"If you haven't thought of it, you're missing some of the benefit you might receive," I said. "Why not think of it next time —and I'll ask Mother Saint Eugene to pray for you."

I have no idea how much this may have helped the man to recover, but recover he did, and there was joy on his face as I turned away from the bed.

Abie also recovered, and in due time he remarked, "Do you remember what I said the first time you talked to me: that I didn't believe there is any God? Well, I've changed my mind. There *is* a God."

"Abie, how did you know?" I cried with delight.

And he replied, "I just know."

No one, I am sure, will ever shake that knowing. For it came from within, from God Himself. And if there are enough people among Christians who love Jesus and therefore love the brethren of Jesus, surely sometime someone will introduce all the Abie's to Jesus Christ, the Son of God.

Or so I hope.

But if not, then maybe Jesus will come directly to Abie and make Himself known to him.

I learned two things in my work at Tilton Hospital, in addition to all that the Lord showed me about healing. I learned the essential decency of human nature, and the utter and absolute evil of war. These men did not complain. They were in the armed services not of their own will, yet they endured what destruction came to them and uttered no word except the little conventional words of grousing about the food or something. About the war itself, they said, for the most part, nothing, but looked out from unbearable memories with blank eyes.

In the old days, war could be thrilling: banners and drums, high courage and great idealism, wonderful hopes of saving our country or making the world safe for democracy. It is no longer so.

There were no Japanese prisoners in the hospital. German soldiers, yes, mopping the corridors with dour faces and a big PW on the backs of their jackets. Italians, yes. No Japanese. Why?

"We threw them all into a trench," a young soldier told me, his face carefully expressionless, "living and dead and wounded—and ran a bulldozer over them."

And after My Lai, one can believe this.

"But what they did," said the young man, "to *their* prisoners of war . . ." And he could say no more.

I know. I was brought up in China. If you want to know in a way made bearable by beauty insofar as anyone can make it so, read A Bar of Shadow by Laurens Van Der Post.

Yet these same little yellow men, after the war, when my son was in Japan on occupation duty, were courteous, kind, and charming. Most people think that was a false politeness and goodness. Not at all! The bright side of the personality was on top. The swing is wider with the Oriental than it is with the Anglo-Saxons. Their bright side is as warm and light as ours and often more so. But their shadow side is darker than any sadism that we can even contemplate. Our mistake is the usual one of assuming that there is no difference between the races. If we could recognize the differences, learn to cope with them, come to love them, and to bring out the good, then we might have a better world. Until we do learn, no amount of warfare will make it better, but will make it progressively worse. For the evil thinking of mankind does not die with them but lives on in the air and attacks another generation in another way.

One of my wards was Ward 17, an officers' ward, and in it was an Army doctor, healed by prayer of some wound or other; I forget what it may have been. At any rate, he was intensely interested in the work of prayer and mentioned it to at least one doctor on the ward—meanwhile, no doubt, pledging him to secrecy. Perhaps it was he who said, as a friend in Moorestown told me, "Nobody need tell me that God doesn't do miracles today, for I have seen three in Ward 17."

Among the three was the miracle of Frederick. He lay in a private cell, which meant, according to the usage of that hospital, that his death was imminent. He was so gaunt and shriveled that he looked like a wizened old monkey. His skin was yellow, the ribs protruded, and the skin fluttered between them as he breathed. There were tubes in both nostrils and attached to both wrists. And usually there was a doctor or a nurse with him. On passing the cell, I always threw him a swift prayer, but did not dare to go within and lay my hands on him. And a general prayer from a distance was not enough. It required an immediate presence and the word of faith and if possible the laying on of hands to provide an adequate channel for God's healing power. One day, however, he was alone and awake. Greatly daring, but compelled by compassion, I went in.

In all these years I have found only one effective motive for healing: compassion. If we desire to heal someone by the power of Jesus in order to glorify Jesus, then somehow we usually fail to reach that person. Jesus is glorified of course through every healing, but only when we are, as He was, "moved by compassion" (Mark 1:41).

"You look like you're about washed up," I said. (I had found that the men liked this direct, unvarnished approach.)

"Yep," he said.

"What's the trouble?" I asked; I could see no wounds, nor could I smell any osteomyelitis.

"Blood clots," he replied, unilluminatingly.

This, thought I, should not be too difficult to heal. Therefore I told him of the power that might help him get well. He was not interested. In fact, he shut his eyes, a clear dismissal. But having got my teeth into this case, as it were, I was not moved to give up easily.

"Listen," I said at last, causing him by my forceful tone to open his eyes. "If you'll just let me try, the way I told you, I promise I'll never mention the matter again, win or lose. Now how about it?"

"Okay," he said wearily, and with a definite lack of enthusiasm. Whereupon he drew back the sheet, and I saw to my horror that his abdomen looked like a pool of dark blood, barely covered by a thin membrane.

"Guts torn out," he said, noting my dismay. "They didn't want to carry me in from the battlefield, but I told them they had to."

Here was a will to live if there ever was one! He had been kept alive for months by intravenous feeding, drugs, and stimulants. If I had seen his abdomen at first, without stomach or any other digestive organ as far as I could tell, I would not have spoken the word of faith. But there it was, and I could not retract it. So I laid my hands on the two sides of this red gaping pool of blood and visioned a stomach and all other organs perfect and called upon the Lord to bring this about.

When I reached home I telephoned every powerful prayer group that I knew and called for help from "the Christian underground" as a friend once called it in her amazement, not having known that there are people all over the land who believe that Jesus lives and heals today and who will respond to a call for prayer. And I myself prayed for a miracle to take place in Frederick. This would require an out-and-out miracle. This was no speeding up of normal healing processes. Nothing could do this except the direct work of God through Jesus Christ.

The next week I passed his room with fear and trembling, but he was asleep and I did not go in.

A week later, two weeks after our prayer, I again passed his room. It was empty. He was not in his bed. But the bed was rumpled, his things were scattered about, and his name was still upon the door. I went on to the common room at the end of the ward where men sat about in wheelchairs, but I did not see him. Then across the room my eyes fell upon a young, good-looking, ruddy-faced man who bore not the slightest resemblance to the wizened old monkey for whom I had prayed in the cell. This young man gazed at me with a twinkle in his eyes and a knowing grin, and presently I noticed that there was a tiny shade of resemblance.

"You can't be Frederick, can you?" I asked him.

His grin broadened. "Yes ma'am, I am," he said.

Remembering my promise, I made no reference to his healing but simply said, "What are you going to do now?"

"Think I'll go to South America and get a job," he replied.

"That seems like a good idea," said I. "My brother once worked there up in the mountains. He liked it." And I added, glancing at my cart, "Have an apple."

He had an apple, and I turned to leave.

He spoke once more, and I looked back.

"Well, but my feet still swell," said he.

"That's only because they aren't used to your standing up on them," I replied. "They'll soon be all right." And with this word of encouragement I went away.

The next week he was not in his cell. He was discharged and at home.

Once I had a brief talk with a chaplain. I recounted to him the story of Frederick, for I knew that he visited in Ward 17 and must have seen the young man.

"Is *that* what happened to him?" he cried in amazement. He referred, not to the healing of the young man's body, but to the awakening of his soul.

"Soon as he could get out of bed, he was down in my office every day," said the chaplain. "He wanted a Bible. He wanted to know all about God and about Jesus Christ."

Three months later, to my utter amazement, I passed that cell in Ward 17 and beheld on the door Frederick's name once more.

Within the cell stood a tall, burly, handsome young man who looked like a lifeguard at Atlantic City.

"You can't be—"

And again he said, "Yes ma'am, I am."

"What in the world are you doing here?"

"Just came back for my ninety-day checkup," he replied. "I did have the yellow jaundice, but it's all right now."

I never saw him again. But I do pray God that He find a way to lead this young man gently in His pasture and protect him from the deadly miasma of an unbelieving church. Perhaps Frederick is one of those who dares to tell the truth, and to help in awakening the sleeping giant of the church into a new life.

14

UT of my work in Tilton Hospital there grew a more mature understanding of the fact that I had been taught all my life: that Jesus Christ forgives sins. This tenet of theology had become increasingly puzzling to me as I learned more and more of the power of faith. For the question was, if the power of right thinking could establish in us the thing that we affirm, then why was the Cross necessary? Why did Jesus not simply pray for the scribes and Pharisees to believe in His truth? Why did He not pray for Pontius Pilate to have the courage of his convictions and acquit him? And most cogent of all, why did we who accepted Him as our Lord and Savior still have within us old darknesses and fears and tensions that were not released in spite of all our faith?

In *The Healing Light, Behold Your God, Dreams Are for Tomorrow,* and most of all in *Twice Seven Words,* I have given my new-old and deeper understanding of this profound subject: the forgiveness of sins. But I have never before told in full my manner of coming to this understanding. I owe it to three people: Sister Leila Margaret, Father Weed, and first of all, Dr. Emmett Fox. I had read his book, *The Sermon on the Mount,* setting aside a few ideas as being untenable according to my beliefs, reserving judgment upon others, but seeing the truths that illumined hitherto dark mysteries. Because I had read this book, I went to hear Dr. Fox (a "teacher of truth") on the only occasion to my knowledge when he lectured in Camden. How marvelously the Lord works! For this talk was on the very subject most on my mind: how it was that through the death on the Cross Jesus could forgive sins.

The vocabulary used by Dr. Fox was different from that

affected by most Christians. And I must admit that the very fact that he did not use the ordinary Christian words made it more of an eye-opener to me. For some of the usual Christian words, while perfectly true, are so common to us that we hear them with the ears but not with either heart or mind. I had to think through his words about Jesus, such as "lowering His thought-vibrations to the thought-vibrations of humanity," and put them into words more acceptable to most Christians, such as "entering into the subconscious mind of the human race." But the very fact of this rethinking sharpened my understanding of many phrases both of the church and of psychology.

This lecture helped me to understand that Jesus' redemption really works. The only book in which I have found this matter treated in a practical rather than a theological manner is a thin book of lectures called *What Seek Ye?* by H. B. Jeffery, another "student of truth."

Even Dr. Fox, however, in his enlightened understanding of this great turning point in history, the redemption of man through Jesus Christ, did not tell me how to receive the power of this forgiveness. And to understand it without knowing how to receive it makes matters actually worse, for then one can do nothing except to try to believe rather miserably that one has this forgiveness and that if one affirms it long enough one will feel better. And that does not seem to be the case. Affirmations are statements of faith that strengthen our character and enrich our life, but they do not, as far as I can see, remove entirely from us the accumulated burden of our own misdeeds in the past.

Once as I was talking along this line with a man of our church, he said, "You need the sacramentalizing of the emotions."

"What in the world is that?" I asked.

And he replied, "Go and see," and sent me to Sister Leila Margaret of the Sisters of Saint Margaret convent in Philadelphia. She enlightened my mind greatly, as I have told in *The Healing Light*, and sent me to Father Weed for a life confession. This opened new doors—it opened the floodgates, it opened the floodgates! I obeyed Father Weed implicitly, making the long trip by bus in to Saint James Church in Philadelphia once a month as he directed me to do. He was there on his knees every Saturday afternoon from two until six, whether he had one or two penitents come to him or none at all. I would take the confessional card and make my small confessions of any wrong words or deeds that I could remember having committed during the last month; and as I had never committed any very outstanding sins (having for one thing lacked opportunity), they were not sensational. Nevertheless, Father Weed would say a few words of counsel and give me a penance (such as reading a certain psalm and saying such and such prayers) and would pronounce the benediction, after which I would kneel in the pew and read those passages assigned to me. Even this must have had a healing effect, for once when I forgot the penance, the usual rush of joy did not come to me until I had reached home, remembered, gone into the church and read them.

There were still, however, areas needing healing that this practice of monthly confession did not touch. I was unaware of these areas until a physician whom I had met at a CFO conference and who happened to be visiting in Philadelphia brought them to my attention.

"What makes you so nervous?" he said as he returned with me by train from New York where I had talked to a small group in Sam Shoemaker's Calvary Church in Gramercy Park. "I studied you. You spoke very well, but you grew more and more nervous until you were keyed as high as a kite. What is it?"

If I had allowed myself to consider the matter, I would have known, for certain aspects of married life were still extremely difficult for me due to my ultra-Victorian upbringing. But I had trained myself to live above this difficulty and it did not come to mind at all.

"Nothing," I replied, thinking that I spoke the truth. "I'm just a very high-keyed person, that's all."

"Oh no," said he. "Oh no! There's something in your memories that makes you that way. If I were to talk to you three or four times I could find out what it is."

My first impulse was to reject this offer and probably with some reason, for it proved rather emotionally disturbing. However, I was set toward learning all that I could learn of God's power, so I agreed. Thereupon, this extremely attractive man of about my own age had four interviews with me, at the end of which I was more or less in love with him (on a high spiritual plane, you understand), but I had learned about the healing of the memories. At his advice, therefore, I used "the tools" I had, and when I went to confession, I would bring up some unhealed memory of my past, connected with some small misdeed or wrong thought, and ask forgiveness for it. And it worked.

The doctor went into the chapel with me several times and prayed with the laying on of hands for the healing of the memories, and that gave me great release—even though in the course of it, I became for a while too much emotionally involved with him and too dependent on him. He had not learned to keep Christ between him and the one for whom he prayed. And this is a very important safeguard.

This had its good results in that in later years when, for instance, a woman would come to me brokenhearted because she had fallen in love with her psychiatrist, I understood and could pray for the feeling simply to die down and go away. I look very dubiously upon the deliberate use of "transference" as a tool in bringing a person "release." For I know that while it may bring a certain measure of temporary release, it is likely in the long run to increase the patient's bondage.

My temporary emotional disturbance, however, was merely a flurry on the surface of consciousness, for beneath it I loved my husband and no other man: I never even thought of breaking the bond of marriage, even though it was founded more on spiritual values than on physical ones. After all, which are more important, and which are more enduring, and which carry from one life to another and then evolve into purely spiritual love?

In spite of these emotional dangers, I still learned from this experience the tremendous and wonderful power of the forgiveness of Jesus Christ. There is, of course, a value in coming to understand our need of forgiveness through the help of a psychologist or psychiatrist. But unless that counselor can lead us through the agony of self-understanding to the bliss of redemption of that self through the entering in of Jesus Christ, we are not apt to be really healed. "This is you, and you must accept it and learn to live with it." These words are completely false for the Christian. This is not you or me. This is only the "old man after the flesh," the one we used to be, the one we would be unless Christ came and redeemed us by bringing to life the "new person in Christ Jesus" lying dormant within us until He awakens it. To say, "This is me and I must learn to live with it," is to be carnally minded, to have the mind on the flesh, the lower physical-mental being we are without Christ. And to be carnally minded is death (Rom. 8:6). But to be spiritually minded—to acknowledge, accept, and dwell upon the new person whom Jesus makes us when He forgives our sins and abides within us through His Holy Spirit—this is life and peace.

So far, my deeper understanding of the forgiveness of Jesus Christ was fragmentary and inadequate. I now realized the power of the confessional when both priest and penitent actually believed in this power. But Father Weed moved to another parish, and shortly afterward, we also moved, and my efforts toward finding another effective confessor did not meet with success. Good "churchmen" would probably say at this point that I must know that the confession was valid whether or not I felt any release. I am willing to accept this statement, but I am not satisfied without the release. A doctor may tell his patient, "This medicine is good whether it makes you better or not," and the patient may accept the fact, but he still wants to be better. I still wanted to be relieved of inner pain and tension, but my experience in working with a lay person along this line had been unsatisfactory, and I did not try it again.

I knew that there was a path through this forest of confusion, and I was casting about for it but had not found it. Then as so often happens, the Lord showed me the clear path, and it was through the need of somebody else, not of myself.

This person was the young man whom I called "John Masterman" in *Oh, Watchman,* and whom I shall call John. He was a friend of Abie's who came to know Jesus while he was there in the hospital.

"What is this that comes through you when you stand by a bed?" he asked me once, even before I had spoken to him of healing. (Did not Jesus say that we should be like a light: like a city set upon a hill whose light cannot be hid?)

So I told him and added, "You must learn how to use this light." His thigh was full of shrapnel and threads and osteomyelitis, and some five inches of the thigh bone had been shot away. He had been in the hospital two years and was twenty years old— finished, so he thought. But he learned, was healed in six weeks, and thereupon made it his business to tell the good news to everyone else in the ward.

Some time later he said to me, "There is something else you have not told me. What is it?"

I then gave him a New Testament and told him to read the Gospel of John. For I thought, "Let's not begin with the Virgin Birth and angels and shepherds and what not."

When I went to the hospital the next week, John said, "You know, that book you told me to read, I read it three times before I got the idea, but I finally did. And then I read another book about Him, by a man called Matthew."

"Oh, oh," I thought. "Here we go." But I only asked him curiously, "What do you think of Jesus Christ?"

"I wonder whether that is who the other one is," replied the young man. "Because when I'm doing my prayers, I often feel that I am not alone."

"I'm sure that is who the other one is," said I. "But what do you think of Him? Do you believe what the man called Matthew said about Him, that He was born of a virgin and that He raised His own body from the dead—He and God the Father?"

John looked at me as if to say, "How dumb can you get?"

"Of course I believe it!" he said. "If even I, who know nothing and am nothing, could rebuild five inches of bone into my leg where there wasn't any bone, just by doing what He said, why shouldn't He· have been born of a virgin? And why shouldn't He have raised His body from the dead?"

Here was a Jew with a belief more simple and more profound than that of most Christians. And why not? God chose the Jews to be the first channels of His power, and not by mistake. He knew their capacities. If only we who claim to be Christians will show them the love of Jesus Christ, I believe they can go farther along the road to power than we can.

Later on this young man said, "I feel that I should be baptized."

"Have you figured it out?" I asked. "If you're baptized, you'll catch it coming and going."

"Yes, I know," said John. "But it's an inner must."

So when he left the hospital, he came down from New York

and visited us on several weekends. Ted baptized him and later on prepared him for confirmation.

But he did not get complete release, even though he led a most wonderful Christian life, forgiving all who had persecuted him or his family and even trying "the game of minutes"—thinking of Jesus every minute.

"There's still something very wrong with me," he said one weekend. "Sometimes my feelings change and I want to hurt people, and I do it, too. I say the rudest, meanest things I can think of, and I thoroughly enjoy myself while I am saying them. Once in the office I threw a typewriter. Twice I threw glasses of water." (John had found through prayer a wonderful summer job. He wrote letters as Betty Crocker! But I did not know how long this advertising work would last if he continued to throw typewriters.)

I prayed for the healing of mental depression, but it did not work because it was a wrong diagnosis. That was not the trouble. I prayed for the forgiveness of a bad temper, but it did not work. John did not have a bad temper. Neither was his trouble "the devil," though some might think so. It was actually the Lord, working in his subconscious mind to bring up old resentments and old fears so that they could be healed.

He returned to New York no better. Therefore I prayed for guidance: "Well then, Lord—how *shall* I pray?"

It came to me first that the trouble was not in the conscious young man but in the little boy within him who had lived in the Gestapo regime.

"Yes, Lord," said I, "but how can I pray for that little boy who lived ten years ago?"

As I listened, the Lord showed me that in the heavenly kingdom, time is relative—Jesus Christ lives in all time, and therefore can go back through time and heal that which is past.

"Yes, Lord, but *how?*" I asked.

And as I listened, there came to me an understanding of what Jesus really did during Passion Week.

This book is a narrative and not an exposition, and a discussion of the redemption of Jesus Christ does not belong here. I will say only that when the understanding came to me, then I knew how to pray for John. I asked Jesus to enter into him, and go back

through time, and heal the memories of fear and resentments—
even those that he had forgotten. I asked the Lord to go back
through all his lifetime and heal even the baby in the cradle—even
the soul of the infant before birth—of any shadow of this mortal
life that may have crept upon him.

And it happened.

"What have you been doing?" John wrote me. "All of a sudden I feel just ridiculously happy from morning until night . . ."

This was not the end of John's journey, nor was it the end of
mine. But it was a great step along the way.

John is now a clinical psychologist. And he has two sets of
tools at his command. He can use either his learned skill as a counselor or his Jesus-given power as a forgiver and healer. Or he can
use a combination of the two. Also, he lectures on healing to ministers and others. If he had been the only one helped, it would
have made worthwhile my two and a half years in Tilton Hospital.

There are those suffering from mental depression: the first
stages of manic-depressive insanity, as I once suffered. These need,
as I did, a simple prayer for the healing of the mental illness. But
there are others—multitudes, multitudes!—who are simply normal people carrying the chains of old memories. Those old memories can be healed, and those chains can be broken. Indeed this is
the reason and purpose for which our Lord came into the world—
God veiled in flesh—to break off the chains from prisoners and
captives and to set at liberty those who are bound.

I learned in talking to people to find out what was binding
them and pray for it to be healed. I do this in a very simple way. I
ask them three questions: "Were you happy when you were a
child?" If they say yes, then I ask, "When did you begin to be unhappy?" And finally, "Why?"

Then I ask Jesus to walk into the past—back through their
memories—and heal all the wounded places and break off all the
chains and set them free. And I *picture* Him doing so, His love
flowing around and around any old wound in the memory until
the feeling connected with it is completely healed, so that one can
remember the very thing that used to make him unhappy, yet feel
no unhappiness, but only the joy of a new freedom.

"Thank the Lord!" I imagine the person saying. "That can't
hurt me anymore!"

And it doesn't.

"But everybody needs this healing of the memories!" you may be thinking.

Yes. And every minister is in a position to pray in this manner, for this is just simply ministry. But not all ministers know or believe that Jesus Christ really does forgive sins. Or if they believe it, they tend to relegate it to the future, thinking of it as some mechanistic or theological thing that takes place at the gate of heaven. It is not. It is a practical, immediate, life-giving act that takes place now and here upon this earth. The Gospels are full of it. The Epistles shout aloud about it. They call it "the forgiveness of sins" and so it is, for all these wounded memories come either from our own sins or from the sins of others against us, needing our forgiveness.

What has happened to the church that this great transformation does not take place when a person accepts Jesus Christ as Lord and Savior? Has He gone away from us, so that His power reaches us no more?

No. He has not gone away. Only last week I went to a meeting of those enthusiastic young ones who call themselves "Jesus people," as indeed they are. There I saw a freeing and a joy and a deliverance that filled the little "chapel," made of a restaurant, with holy ecstasy. These young people had experienced the healing of the memories. Their faces glowed with the joy of it. They were healed not only in the mind but also in the body, being set free from the chains of drugs and that without any withdrawal symptoms. I know. I was there. I heard their testimonies, though the strongest testimony was not in their words but in themselves: their whole person free and glowing with new life.

For forty years I have talked and prayed and worked in churches, and new life does spring up here and there, yet these young people say that the churches are dead. Compared to the burgeoning and glorious new life that I found among these hairy young ones in their desert restaurant, the churches *are* dead—though one hopes and prays always that they will come to life again.

But God is not dead! Jesus is most vigorously alive, and since it is His will to bring us the kingdom of heaven, wherein sins are forgiven and souls are healed, He will find ways of doing so, whether we like those ways or not!

Meanwhile, my days at Tilton Hospital were drawing to an end. I did not want it to be so, for in spite of the grueling pain of it, I loved this work. Even beholding the agony of the world seemed to have a healing effect on my spirit as well as on the bodies of those for whom I prayed. Maybe it was comparable to the purpose of tragedy on stage, which is, according to the classic definition, "to purify the emotions by means of pity and terror."

But the work was beginning to affect my body. For several days after working in the hospital, I would feel a bit of pain around the heart—walking some ten miles a day, pushing a heavy cart, and at the same time pouring out spiritual power was draining too much strength from the body. We do live in these bodies at the present time! We carry this treasure of the power of God in earthen vessels, and it is our duty to take care of the vessels. Some people ignore this duty, allow themselves to be burdened beyond endurance by the troubles of others and find that the body collapses. There is a fine balance between telling ourselves that we can do all things through Christ who strengthens us and in deciding how much of His work He wants us to do.

But I could not bear to stop. Each week I would toy with the thought of resigning, and then a young man would look at me with the wistful eyes of a child from out of the broken body of a man and would say, "When are you coming again?"

Then one day I was summoned out of my ward to the office of the local head of the Red Cross and into the presence of an enraged female of uncertain years. I had been working on another ramp than my usual one and had apparently grown careless. A doctor who did not know me came up behind me, caught me in the act of praying for healing for a soldier, and reported me to the Red Cross. And I have never before nor since heard the equal of the stream of vituperation that issued from her lips. She was a faithful member of a church that did not believe in healing, that was the trouble. For from the days when heretics were burned at the stake, no one can be more utterly condemnatory toward an aspect of Christianity that they do not believe in than can another Christian. There was nothing I could say. It would be impossible to defend my prayers by saying, "But they really are healed," without getting some soldier into trouble. So I said nothing, but handed in my uniform as commanded (incidentally, I had paid for it myself), and departed, never to return again.

While my dismissal could have been done in less summary fashion, I do not blame the woman mentioned above. She was only carrying out orders. There was some reason for these orders, of course. They were meant to protect the men from fanatics and from those who might get them emotionally disturbed. And by the church as a whole, which still did not believe that Jesus heals today (Thank God, they are now beginning to believe it!), I suppose I could be classed as a heretic.

So when one traces this tragedy back to its source (and it *was* a tragedy), one traces it to the church, yet unawakened to Christ's power.

There was, for instance, an Army chaplain on the West Coast who wrote to me plaintively saying that eight men in his hospital had asked him to pray the prayer of faith for their healing and he did not know how to do so. Would I therefore come over and help him? In due time I came. We prayed together for the eight men, four white and four black, and they were healed, every one.

"I suppose I should learn to do this," said the chaplain, looking extremely unhappy over the whole thing.

"Looks like you've got to," I agreed with a grin and left him some suggestions and some books. He learned. He was very discreet and did not even use the laying on of hands, but only the prayer of faith, together with the power of real conversion to Jesus Christ. He was far better at the latter than I was, having the training and the authority of a minister. He became known throughout the hospital. When the doctors had to perform a difficult operation, they would often ask him to stand outside the operating room and pray. When a nurse could not get a patient quiet, she would send for the chaplain. On one occasion the chaplain first converted and then prayed for healing for a soldier dying of cancer and the man recovered in six weeks, bought an old jalopy and disappeared. But before he left, a doctor asked him, "What are you doing? I don't understand your recovery."

"It's the chaplain," said the soldier innocently, not knowing that chaplains are not supposed to pray. "He's praying for me, and I'm getting well."

This was reported to the hospital authorities and they referred the matter to the church from which the chaplain came, asking, "Does your church believe in healing?"

The answer came back, "No."

Whereupon the chaplain, no longer young, was dismissed without even a pension and for a season sold pots and pans from door to door.

All of this I reminded myself as I endeavored to forgive the head of the Red Cross—for at first I was very angry, and my husband was even more so! But I had to forgive her—and quickly—for someone was coming to see me for healing prayer. And if I remained angry, that person would not be healed. Moreover, I reminded myself of the words of our Lord, who knew that in the course of history such things must happen, and said, nevertheless, "Rejoice and be exceeding glad, for so persecuted they the prophets which were before you" (Matt. 5:12). When I remembered the sad fate of some prophets, I knew myself to be extremely lucky and did not know whether to laugh or to cry.

But why *rejoice*, I wondered. Merely because I was by way of being a prophet? This to me was no big deal. I would still have preferred to be a well-known dramatist or at least a writer, and to have a lovely garden full of flowers and time to tend it. Why rejoice?

It did not come to me until this moment that one can rejoice because those things told by the prophets are true, and the time will come when the whole church will awake to the fact that Jesus heals today—both soul and body. Or if the church will not awaken to the truth, then the church will perish of dry rot and the Lord of heaven and earth who is Jesus Christ will Himself find those outside the church who will come to Him by thousands, by thousands, and He will be their Lord and they will be His people.

At any rate, I had a day in which to forgive the embattled lady. It was Sunday, and with the help of the Eucharist and of determined prayer, I got over being angry in time to pray for the troubled person who came to me on Monday.

15.

WHEN one door closes to us in life, another door always opens. Therefore we should not look back grieving at the door that has closed, lest we fail to see the opening of the new door.

My new door was the inspiration to write, and it grew directly out of my years of working in Tilton Hospital. Now writing was my original desire and my original intention in life. I had studied every course in writing given at my two colleges. Moreover, I had at two different times taken a year's correspondence course in commercial writing. But for years I had been so busy in teaching and in praying for those in trouble that writing had simply been laid aside. I had never decided to give it up. It had just been pushed out by necessity; and when I realized with great sadness that this was so, I consented to it for the sake of the Lord's work.

True, from time to time I dashed off some little play or skit for the Woman's Club or somebody, but these were very small things. One morning I asked the Lord which of two small things I should write. And the voice said clearly in my mind, "Neither. Write a novel about your experiences in Tilton Hospital."

How wonderfully the Lord works all things together and turns them into His glory! Writing *Oh, Watchman!* was sheer delight. It teaches actual ways of presenting prayer and healing even to non-Christians. It is a parable or a series of parables.

If anyone says to me, "But how can I present this matter of healing to a Jewish friend? Or to someone who knows nothing at all about God?" I can say, "Read *Oh, Watchman!* and see." The hero, Timmy, is a composite character, but all the others are drawn from life. One, John Masterman, the clinical psychologist,

is filled with all the gifts of the Spirit, particularly the gift of healing, both of mind and of body. He is original and powerful in his
methods, looking to God much more than to Freud or to any
other teacher. I have just been working with him as a co-leader in
a School of Pastoral Care and have watched him run two miles
every morning, remembering, as I did so, how he lay in traction
with one leg full of osteomyelitis and minus four or five inches of
the thigh bone.

As I study God's working in my life, I perceive that He had
more than the actual book in mind when He said, "Write a
book." It was for the comfort of my family and of my own soul
that for a season I refused invitations to lecture and stayed at
home to write. Writing is my joy, whereas lecturing and healing is
from the beginning to this day a terrifying challenge and a fearful
burden to me. It amazes me to hear other people in this work say
that the more they give out, the more God's love flows into them,
and they feel better when they have finished a healing mission
than when they began. Are they really telling the truth? And if
they are, then the question arises, "How much are they really giving?"

It may be all right merely to say words, but that is not what I
do or what God allows me to do. I prepare for a lecture with much
prayer and careful thought. Moreover, in this work, as I have explained in a previous chapter, there is a mysterious flow from mind
to mind that brings about the actual power of God in the church
and frees Him to do His healing work.

In prayers for healing, especially with the laying on of hands,
this flow of power through the one who prays into the one who
needs healing is tremendous. I give out far more than I can at that
time take in. I cannot help it. If I do not allow myself to be used
as a channel, then nothing happens. And when I have finished the
assignment, my strength has been drained to the uttermost.

On the other hand, when I write, the inspiration comes from
God, but it comes into my own mind and is not immediately dis-
persed to others. Therefore, I myself am fed and recharged with
life, and even if the conscious mind and the body are weary simply
from the work of concentration, the inner being is deeply comforted and is strengthened. When I write, I am in my own way re-
building the Kingdom within, while when I lecture I am labori-

ously laying bricks in the foundations of the Kingdom without. I build the Kingdom within through constant prayer and listening. In fact, in writing novels I *hear* the words my characters speak, and I *see* their movements, and simply write down what I see. This, however, does not mean that the writing is perfect! Far from it! Never, so far as I know, are we relieved of the responsibility of using our own minds. It is still necessary for a writer, no matter how inspired he may be, to develop and use to the utmost his critical ability.

One does not do this in writing the first draft, for that would stop the flow of creativity, but after it is finished, then the more laborious part of one's work begins. Then one deliberately turns the mind over and releases its critical aspect. One becomes an editor rather than merely a creator, and one probably rewrites and corrects many times. Certainly I did this in writing *Oh, Watchman!* and even then it was not ready for publication.

If I had any happy dream of sending it to a publisher and having them write me in ecstasy, accepting it, that dream soon died. I was advised to find an agent. The Lord provided Ruth and Maxwell Aley, literary agents, through a friend in the CFO. They were interested in healing—with good reason, for Maxwell had Parkinson's disease, and while prayers eased him and prolonged his days (a mixed blessing) he did eventually pass away. Ruth and Maxwell studied the book and advised still further corrections. And a wonderful friendship developed from this relationship.

God worked out the question of a publisher in a most unusual manner. Ruth and Maxwell and a lovely praying lady, Grace Bouret, met in Ruth's kitchen on the ground floor of their tall old home in New York. Ruth wrote on slips of paper the names of twelve possible publishers and put them into a stainless-steel pot, and we closed our eyes and drew out a paper. On it was written J. B. Lippincott.

"This can't be really guidance," said Ruth. "Tay Hohoff is the fiction editor there, and I don't think she is interested in spiritual things. Lippincott was the very last name I wrote down, just to round out the twelve."

Nevertheless, having asked for guidance, we followed it. Ruth and Maxwell sent the manuscript to Lippincott, and after some weeks of deliberation they accepted it. I was flying to Tucson at the time, and during the flight I suddenly knew that they had accepted it. Waves of unbelievable bliss flowed through me. This was the fulfillment of my heart's desire. It was a testimony of the Lord's love for me, that after giving myself to His service for many years He was now giving back to me that which I had given up for Him: the joy of being accepted as a creative writer. "Wait on the Lord . . . and He shall give thee the desires of thy heart" (Ps. 27:14; 37:4). In that delight while flying across the continent, there came to me the plot and the theme and even the title of the next book, *Lost Shepherd.*

When I arrived at Tucson and was met by my friend Marion Lovekin, she held in her hand the telegram stating that the book had been accepted. Years later I found out what had caught and held the attention of the editor, Tay Hohoff, who was also to become a real friend: she had herself gone to Tilton Hospital once a week and had taught classes in writing. She had even met John Masterman. Therefore she recognized the descriptions of the hospital and the young man chained in that life as absolute truth, not only in the words written down, but also in the emotional content of those words.

Again, how wonderfully the Lord weaves together everything in the pattern of our lives! If we make a mistake in the human part of our weaving, He alters the pattern a little to accommodate the mistake and makes of it something even more beautiful and useful!

I still remember that visit to Tucson as one of the most happy and glorious times of my life: it was wonderful to sleep in Marion's little guesthouse, to get my own breakfast and eat it out of doors under the blue sky, and to spend the day in delightful company with much prayer and fascinating drives in the desert and in the mountains. Marion had been very ill with an intense irritation of the nerves all over the body, polyneuritis. This pain in the body was caused by bitter memories of a painful past, and we prayed together for the healing of those memories. Some years later she was helping me in a mission in Los Angeles and suddenly one day she said, "Why, Agnes, this is Los Angeles!"

"Of course it is, you goose," I replied. "Where did you think you were?"

"But Los Angeles was the place where I was the most unhappy!" she exclaimed. "For years I couldn't even think of this city without getting sick at my stomach! And now I've been here three days, and I didn't even remember it!"

"Of course," I said. "Didn't we pray for the healing of the memories?"

So I returned home in the joy of the Lord and started writing *Lost Shepherd*, the one of all my books that I myself like the best and that I most enjoyed writing.

Meantime, our days in Moorestown were numbered. For five years or so Ted had been dissatisfied and restless. The church was filled with power, healing occurred during the church services, and everybody loved their minister. But Ted said that he had done everything that he could think of in that place, and he wanted to try another. Indeed, so great was his unease that he developed a chronic indigestion—which ceased immediately when he moved!

By that time I had come to love the glory and beauty of the church, with God's gentle light visibly enfolding the cross on the altar and with the breath of the Spirit making the whole church a place of rest and of healing. Moreover, this was home to the children. Young Ted was still away in the armed forces, being continually retrained for some other branch of the Scouts and Raiders. Tookie was working in a bank in Camden to save money for college and came home each evening by train. Jack was as yet in high school where he kept himself busy by studying philosophy, computation, surveying, and chess during class time. (Apparently his mind was such that he did not need to study his high-school books.)

I did not want to go away. But we would have gone if Ted could have found another church. However, Ted, the best pastor I ever knew, was probably the worst general churchman. He hated meetings and simply would not go to them. Other ministers drove cars full of women to diocesan women's meetings. Not Ted! If they wanted to go, they could get there under their own steam while he stayed at home and took care of his little flock, which he did more and more effectively. Though shy about prayer in the beginning, he now had reached the stage when he never made a parish call without prayer for healing or for a blessing on the house or the new baby or the business—and people loved it and loved him. But all this did not make him known to other churches in the state or to bishops and archbishops and all the company of heaven.

So we stayed, and Ted fretted, and the war lumbered heavily to a close. The last summer of it came, and there was the horror of Hiroshima and Nagasaki. I could not accept the theory that this devastating act of unloosing a new weapon of war for the killing of men, women, and children was necessary to end the war. To this day I do not believe it. For I know the Orientals. According to the newspapers, the Japanese had asked for terms of surrender: they had asked, "What will you do to us if we surrender?" and to them it was quite possible that we would kill many of them and rape their women and destroy their homes. We might even have ravaged and burned the land, as Sherman ravaged and burned the South after the Civil War. If we had outlined for them exactly what we intended to do—just what we did do, which was actually extremely merciful and accomplished for the country more good than harm—they would have surrendered without the horrible example of man's savagery shown to them at Hiroshima and at Nagasaki. We did not realize that all we needed to do was to answer their questions. This goes back to the subject mentioned more than once: we assumed that there was no racial difference between the Occidental and the Oriental. And there was and is and always will be, praise God! For it is to His honor and glory and delight that human beings should be diversified, just as it is to the honor and glory and delight of a gardener that the plants and flowers in his garden should be diversified.

So this war ended in a gloom and in a foreboding as one remembered the words of Scripture: "All they that take the sword shall perish with the sword" (Matt. 26:52).

We were in Alstead when it ended. Tookie and I went up to our neighbor's house over the hill above to listen to the radio. (We never allowed a radio to disturb the peace of our own little house.) Jack, as I recall, was surveying for my brother H.M. to earn the money for college, and Ted was still away—in Calcutta, as it happened.

When the news of surrender came, we tore down the rocky stretch honored by the name of a road, though it more closely resembled a stream bed. We saw our neighbor down the hill driving a truck loaded with hay and called out to him, "Heman, Heman, the war is over!"

And Heman, a Quaker, remarked dourly, "What war?"

He spoke with great discernment. The conflict between nations was for the moment stilled, but the conflict between the devil and God was not over. It had not as yet even reached a crisis. For the evil of anger and lust and cruelty engendered by war still lived in the air.

Shortly after this, we closed the little house that to us was the gateway to heaven with its steep shining meadows and its still lake below. We loved it. We loved every blade of grass that grew on our own land, now increased to twenty-three acres—fields and berry pastures and woodlot. We loved the little gardens that I had made within the stone walls of the lower lawn (formerly a cowlot). We loved the barn that Ted had repaired and beautified and filled with delightful tools. The fragrance of old wood and apples delighted us. Our hearts were heavy as we drove away, into the flat fields of New Jersey, redolent with wilting cabbage and oil drums. Yet as we drove, part of me came back to life, ready to arise again into the work of teaching and healing.

Ted, however, did not rejoice in returning to Moorestown. His indigestion troubled him more and more, except during those times when he and I were away doing missions. It became evident that we would have to leave. Ted, being at that time nearly sixty, conceived the idea of a partial-retirement place where he could run a small church and have more time for missions. Bishop Appleton Lawrence, of Western Massachusetts, found for him just the right place at just the right time, the time of Jack's graduation from college and Tookie's marriage.

Bishop Lawrence, who became a most beloved friend of the family, offered Ted not one little church but two: Trinity Church, Westboro, and Saint Paul's Church, Hopkinton, six miles away. Both were actually missions, and neither owned a vicarage. Westboro, however, had an apartment used for that purpose. The mission owned an old white house on Main Street with a barn behind it. This barn had been made into a tiny church, quite cozy and warm though not architecturally stimulating. The lower floor of the large house contained the vicar's study and two Sunday-school rooms, and the upper floor was a very adequate vicarage.

But I hated it.

That, however, was neither here nor there. I had given my consent to moving, and to Westboro we would go. There was a small incident that made it easier for me to say, "All right, let's move—now." The Moorestown vestry felt, quite rightly, that it was time to put in oil furnaces instead of the old coal ones, and the only place for the oil furnaces was my tiny garden. (They made it into a parking lot holding about two cars. And Ted's lovely lily pond, in a corner of the parish house, was made into a parking lot holding one car. Thus the world goes.)

Great was the consternation of the vestry when Ted resigned. In fact, one vestryman went home and had a heart attack from which he did not recover. They could hardly have been more stunned if God had resigned from the throne of heaven. Yet it had not occurred to them to make the changes that would have kept him challenged and made him feel appreciated.

As Ted brooded on this later on, however, it came to him that the original mistake was his own. He should have acknowledged his own worth and put a higher price on his services. He should have enlarged the vestry's horizons by enlarging his own. He had thought that when he tithed his minuscule salary it would be a lesson to them, and they would follow his example and tithe their own. But, as he came to see too late, it was not so. Ted's father had suffered greatly from a parish that paid him a very small salary and that usually overdue, which he had to stretch to support seven children. Ted had been deeply hurt by this and had, in fact, never really forgiven that old neglect. Therefore, the thing that he greatly feared had come upon him, as it came upon Job of old. My own feelings about money were quite different, and therefore, the Lord had supplied our needs from other sources.

But I was never able to set Ted free from this one thing: he did not believe, ever, that God was the least bit interested in money. He apparently still felt, as I had felt before I learned better, that one could work for money but must not pray about it!

However, as I have said, God uses even our mistakes. Ted felt later on that it was a mistake not to state his worth and his requests to this vestry whom he really loved and who simply did not understand. But God used that mistake for His purposes, for when we moved to Massachusetts, the doors opened for a new kind of work for Ted as well as for me: the School of Pastoral Care. And this has done more good for the church at large than any one parish could have done.

The last two months in Moorestown were very difficult. I knew that I would not miss the town itself very much, for my soul had never felt at home there. But I would be lost without my Bible class and the two or three prayer groups that had grown from it. They prayed for me and for my intentions as well as I for them and theirs. We could call each other and find help for every problem. Once I called Didi and asked her to pray for a cook, for I had a trip on the horizon and Elizabeth was not available.

"Oh fine!" cried Didi. "I'm awfully good at praying for cooks." And sure enough, that very evening a dark, friendly face appeared at the door and there was my helper.

I would miss the church, for it had become a battery of power. Also I would miss Philadelphia, which I loved. Every Friday afternoon, by dint of waiting an hour or two at the peanut gallery entrance and paying fifty cents, I stepped into heaven by way of the Philadelphia Orchestra, directed then by Leopold Stokowski. After some years, the congregation came to know that I saved Friday afternoon for the orchestra, and if someone could not go, she would give me her ticket, and I then sat in state among the elite. Actually, the peanut gallery had some advantages: only real music lovers would climb those steps to heaven, so one sat in the midst of delight. The acoustics in that hideous old Academy of Music were wonderful throughout the whole vast auditorium, but they were best of all up there in the highest and farthest seats. Waves of joy and inspiration would flow through me, and my programs were penciled over all the margins with lines of blank verse.

Also, I would miss the Pennsylvania Railroad! No matter where I wanted to go, North, South, or West (for one could not go far toward the East without toppling into the ocean), I hardly needed to check on trains, for every half-hour or so one would come thundering in, its headlight illumining dark tracks, and the roar of it delighting my soul. True, the first page of this book tells of an infantile fear of trains. But apparently the Lord healed that fear. And I notice that when He heals a fear, He puts in its place an absolute joy in the thing that was once feared. For instance, as a child in Kuling I remember a terrible fear of thunderstorms, gradually healed by repeating John 14:27 at my mother's suggestion. And to this day I love thunderstorms and go out of doors the better to enjoy their glorious burst of sound as it shakes the air.

Moreover, I would miss the great nearby cities of Washington and New York. New York I particularly loved, for in those days before a mantle of dirt began to enfold it, New York was a truly thrilling city, full of the delightful smell of the sea and the beauty of tall buildings and lovely parks. Ted and I would take certain Sunday-school children for a day there as a prize for excellence, going over on the Staten Island Ferry from which the breathtaking city seems to rise out of the sea. And I would go alone for a lecture in Calvary Church or the Marble Collegiate Church or the Church of the Heavenly Rest. On these trips I became better acquainted with Grace Bouret, the friend of Ruth and Maxwell Aley. She was a remarkable woman and did much healing—for which, tragically, people cared so little that later on she died in poverty and, indeed, of starvation. At this time, however, she was filled with power and beauty, and the glory of the Lord filled her tiny apartment.

I remember standing on the sidewalk after a meeting with her and being so uplifted into another world that I absentmindedly stepped into a taxi, though I had been waiting for the Fifth Avenue bus. The taxi driver was a somewhat greasy Italian and was evidently in much distress, for he coughed and moaned and groaned continually. I was in prayer for him (for one gets in the habit of praying for everything) when he delivered me at the Church of the Heavenly Rest and asked for his fare. I handed it to him and turned away, still not quite in this world.

"Hey, Lady!" said he. "Didn't you forget something?"

I brought my mind back to earth and said, "Oh, yes! Tip!" and gave it to him. "I was just thinking," I added, "that if only there were some place where I could see you alone for a few minutes I could soon stop that cough." (I knew of course that it would be God stopping it, through me, but I did not have time to explain that to the taxi driver.)

"Yeah?" said he. "Could we go in there?" And he looked expectantly at the holy facade of the church.

We entered the door into a hall, encountered a somewhat

dubious secretary, and secured permission to use the chapel for a few minutes.

"Now I haven't got time to explain," said I, being used to this crude approach and nervously sensing curates and vicars and rectors and vergers descending upon us. "You just sit down in this pew and let me put my hands on your chest and think in a way that I know."

I removed my hands after about three minutes of silent prayer.

"Gee!" said the taxi driver, "I don't have to cough anymore."

"Sure," I replied. "Is the pain all gone?"

He arose and tentatively waved his arm around in a full and vigorous circle.

"When I do that it still hurts a little," said he.

"Then don't do that," I instructed him.

He came forward and took my hand and shook it fervently.

"You're a funny lady," he said. "I never met a lady like you before."

When I recounted this incident to Ted, he remarked with feeling, "*That* may well be."

So the taxi driver departed, and there came in scores of ladies dripping diamonds and furs and a few somewhat the worse for wear. But I had more fun with the taxi driver . . .

Now of course I could come down from Westboro to New York, but not with such ease and joy; though I did come down particularly to talk to Tay Hohoff, my most admirable editor. For by the grace of God, I was at this time writing *Lost Shepherd*, to my great delight and comfort.

In spite of the writing, however, during the last two months in Moorestown I developed a pain in my chest and around my heart. As soon as we left the town, the pain departed. Therefore I knew that I had been picking up the pain of our friends who were heartbroken that we should go away from them—the pain of Ted's sister living in Philadelphia, that we would no more come to the tall brick house and have Thanksgiving dinner with her and her doctor husband—the pain of Ted's brothers and many others, who used to drive for miles to the Christmas Midnight Service and knew now that they would never again enter into that pageant of wonder and beauty and holy worship—the pain of the sick and the aged to whom Ted was the very fountain of life. He told them that another minister would come to take his place, and that the new minister would be to them what he had been. But it was not so, for the new minister had been taught nothing in the seminary about healing or about the power of the prayer of faith.

So the day came, and we drove away toward the north, wrapped in the grief of others, but comforting ourselves with the thought of New England, and, most of all, with the remembrance that Alstead would now be very near to us, and we could enter into that haven of peace and beauty time and time again, not for only one month during the year.

And so it was. In all the strangeness and newness of Westboro and of the tiny church in Hopkinton, there was our own place in Alstead, peacefully dreaming among the green hills and waiting for us to walk over the little lawn, to turn the key, and to enter into rest.

Ted never returned to Moorestown again. He would accept no invitation to preach upon a festival day or to supply on a Sunday or to marry anyone, bury anyone, or baptize anyone. It was not fair, he said, to the new rector, and thus was not fair to the church.

When we had departed, we had departed.

16.

O we moved. Our furniture was carried out of the big stone rectory and laboriously hoisted up the narrow stairs and into the upper story of an old New England house. We were all alone there for the first time since leaving China. Ted was at Yale Law School, Tookie was married, and Jack had entered Kenyon College. How wonderfully the Lord takes care of these changes in life! When the children were small, I thought that I would die of lonesomeness when they departed, but now that the time came, I found it very restful! Both of us felt at home almost immediately in the little town of Westboro, far more than we ever had in Moorestown. We brought one friend with us: Ernestine Bradley, who had followed me from a CFO to Moorestown four months before we departed, in order to be, as she called it, "my secretary" and help me with my work. She was never a secretary in actuality, for I found it better to take care myself of business letters and arrangements. But she answered many of the prayer requests, and was, moreover, a gay and delightful friend and prayer partner.

We made other friends very quickly. Every week I invited two couples to dinner in the little upstairs rectory, and as I had, thanks to my husband's patient encouragement, become by this time a very good cook, this met with favor. In Moorestown everyone had called Ted, "Mr. Sanford," but here, to his great delight, they quite spontaneously called him "Ted." He himself had been very formal in Moorestown. He unbent in this simple, half-country atmosphere, and thoroughly enjoyed his life among his own New England people and near to two beloved brothers living in Walpole. I also enjoyed it and felt the change very little, partly because the main part of me did not change: I was still writing and rewriting *Lost Shepherd* and so was living in another world. No sooner had that book gone to the publisher than the Lord began to give me the content of my next book, and in a rather odd fashion.

I was still traveling a great deal, doing lectures, missions, and CFO camps, and on trains and planes my mind spontaneously rocked into little poems and jingles of a rather childish nature. I would jot them down on plane tickets and backs of envelopes, and when I got home, I would type them out. They are not bad! A number of them have been set to music and used in primary school or Sunday school! I did not even realize why the Lord was giving me these poems until they were nearly all written! Then it occurred to me that they would make an excellent framework for a book on prayer for children, and so *Let's Believe* was written, based on my lectures in the daily vacation Bible school in Moorestown. Thus the prayer that I had made long ago for fifty dollars, answered at the time by the offer of conducting the Bible school, is still being answered each year as a royalty comes to me on that book!

I am fascinated by the infinite variety of the ways in which the Lord deals with us. For instance, my next book, *Behold Your God*, I wrote at the request of my brother H.M. who said, "I wish you would write sort of a commentary on the Creed and give the biblical references for everything you say." That time God chose to speak to me through my brother. If we expect God to give us guidance always after the same pattern, we miss a great deal; for apparently He delights in variety and can speak in words to the mind or through a person or through the circumstances of life or through the beauty of nature.

My only problem in Westboro was the apartment. I talked my conscious mind into enjoying it. But I could not persuade the unconscious part of me, which reported its uneasiness by producing a pain and tightness through the chest. It took a trip to England to solve the reason for this and find the answer.

As we sat at table in our dining room one day, the phone rang, and I received a cable asking me to come to England and speak at a "Healing Advance" at High Leigh, conducted by the London Healing Mission. Ted was as excited about this as I was, and to England I flew. This first trip was a bit overwhelming and I did not feel quite at home at High Leigh. I looked with dismay upon a group of ladies sparsely interspersed with an occasional man, most of the group being "of a certain age." Moreover, I found the atmosphere perturbed by considerable agitation concerning the advantages of communism, stirred up by only a few, but disturbing all of them. I had to change my lectures from healing of individuals to the healing of the world by prayer. The Lord used this, particularly for one person, a doctor who gave his life at that time to the Lord's service and who has ever since done healing, not only through medicine, but also through prayer.

During this conference I met a lady who invited me to her home for the weekend and who gave me the answer concerning the pain and tightness in the chest.

"Don't you see," she said as I described it, "your chest feels tight—feels hemmed in and hurts because your spirit feels tight and hemmed in. You cannot live in that apartment. Your spirit is demanding a larger place."

Ted and I had considered building a house. We had even looked at available lots and had found a beautiful one on Mill Road. But we had decided that building was too expensive. My English friend, Mrs. Davidson, however, convinced me of the need for our own house, and I flew home and went promptly to a real-estate agent. This lovely lady laughed at my fear that we did not have enough money, and explained to me that one did not have to pay the full price down upon buying a house—a fact that Ted and I had not grasped, both of us having always lived on a cash basis.

We did not immediately find a house that pleased us. Meanwhile, my friend wrote from England, "What kind of house do you want? I cannot pray for it until I see it in my mind."

I did not know. I was expecting just to stumble upon one and recognize it as I had done at Alstead. So I looked over a collection of house plans that Ted had gathered over the years and found a sketch of a little story-and-a-half New England cottage set upon a hill, and this I sent to Mrs. Davidson in England. Shortly thereafter, Dorothy, our real-estate agent, said, "I want to show you a house on Mill Road." There it stood, a small white story-and-a-half Cape Cod cottage, set upon a hill amid huge oak trees, through whose branches one looked out upon meadows where cows grazed peacefully among buttercups and daisies. Moreover, this house was built on the very parcel of land that Ted and I had liked two years before! And most amazing of all, the owners had been away when the foundations had been dug, and the builders had made a mistake. The foundations were ten feet farther from the road than the owners had desired—but exactly where Ted and I wanted them! Truly, our Father does take care of us when we dare to pray the prayer of faith!

We moved in just before Christmas, with happy hearts even though the vans struggled up our steep drive over snow and ice and through howling winds.

Meanwhile I was still traveling, sometimes with Ted but more often without him, leaving him to the tender mercies of Ernestine and many friends and the Merry M, a small, inexpensive restaurant a block away. I was always and increasingly tired. One night I dreamed that I simply could not climb up to a pulpit but fell and lay exhausted there on the steps. Then in the dream, my spiritual body arose out of my physical body and stood in the pulpit and gave forth the power of God—as one always tries to do in lecturing.

Yet I continued to go from city to city in the United States and in Canada, to proclaim the truth: that Jesus lives and heals today. In this one way I know that I really love the Lord. It is not in my nature to feel the joy of a gushing emotion toward Him, though I wish that were so. But insofar as I know what He requires of me, that I try to do, for His sake.

One of these trips included four days in Tucson. The proposed lectures there did not work out, and Marion Lovekin wrote me that her guidance was that we were simply to have a rest time and a prayer retreat in this beautiful city. So I traveled there by train, feeling utterly exhausted and asking God again and again why He did not give me the strength to do what He wanted me to do. On arriving at Tucson, and talking and praying with Marion and her prayer partner Mildred, I found that both of them had reached a similar state of weariness.

"I dreamed last night," said Marion, "that the three of us were toiling up a hill and were laden down with other people's burdens. We had them on our heads and under our arms, and we simply could not get up the hill for the weight of them. Yet we felt that we could not drop them."

"That's true enough," I said. "But what are we going to do about it?"

We prayed for strength, and no strength came. We prayed for the healing of various small ills that weariness had brought about in our bodies, and we were not healed. Finally at the end of three days we ceased praying the prayer of faith and prayed the prayer for guidance.

"Well, then, Lord, what *do* you want us to pray for?" we demanded.

A voice spoke within all three of us saying, "Pray for the Holy Ghost."

This amazed us. We had not the least idea what it meant. We were not apt to speak of the Holy Ghost anyway, but addressed the Third Person of the Trinity as the Holy Spirit. We assumed, as most good Christians do, that we had this evanescent sense of Christian brotherhood or whatever it was that these words meant. Nevertheless, we obeyed. And the Lord sent an angel to enlighten us. He did not appear in the guise of an angel, but only as a doctor, and one interested especially in his particular field, the inside of the head. He was also interested in the mysteries of the human mind and spirit, though whether he was even a member of a church I do not know. But he said something like this: "I believe that within the head there are centers of spiritual perception that are dormant, or nearly dormant. I find the pineal and the pituitary glands to be somewhat flattened, like balloons that have lost part of their air. Moreover, I find between them a canal or channel that apparently used to be open like a hollow tube, but that is shrunk and closed. I believe that modern man has so over-rationalized and under-spiritualized that even these centers of receiving a direct current of the power of God are no longer in use."

I cannot prove the truth of his remarks, but this I know: they gave us a sense of expectancy, because he said in conclusion, "I believe that it should be possible for a person to receive such a powerful injection of a spiritual energy that these glands would come back to their full functioning and even the channel between them would be opened."

That night we went into Marion's prayer room and addressed the Almighty upon this matter.

"Lord, we don't know what You mean by this, 'Pray for the Holy Ghost,' " we said. "But whatever You mean, we are going to stay right here until we get it, because if You want us to do Your work, You have got to give us the power to do it."

We did not get this prayer out of the Prayer Book, but nevertheless it seems to me completely right. We were praying, in our ignorance (for none of us knew that the gift of tongues existed outside of the Bible), not for any gift nor for a mere spiritual experience, but for the one thing that Jesus promised His disciples in His last talk to them before He departed in a cloud of light. "Ye shall receive power after that the Holy Ghost is come upon you" (Acts 1:8).

Moreover, though we did not realize it at the time, our preparation paralleled that of the disciples. We had used what faith we had and had gone forth, as had the seventy whom He appointed to tell the good news that Jesus lives today, and to heal. Also, we had searched our souls and confessed and repented of whatever sins and weaknesses we found there. And finally, we had been in a prayer retreat for four days, waiting upon Him.

We prayed for each other with the laying on of hands, two for one, two for one, two for one. And the power of the Spirit fell upon us immediately. First of all, we felt a deep and intense burning in the middle of the head and with it a drawing feeling, as though the hair were brushed the wrong way, or as though one had on a hat that was too tight.

It was the same feeling, though not quite so intense, as that "illumination" that fell upon me as I meditated alone beside the lake in Alstead long before. I wonder whether this was actually the "cloven tongues as of fire" descending from the Father and the Son and bringing to life within the very flesh the capacity to receive the power of God. It seems so, for we were healed immediately, every one of us, of all the small weaknesses that had troubled us. (Matters such as the wearing of glasses were not healed, nor were we given the permission either then or later on to pray for these minor things.) I felt for the only time in my life, except for the dream recounted in an earlier chapter, the radiation of a spiritual power all over me, from the top of the head to the soles of the feet.

In addition to these all-pervading currents of the power of the Holy Spirit, we were at that time given the three specific gifts that Jesus Himself promised. First of all, the gift of joy; we were swept with a joy transcending any that we had ever known before. This heavenly rapture came, not from the mind, but from the heart— from within, like a well of water springing up unto everlasting life, even as Jesus told the woman at the well in Samaria.

We next became aware of having been given a new gift of the understanding of truth. It swept over us all night long, for we slept but little, being so filled with light and so illumined by the Spirit that sleep was unnecessary. As I lay there, unsolved problems and perplexing mysteries came up into the conscious mind one after another, and with each came the solution, so that I cried, "Oh, I see!" Indeed, as prophesied long ago, we heard within us a voice saying, "This is the way, walk ye in it!" (Isa. 30:21).

And finally another change took place in me immediately, though it was not perceived until later. This change was wrought by the gift of peace. Everything that I did, either with the mind or with the body, could now be done with about half the energy that it once required, and in about half the time. I could write and not be weary, and I could cook and not faint. I could now serve a dinner in half an hour instead of in an hour and a half. How perfectly amazing and how completely delightful! Apparently the Holy Spirit does not require us to float around continually on a rosy cloud praising the Lord, but to praise the Lord in our everyday lives by doing our ordinary work with precision and speed. Apparently the Holy Spirit at this time invaded and pervaded both the conscious mind and the heart or subconscious, soul, spirit, or whatever one may call the inner intelligence of mind and body. Thus everything in mind and body was "quickened," made more alert and more efficient.

This experience was kept a secret between me and the Lord for many months. I thought it something so far out, so strange and mystical, that nobody would understand it and people would brand me a fanatic if they knew of it. Least of all did I mention it to Ted, for he did not like that kind of thing at all, and by mutual silent agreement we did not talk of the spiritual aspect of me and my work. He knew that it existed, but he also knew that there was another facet of my nature that loved earth and sea and sky and our beautiful little house set on a hill, and it was this aspect of me that he cherished. This was very good for me, because if he had been as spiritually adventurous as I was, we might have flown off together, high, wide and handsome, in no one knows what sort of divergent paths instead of remaining as we did in the bosom of the church, there little by little to plant the leaven of God's Holy Spirit.

From the point of view of "sharing" every thought and every fancy, our marriage might have been considered an inadequate one. But for spreading the kingdom of God, it was a well-balanced and efficient partnership. Ted was a man of great reserve; and every man has a right to his reserve and to the secret place within himself—and so does every woman.

However, though Ted did not comment upon the difference in me, others did. For months, and indeed for years, people would say, "What's happened to you? You look ten years younger than you did ten years ago!" For the light remained. The peace of God continued to develop in me a better coordination of spirit and mind and body, and the joy of the Lord still bubbled up as from an unseen spring within, sometimes more, sometimes less, but never completely gone.

Some months later, as I have recounted in *Behold Your God,* I attended a confirmation service. And for the first time, I saw what it was!

"Why, the bishop is doing what we three people did in the desert!" I thought with unbounded surprise. "He's praying for the Holy Spirit!" But nothing happened, at least not anything that one could see. There was nothing wrong with the service of comfirmation except that it was perhaps somewhat understated, with due churchly caution. But through the dullness of the ages, the expectancy had worn thin.

Six months later I received a very disturbing letter from Marion. It was full of hallelujahs and praise-the-Lords and stated that she and her sons and Mildred had attended a Pentecostal group and now spoke with tongues.

I am sure my hair stood on end with horror. This was the end of our journey together into the kingdom of God, for I would never do a thing as weird and completely off base as this. I wrote her to this effect, with some vehemence, but she replied with equal vehemence and with disconcerting arguments out of the Bible. Finally she wrote, "You are a Bible teacher. How then can you refuse even to contemplate something that is right out of the Bible?"

"Very well," I wrote back rather grimly. "Next time I go west I will stop off at Tucson and let you two pray for God to give me whatever gifts of the Spirit He wants to give. But I do *not* want the gift of tongues, so don't expect me to sound off, for I'm sure God would not give me any gift contrary to my will."

In due time I arrived at Tucson and met with the two women and one of the boys, the others being away at college. We sat in a circle and prayed together, and presently they began to speak in languages that I did not know, although quietly, without hysteria or any upsetting demonstrations. I might have been in China hearing a number of people speak different dialects of Chinese. Finally, they laid their hands on my head and prayed as I had asked them to pray. But immediately I desired the gift of tongues with a great longing! And in another moment I spoke as they had spoken, in words that the conscious mind did not understand. Within me there was a great melting, even unto tears of joy and of comfort. I felt as though the love of Christ, already in me, now moved down, down to a deeper level, and I am sure it did! For speaking in tongues is simply the Spirit reaching and touching something in the deep unconscious, or as the Bible would say, the heart, so that out of the heart the tongue speaks a language that the conscious mind does not understand but that the heart knows. Hence the feeling of the nearness of God, so that "He that speaketh in an unknown tongue speaketh not unto men, but unto God," as Saint Paul said (I Cor. 14:2).

That night I did not lie awake too filled with joy to sleep as I had on the occasion of my baptism in the Spirit, but I awoke toward morning with a strange drawing feeling about my lips, and I thought, "Now what is happening to me? Has this made me nervous?"

Then I remembered my friends saying something about "the

movement of the Spirit about the lips," and so I let my voice come forth and again found myself, all alone in the guesthouse, speaking in tongues. For I was still not sure what strange thing might have happened to me and was in grave doubt as to whether it was "sound," in the words of my childhood. Never, never would I speak of this to anyone, I decided. Never.

For three months I adhered to this resolution. Moreover, I did not during this time use this gift of the Spirit at all. I was not going to give way to an impulse which I did not understand, lest it come not from the Lord, but from the devil or out of my own pervid imagination. However, at the end of three months I was in Florida on a mission, without Ted this time, and was enjoying the delightful company of an old friend, Grace Munsey, far more advanced in the line of visions and revelations than I. Knowing that she was so far out herself that nothing could startle her, I mentioned to her this strange experience of giving tongue to sounds that seemed to be a language that I myself did not know.

"Why, Agnes," she said, "I've had the gift of tongues for twenty years!"

"But Grace, I never heard you speak in tongues!"

"Of course not," said Grace serenely. "This gift is for my own personal use. Like visions. I never speak in tongues in a public meeting."

"But what is the use of it?" I demanded. "When you can't understand what you are saying?"

"The other one of you understands."

"The other one?"

"Your subconscious mind or your soul or your heart—something within you knows what you are saying! I guess it's your spirit really, because Saint Paul talks about 'praying in the Spirit.' This brings you nearer to God, of course. That's why you feel such joy within. Didn't you?"

"Oh yes, but I thought maybe I was just getting a bit manic. You know when you've been in depression you have to be careful not to get overstimulated—"

"Jesus can take care of that," said Grace.

"But what if I should be teaching my Bible class and all of a sudden I let fly and spoke in tongues?" I further demanded.

"That would never happen," said Grace serenely. "Saint Paul

said, 'The spirits of the prophets are subject to the prophets' (I Cor. 14:32). This gift is always completely under your control."

"Always?"

Grace pondered this for a moment. "I've heard people say, 'I just couldn't help it,'" she replied; "'the Spirit made me speak.' But I don't believe it. I don't think God forces us to say anything. We may be so filled with the Spirit that we have a strong impulse to speak, but we are always in control. The choice is always ours. People doubtless think they are telling the truth when they say, 'The Spirit made me.' But I'm not sure that they quite understand themselves."

This I believed, for here was this woman whom I had known for ten years and yet who had never urged upon me the gift of tongues. God uses the zeal of some people—that I know—but He uses the silence and the discretion of other people. While some people can be moved only by zeal, others cannot be completely won unless that zeal is mingled with discretion.

From this time forth, I permitted the Spirit to speak through my spirit in my morning meditations. When Ted had driven to his office in the parish house, I would repair to the small study back of the breezeway and there look out upon white birch trees on our little hill, ice glistening upon them in the winter and crocuses lifting shining heads beneath them in the spring. And this became my altar, as indeed it is, for the whole earth is the altar whereon God pours out His life and love.

As soon as I gave permission to my own inner being to speak with tongues, a strange language would flow forth from me, and my heart would lift and lighten with joy. When I listened to the little sounds of this language, they seemed to me silly. I would begin to wonder whether it was a real language or not, for I could not identify in it any trace of any Romance or Oriental tongue. I decided that it did not matter whether it was a real language; it rested my conscious mind and lightened my spirit, and I should not try to analyze it.

It seemed to me more and more certain as time went on that this tongue was for the edification of the spirit, not of the conscious mind, for after I had ceased speaking, inspiration would come to me. Indeed, much of the latter part of *Behold Your God* was given to me in this way, for I would ask a question concerning the mysteries of Jesus Christ and apparently while I was speaking in tongues, my spirit would receive inspiration, and I would write it down.

Once, years ago, I was invited to speak at Central Bible Institute, the Assemblies of God seminary. The large audience was discreet and quiet. After my talk, the minister led them into a time of prayer. They prayed together, in a gentle murmur very sweet to hear, like bees over a clover field. Then one person arose and gave a "message" in tongues in a wailing tone of voice that I personally find rather unpleasant. However, when she ceased, someone else arose and "interpreted," giving a beautiful message of faith and hope such as one can find in the Psalms. This happened a second time and a third, different ones speaking each time. The Lord gave them not more than two or three public messages, and then only when there was an interpreter, just as Saint Paul recommended in I Corinthians 14.

On the other hand, I was once some years later in a "Holy Spirit group" in a distant city and found their system to be that each one in turn prayed in tongues and then interpreted his own utterances. It struck me that the interpretations were all the same, namely, that they gave thanks that the Lord had sent them this lady to speak to them. I was not impressed.

Some of my readers may at this point be shocked that I should test and weigh the value of these messages. I find this advice in the Bible: "Try the spirits (or the messages given by the Spirit) whether they are of God" (I John 4:1).

No one in Westboro knew that I had this gift, not even my husband. I tried to tell him, but he threw up his usual delightful barrier of disinterest and a bit of raillery, so I kept it within myself and pondered it in my heart for many years.

This was good. For it gave me time to absorb and digest this revelation of God before I explained it to others. Meanwhile I began privately to speak of it to those whom I deemed ready for this new outpouring of God's power. I "laid hands suddenly on no man," but first had sessions of counseling and teaching and prayed for the forgiveness of sins and the healing of the wounded memories—cleaning house, as it were, for the newly expected Holy One. Finally I would pray for the baptism in the Spirit, not emphasizing tongues, though of course rejoicing when it accompanied the deeper gifts.

Indeed, many who receive the baptism nowadays are led into the experience of the Holy Spirit by someone who was brought into it years ago through me. However, in the beginning, I would instruct others to keep the gift a secret. This was wise at that point, for most of them, being ministers, would have been rejected by their congregations if they had immediately leaped into their pulpits and spoken of tongues. I could sympathize with the congregations as well as with the minister, for had not I felt that very same way myself?

"You can testify," I would say to a minister. "But testify by your life rather than by words. 'By their fruits ye shall know them' (Matt. 7:20). When people see more and more that God heals through you and that God's light shines in you, the time will come when certain ones will say, 'What *is* this that you have?' Then you can tell them, trusting them also in the beginning to do miracles rather than talk about tongues. What I hope is that it will spread through your church so quietly and so gradually that when it comes out in public, your people will accept it." And in some churches this did happen.

There was another value to this slow approach, and that was the deepening of the power. Let me illustrate this by a story about the first Catholic priest who came to one of my conferences. I am sure that we thanked in our hearts that great man of God, Pope John, whose wisdom and love opened the doors, that Roman Catholics might pray and study with other Christians. Later on Father McNutt attended a CFO where I was a leader, and told me the first day that he desired the baptism in the Spirit. Knowing that there were other groups doing this work of prayer after the day's program, I advised him to attend one of them. The next day he came to me in great disappointment.

"It didn't happen," he said. "Oh, I spoke with tongues; that was no trouble. But nothing really happened inside."

"Well, then, I had better pray for you," said I. We went with two others into my room, and there, with the laying on of hands, I prayed for the real entering in of the Spirit of God—into the heart, into the soul, into the unconscious. And it did happen! He was so overwhelmed with holy joy that he laughed aloud, not in any hysterical fashion, but in a deep outpouring from the heart.

"Oh, this is the way I thought it would be!" he cried again and again. "Oh, this is the way I thought it would be!" He has since led countless others into this experience.

This man's first experience in the group, wherein he spoke with tongues, was by no means useless, I am sure. It was authentic, but it was not deep enough. It did not really penetrate the psyche. But very likely it opened the door for the deeper experience, and I am not by any means criticizing it.

The danger of not going deep enough is the old danger of Christianity: pride, inflation, the feeling that one has now attained and is now made perfect; and there is nowhere to go from here. There is no greater danger than this in the whole of the Christian life.

Nevertheless, the Lord uses different people in different ways, according to our circumstances and according to our gifts. For instance, Billy Graham is an evangelist. I have no gift for this kind of preaching, but I rejoice in his work and often build on a foundation that he has begun. And often I have built a house of faith in people that Dennis Bennett and many other more forthright speakers have crowned with the crown of the Holy Spirit. I delight in their work and give thanks for it even though my own seems to be to take the middle path: zeal with discretion and discretion blossoming forth into zeal.

I look back over the years with a certain sadness, for I had hoped that by this time the churches wherein I have always worked would be filled with the glory of God. I had hoped that the love of Jesus Christ in the churches would create such an atmosphere of faith that many simply sitting in a church service would be healed. And I had dreamed of the day when out of the churches would shine a light that would illumine the nations and bring in the kingdom of heaven.

Alas! Jesus was more realistic. Just as He said, some of the seeds that I planted withered away because the soil was too shallow to sustain them. Some of them sprouted but were eaten up by the birds of humanism and socialism and various other isms. Some grew vigorously until the hot sun of the devil's wrath burned them out—often using as his tool the unholy fire of spiritual pride. But others do remain. There are churches where the healing power of the Holy Spirit accomplishes miracles. There are churches wherein the light shines. And the most amazing thing is that some of the seeds that many of us have so striven to plant in the churches have somehow been transplanted and have taken root elsewhere, helping to open the door for a tremendous revival that is taking place almost everywhere except, alas, in most churches!

For the Holy Spirit of Jesus Christ is coming again in His glory, and there is no holding Him back. A new day is dawning. A new age is upon us: the day of the Lord; the kingdom of heaven. The Son of righteousness is rising and nothing can stop His coming, just as nothing can stay the sunrise from creeping over the mountaintops. I see it from my bedroom window on awakening: the San Gabriel Mountains, dim and misty with fog from the sea and smoke from the city; then a faint dim gold light upon the highest peak; then the sunshine brightens and creeps over the whole range, lighting ridges here and there and turning the tree-tops into golden glory. The houses beyond my canyon cast long shadows, but soon they also will be lit by the ever-rising sun and will stand forth bathed in its radiance!

Some churches are now awakening into this glory of the Lord, this coming of His Holy Spirit, this actual mutation of human beings into the sons of God. Other churches are still casting long shadows. But even if they shut out the rising sunlight of the Lord, and even if the shadows of their bony structures still remain, the light of the new day cannot be held back. The Son will rise just the same. *Jesus is coming again!* And if the wise and prudent will not see Him, being enamored of their own humanity, then He will reveal His divinity unto babes.

17.

MY life in Westboro was illumined by the light of the Holy Spirit from God above and by the light of the creative life of God from the earth beneath. The earth sustained me, just as the Spirit illumined me. Never before in my life had I lived in our own house, but always in a mission house, a manse, or a rectory. I would not have believed the difference that it made to own the charming little cottage and the acre of land around it, shadowed with huge oak trees as it sloped down to the winding road. The lawn ended with a steep bank edged with a rock garden where in the spring, to my wonder and delight, small hidden flowers put up green shoots when I removed their covering of sodden leaves, and lifted their gold and purple heads in bloom. There were no flowers planted behind the house, but only a little lawn and then the woods of white birches growing up the hill. But I planted flowers all around the house—lilies of the valley and ferns in the shadowed backyard, spring bulbs between the bushes in front of the house, and rhododendrons and laurel up through the woods. The latter was Ted's venture, for he loved woodsy plants. Thus we created a bit of paradise, cuddling the house in its arms as it were, while crocus and scillas sprinkled the lawn in early spring.

This was my delight. Strength came into me from the earth as I dug in it, and joy flowed from every living thing about me—except, I must confess, mosquitoes. Moreover, this was my springboard into writing. Ideas do not come to me readily when I sit pencil in hand in my study, but they come from the world around me as I live and rejoice in it and coax it into beauty.

I used to say, "It is as though God spoke to me through the earth and the living things that He has put upon it."

Now I say, "God speaks to me through the earth and the living things that He has put upon it." Because He does. And as I love them, God's life seems to be increased in them, and they grow for me as they are loath to grow for many other people.

In Westboro, also, I established a more ordered rule of life than ever before. I did not start a Bible class or any work in the people of the parish, for it was not necessary. It was a small parish, and Ted took care of it in a wonderful way and needed no helper. Indeed, for the first two years he also took care of another tiny country parish in Hopkinton, and it would be hard to say which he loved more. From this time I definitely decided that writing was my main work and established a rule of life: I wrote in the mornings and did nothing else at that time, not even answering the telephone or going to any "morning coffee" or church meeting save only church on Sunday—or, rather, two churches on Sunday; for I would drive with Ted to Hopkinton for a nine o'clock service and back to Westboro for another service at eleven. I did not become bored with this. It was a joy to be with Ted, and he held the most dignified and beautiful services I have ever known. Every Saturday night he went into the church alone and rehearsed the whole service. And he not only trained his lay readers himself, but also had me train them in voice, diction, and pronunciation.

Save for Sunday morning, however, I wrote. Gradually people learned that these were my office hours, just as though I went to an office in town. Thus I limited the periods when I could take prayer appointments, seeing only two or three people a day. There were many reasons behind this change of pace. The most obvious was financial. The exigencies of my life and the demands of my spirit were such that I required space and beauty wherein my soul could expand, and help and conveniences about the house in order to free me for the work of mind and spirit. Therefore I was most grateful that the Lord gave me back my trained work of writing, for this is a real and honest job for which one is paid. Moreover, I am sure that, in the long run, my books help far more people than all my personal work could ever do.

Another joyful aspect of life in Westboro was that Jack, having finished college, decided to enter the ministry and went to seminary at Cambridge, whence it was easy to spend weekends at our home. Sometimes he came Saturday night with a carful of young men who enjoyed a buffet supper and sat about the living-room floor asking questions about prayer and healing. For years my Bible class in Moorestown had prayed for seminaries, that they should teach the truth of the Gospels and send their young men forth to do the works that Jesus did. However, even to this day I have seen very little answer to these prayers. Against the barrier of an almost complete disbelief in prayer, the tiny bit of light that may have dawned on those Saturday evenings could make but little headway. At the end of Jack's second year, such was the crushing weight of disbelief and cynicism in the seminary that nine young men, including Jack, left it, being on the verge of breakdown from the struggle. Jack regained his health and deepened his understanding through a year's outdoor work surveying for H.M. in California, and eventually studying under Dr. Fritz Kunkel, a wonderful Christian psychologist. But the other eight were lost to the work of God's church because they were not taught or even allowed to obey Jesus: to pray and to teach and to heal.

Meanwhile the power of God increased in Trinity Church, Westboro, so that the whole atmosphere of that little building (once a barn) was joyous and uplifting. I noticed during the first year that as I sat in the tiny choir during a morning service, praying for the congregation, waves of nausea were apt to sweep over me. These disappeared immediately as soon as the service was over. My guidance was that I was registering some disturbance of soul or body from someone else there. As soon as I knew this, the problem disappeared, for I learned to lift it to the Lord in prayer, saying: "Lord, I don't know whose trouble I am catching in this way. But You know. So I pray that Your light and life and healing will at this moment enter into this person making him (or her) well in soul and mind and body." And my uneasiness would disappear.

While I did not have a regular class in Westboro, I did once give a series of ten lectures in the church. These lectures followed more or less the outline of *Behold Your God*, which I was writing at that time. I asked those attending to divide their lives into ten periods. And each time we met, I prayed for the healing of the memories of one period of their lives, beginning at the present and going back into time. Marvelous healings took place in this manner. One woman told me afterward that she was healed of cancer, though at the time I did not even know that she had cancer. Another one reported a healing of a very strained relationship between her and her mother. This was a group effort, and I work usually with individuals. But if one feels the need of a "sensitivity group" or an "encounter group," I would highly recommend some such method as this, looking up to God and not down into oneself, reaching for the highest in one rather than for the lowest, rising to the Spirit level instead of sinking to "gut level," as some rather disgustingly say.

The Lord has the most extraordinary ways of doing what He wants to do through individuals, either because of them or in spite of them—if only someone will pray to Him with faith. Seminaries proving singularly unresponsive to suggestions concerning faith, the Lord began an answer to the prayers of many people in a way of which Ted and I had never dreamed.

One day there appeared at the door a young man stating that he represented a foundation (a small, anonymous one) and that it was his duty to find places where the money might do good. He said that he had read *The Healing Light* and that the foundation was interested in healing work, and he wondered whether a grant of money could in any way further my work. I could not think of any way at all. Our immediate needs were supplied by Ted's church and my writing and lecturing, and we did not need to be subsidized.

So he went away for a season. And I returned with joy to my writing, not knowing that the young man was a messenger from God. When he said on departing, "I still think there is something that you need to do with money," I did not believe him, but smiled sweetly and let him go.

Even with the help of the Holy Spirit—for I would ask questions of Him and receive the answers first in tongues and then through the interpretation of tongues—the writing of *Behold Your God* was not easy. Just as I had needed to study through the whole Bible in the light of my new understanding of God's living power, so I now needed to study through the whole Christian creed in order to deepen my understanding of it in the new light of the Holy Spirit.

I found that it is all true, but it transcends truth. This is precisely what Jesus said would happen: "When he, the Spirit of truth, is come, he will guide you into all truth. . . . He shall receive of mine, and shall shew it unto you" (John 16:13, 14). This does not mean merely that the Holy Spirit will help us to understand the words of Jesus quoted in Scripture, for in the preceding verse Jesus said, "I have yet many things to say unto you, but ye cannot bear them now." Put these three verses together, and you will see that Jesus expected the Holy Spirit to reveal to us new aspects of truth, never contradicting the words that Jesus spoke in Bible times, but adding to them. He could not tell us all that He knew until after Pentecost, when the Holy Spirit came to lead us continually into all truth. And He is still leading.

About this time the Spirit began to show me that intercession for individuals and for ourselves is not enough, but that we must also pray for the healing of this little earth that we live upon.

What is the use of praying for healing of those ill with lung infections if they cannot breathe our polluted air? What is the use of praying for the healing of cancer if the very water that we drink and the very food grown upon the earth tends to poison the body? This prayer for the earth, moreover, is precisely the prayer that Jesus Christ told us to pray, and it is what the Christ Spirit within us has been urging us to pray: "Thy kingdom come. Thy will be done on earth as it is in heaven."

My first inkling of an interest in what is now called ecology came from a lecture given at our parish house by a specialist in genetics. He spoke with great fear and horror of the dangers implicit in the test explosions of the atom bomb. The splitting of the atom, he said, might bring about terrible effects upon human genes, resulting in sterility, or worse—in the bringing forth of more and more deformed or subnormal children. Moreover, he said, this effect would be cumulative; it would increase as time went on. Nor would it be limited to the place where the bomb exploded, but would permeate the atmosphere of the world, particularly of New England whither the prevailing winds would tend to blow it.

—— 232 ——

He desired us to use all our influence to prevent the beginning of atomic test explosions. My only influence was in prayer, and therefore, I actually prepared a pamphlet on this subject, calling on all those who believed in the power of prayer to unite in praying that the president would not order these test explosions. I planned to send out a great number of these—quite contrary to my usual custom of speaking only when I am asked to speak. But a very strange thing happened. I had prepared these with much care, and copies were all over the house: rough draft, first copy, second copy, etc. But on the morning when I planned to take my completed copy to a printer in Worcester, not a single copy could be found. They had disappeared, every one of them, and not one of them has turned up to this day. I took it that I was not meant to undertake this venture, that God must have removed them in order to stop me from possibly making a fool of myself. But sometimes I wonder uneasily whether it was the enemy and not God who had thus apparently "spirited away" these papers. I have no explanation concerning this mysterious disappearance; any who read are welcome to come to their own conclusions!

However, though frustrated in my attempt to request prayer from many people, I myself began at that time to extend the scope of my prayers beyond the narrow circle of myself, family, and those who requested prayer, and to pray for the healing of the earth itself.

I tried this first in praying for hurricanes to quiet down and gradually go out to sea. A prayer partner and I would make a decision as to when we should pray this prayer deciding on an exact picture of where the hurricane should go, lest it simply stop blowing and dump all its rain in one place on the earth. (This did happen once, before we learned to improve our mental image of the swing of winds and clouds.) As our prayers were answered, radio announcers would say that they did not know what had happened, but the predicted hurricane was going out to sea, and there would be little or no destruction after all.

We then tried praying for the ending of a five-year drought (maybe too many hurricanes went out to sea!) and found this more difficult. One can understand the reason. Few people are sensitive to the needs of the earth for moderate rains in due season, and at almost any time some people are praying for a sunny day so that they can have a pleasant trip. This brings up a very important point: if we are going to pray for the earth, we must be willing for God's healing to come to it at whatever time is best, whether or not it suits our personal convenience. It required a real discipline not to say, "Oh Lord, please don't let it rain today, because we want to go to Alstead," but even that act of self-abnegation one learned to make if the earth needed rain!

Alstead was our little bit of heaven on earth, and thither we would start with a sense of high adventure on Monday morning, or even on Sunday afternoon when all services were over. We might make this trip first in late April, taking along some old wire bedsprings in case the car stuck in the mud of our tiny road. The meadows would be stark and brown and the gardens covered with sodden dead leaves, but tiny, pale green leaves would be showing on the birches, and there might be a shadbush blooming among the trees that overhung the wall below our fields. We would feel as though the land itself awoke and welcomed us home with as much joy as our nearest neighbors half a mile or so down the road would welcome us when we strode up to their front door.

When night came down, we would welcome the dark—the complete black, velvety dark with no light showing anywhere at all, for the neighbors' lights were hidden by hills and trees, and there were, of course, no street lights. One of my games was to walk down the road in the dark without a flashlight (for I eschewed these symbols of civilization), finding the way by the feel of the rough road under my feet and the path made through the sky where the dark road parted the trees. As the season wore on, the milkweed bloomed by the roadside and clover in the field and small, shy wild flowers in the brook. I could also tell on the darkest night just where I was by the fragrance of my mother earth—pine trees or meadows or milkweed or goldenrod.

Land in this area was very cheap. So we added to our fields the neighboring meadows and woodlots until we owned twenty-three acres of mowed fields, berry pastures filled with blueberries and blackberries and wild strawberries, and woodlots where Ted sawed wood for our big roaring fires. The joy of Alstead was as great as the joy of Kuling had been in my half-forgotten childhood. No strangers and foreigners were to come near us here—no uncircumcised Philistines were to disturb our sanctuary, for in this one place Ted insisted that we be alone.

Family, however, were not among the Philistines. Some summers one of Ted's brothers would rent a cottage down by the lake, and we would go there to swim, and they would come up the hill to pick berries. That was also a great joy, for we did not own land beside the lake nor could any be bought. Our neighbors at the end of the millpond very kindly permitted us to swim from their land, and this we gladly did, but sometimes with a bit of shyness, not knowing who else might be there and whether strangers would welcome us.

There was one summer's day, however, in early June when Alstead gave us no joy. It was very hot, and there was a vicious wind blowing—a searing, tearing wind like a blast out of an oven. There was uneasiness in that wind, and I did not know how to pray about it. If I were ever to feel such a wind again, I would know!

As we drove home the next morning and passed through Shrewsbury we were stopped at every corner by policemen who asked our destination and let us go on. Then we passed the high-school building and saw it hung with Red Cross and American flags, and still we did not guess what had happened. Not until we reached the edge of town, where we saw houses flattened and fields strewn with planks and debris did we realize there had been a tornado. I confess guiltily to a bit of joy in the hope that it had hit Shrewsbury and not Westboro—but that joy was short-lived. We were stopped on the edge of town amid fallen trees and roads strewn with torn leaves and were forbidden to drive further.

"How can we get through to Mill Road?" we asked.

"You can't. It's all blocked with fallen trees."

"But we live there!"

"Well, go around to the other end of the road and maybe they'll let you try it."

To the other end of the road we went and found it partly cleared. But we could not see our house from the road. We left the car and scrambled under trees and over tree trunks and found the house still standing. But all of the huge oak trees that had made our place a delight and a joy were torn out of the ground, the whole root structure standing up in the air like huge pancakes.

The house was intact except for a few cracks and broken glass all over the upstairs floor. If we had been at home with windows and garage door open, very likely the garage would have disappeared entirely and roof and furniture would have been chewed into fragments and blown away.

We had no gas or electricity for four days. That first night the Red Cross brought sandwiches and coffee to the house. But after that, I built a stove in the fireplace with bricks and racks out of the oven. It was rather fun to prepare meals in the living room.

"Where was God's protection?" the reader may ask. And I reply, "There. Right there!" The house was safe, and in due time insurance took care of our damage.

But we had lost all of our trees. We cleared and replanted the lawn to cover the holes left by the oak tree roots. We did not plant other oak trees, for they would not grow up during our lifetime nor the lifetimes of our children nor our children's children. Instead, we planted a crabapple and a pink dogwood and many lilacs brought from Alstead. And the loss of the trees opened vistas hid from us before: meadows far away where cows grazed peacefully among daisies and buttercups, with a glimpse of small blue hills beyond—the edges of the woods where, in the fall, oak and maple painted a magic carpet of flame and crimson—the two pretty little cottages across the road with their gardens of day lilies and iris and climbing roses. In time, this became more beautiful than the trees that we had lost. Moreover, I strewed drifts of yet more crocuses and scillas here and there upon the lawn so that as soon as the snow melted their little shining faces would smile in the sunlight and say, "Spring is here."

Still, we had lost the trees. Ted grieved greatly and, in fact, was much more upset by this whole disaster than I was. It is an advantage to have been born in a country where all life was risk and danger. One knows that it is part of living. Nor does it work out that all the evil people are destroyed or vexed and all the good people lose not even a tree. In the first place, it could not be so, since we are all part of the same human family. In the second place, those who profess Christ are not necessarily free from the persecution of the spirit of destruction. The more we exert the power of God for saving souls and bodies, the more avidly the enemy is apt to pursue us. It is a battle! In fact, the whole Christian life is a battle. It is so described both in the Bible and in the Prayer Book, and in infant baptism we promise to "fight manfully under His banner against sin, the world, and the devil," as sponsors for the infant. His banner will, in the end, triumph, and His will be the victory, but that does not mean that there will be no battle.

Nor does it work out in a battle that only the bad soldiers are wounded or die. Even a good soldier can be wounded. And it may be that Ted was wounded in this battle with the trees, for all the next day he worked with saws and hammers in a temperature of 103 degrees. (The whole tornado had taken exactly six seconds and was followed immediately by brilliant and very hot weather.)

When the lawn was cleared, we went again for a rest and for the refreshment of our souls to Alstead, where young Ted and his wife Diana visited us for a few days. Whether it was due to the shock of the tornado or whether it was simply overexertion, my husband had a strange half-fainting spell from which he soon recovered—and we did not know that it was a heart attack. Faith has its dangers. One can become too hopeful and can thus fail to take due precautions. Ted was soon well except for a bit of difficulty in breathing, which in our ignorance we attributed to hay fever, for he had been mowing the hayfields—again in the hot sun —and refusing to stop and rest.

A strange thing happened when we left Alstead on our last trip that summer. I looked at the shining meadows rising up to the forest of oak and pine, and something within me seemed to say, "You will never see it again." My heart sank into a bottomless pit of darkness and grief. All the way home I fought this ominous foreboding—this sense of an approaching doom—and would not ask myself what it meant. More fervently than ever, I prayed for Ted's complete health and strength. Resolutely I threw my mind ahead and visioned the two of us happily engaged, each in his creative activity from morning to night—Ted building and hammering in the barn, while I dug and weeded in my gardens. I suppressed my feeling of doom and lived above it, but it would not go away.

And though the end was delayed, it was a true presentiment. I never again saw Alstead with the same eyes of perfect delight, and with the luxury of living carefree in the sun. For Ted never quite regained his full strength. Nevertheless, he would mow the hayfields and gouge up stone with his crowbar, and nothing could stop him. True, he went to a doctor for a checkup and was told that he was no longer young and must take care of his heart and cease doing certain things. But he would not cease. And when I pleaded with him to heed the doctor's words, he would at first laugh and tease, and finally would say with decision, "This is my own life and I will live it the way I please."

But wonderful are the ways of the Lord, for in spite of declining strength, in the nine years left to him he accomplished the greatest work of his life.

The young man from the foundation returned, as he had promised to do, and this time at last I really considered his words and took them to the Lord in prayer. "Is there something," I asked God, "that You would really want me to start or implement with the use of money?" Long ago I had decided never to open a healing home of any kind. Indeed, I had turned down four or five offers of someone's house or country estate to be used for this purpose. I did not want to be tied down to any such thing. Besides, I found that Jesus did not start a healing home, but went to people where they were. And since I expected them to be healed by prayer, why should I want a home for them to live in? They would be much better off to learn to be well in their own homes, as I had done.

As I prayed, however, it came to me that the most important thing that could be done in the whole world would be to start some kind of school for ministers wherein they could learn those things that the seminaries did not teach them, namely, to do the works that Jesus did, according to His commands. I myself did not want to become involved in a school, but if it was best for God's kingdom, I would again give up writing, and if Ted was willing, would enter into this work. It depended entirely on Ted's willingness. He was an excellent organizer and very much a man's man. So when the representative of the foundation again appeared on my doorstep, I mentioned this idea to him, and it was met with the greatest enthusiasm. The foundation, I gathered, would build a building for this purpose and would take care of all expenses. So there remained, as I thought at the time, only Ted to agree to it.

He was as reluctant as I, for he loved his ministry as I loved my writing, and we did now know whether he could go into this work of teaching ministers and still run his church.

We did not need to decide immediately. The representative would first broach this idea to the foundation and see whether the director was interested. He was interested. I had rather hoped that he would not be.

"Oh, you can still write!" their representative had told me cheerily. "You can meet with the group during the day and do your writing in the evening." But I knew that I could not, for I cannot write without giving it my undivided attention.

However, if this was the answer to all our fervent prayers for ministers, it would have to be done.

So we went a long journey by train to talk to the director of the board. Difficulties developed during the conversation because Ted, with his usual caution, contemplated about one School of Pastoral Care a month, while the director and I thought of this as being an almost continuous venture. It was finally decided that the board would first give us a small grant that would underwrite the work for about three years: secretary, travel expenses of leaders and those attending, and some small recompense for us and the other leaders. Meanwhile, their representative would attend one of the schools, see how it went, report to the board, and make further plans.

This period of waiting was not easy. Both of us in our different ways were beset with fears and qualms and certain regrets. For Ted, this would mean resigning from the little parish that he loved, for the foundation demanded that he do so in order to give his full time to this new work. For me, it involved giving up again my life's desire of writing. We felt, both of us, that this new venture of teaching ministers the area of the faith that seminaries omitted was the most important thing that could be done for God's world—and I still think so. But we thought, as did Moses, "Lord, send whomever You will send, but not me." It still amazes me that we should have been chosen by the foundation for this work, for neither one of us was at all the go-getter type.

There was another difficulty: I was the one to whom the offer was originally made, but Ted being the man of the family naturally assumed that he would take control and run it according to his ideas, which were much more conservative and more inclined to agree with the establishment than were my more feminine and free concepts of this work. For instance, he said, "I will invite Dr. ———— to lecture," and when I replied, "But Dr. ———— does not believe in healing, does he?" Ted responded, "Maybe not, but he's a big man in the church."

Perhaps Ted was right. Possibly we should have first invited the big men in the church and then tried to convert them to healing. But what if they were not converted, and the School of Pastoral Care went the way of the establishment and forgot healing altogether?

Another difficulty arose at this point: Ted and I, both of us brought up in the old tradition, were not accustomed to talking things out, to arguing, to getting angry with each other. Perhaps we were entirely wrong in abstaining from quarreling. But we built and maintained a marriage of mutual respect and love that survived all our differences, and whether we could have done this by confrontations and arguments I do not know.

"Why don't you talk more about how I'm going to run this school?" asked Ted one day.

"Well, I guess I don't know what to say."

"I know how I ran Proctor School in China," said Ted.

"But this is different," I replied. "This is a *cooperative* venture. We are supposed to run it together."

Poor Ted. He had never cooperated with anyone in his whole life. For instance, he had refused an assistant minister consistently, saying that he preferred a good secretary who would simply take orders.

The conversation dropped at that point, but next time the subject came up, Ted said "we" instead of "I."

In doubt and perplexity we awaited the foundation's decision.

During this time of waiting, the Lord gave me a dream. I was walking down a moonlit path outside Marion Lovekin's house in Tucson, where I had first received the Holy Spirit. There was a numinous quality in the whole dream. It seemed real, yet unreal. The night was dark, and I could see nothing except the path, dim among trees and bushes. And there, diagonally across the path, lay —a thing. It seemed huddled and shapeless, yet as I drew near to it in the dream, I cried, "Oh, it's a man!" It was indeed the remnant of a man, age-worn, emaciated, and lying at an odd angle as though there were no life in it. "But it's dead," I breathed in the dream.

I gazed in pity upon him and saw that there was yet in that wizened body a spark of life. At that point, I felt a surge of power enter into me and pierce down my spine—a burning such as I had felt in the head when the Holy Spirit came upon me. And I said to this half-dead creature, "In the name of Jesus Christ, arise and walk."

He arose and stood in the middle of the path. The flesh grew upon him. Light came into his eyes. He stood tall and virile and full of life.

I did not know the meaning of this dream until I related it to one of the ministers in the first School of Spiritual Healing, which we re-named the School of Pastoral Care, as being a less alarming name for clergy to contemplate.

"That man in the dream represents the church," said this minister. "He is not dead but almost appears dead to one who passes by. He lies not in the middle of the path but at an angle to it. When you spoke to him the words of faith, he arose and came to life and stood no longer beside the way of life but directly upon it."

I pray God that this vision will yet be fulfilled.

18.

E began the School of Pastoral Care in Lasell House, a large, handsome mansion given to the Diocese of Western Massachusetts. During the period of consideration, we had visited a healing center run by a medical doctor in Hemet, California, with the idea of possibly joining our effort with his very fine work. His house and cottages were strewn about a mountainside with a full view of snowcapped Mount Jacinto and all its glorious range of mountains. Just to look at them lifted the heart. On the other hand, Lasell House at that time stood alone and wistful, as an old house will stand, and the feeling of it was cold and dark.

But it was evident that Ted could never stand the far reaches of the desert with its heat and dust and the speed of the life that surrounded it. So one must needs step out into the unknown in Massachusetts not knowing whither that step would lead.

One good thing came, however, from our visit to California. The foundation considered starting a Department of Religion and Health in some hospital for the purpose of promoting cooperation between chaplains and doctors and perhaps analysis and documentation of the work of Christian healing. Their representative asked my advice concerning this venture, and I recommended the Good Samaritan Hospital in Los Angeles and my friend, Bert Hause, the chaplain. And so the work was started by the foundation, was soon taken over by the hospital, and continues to this day.

Our bishop at that time was the Right Reverend W. Appleton Lawrence, a saint of the Lord and a good friend to both of us through all his life. With his blessing and his warm and loving presence, we held the first session of the school with some twenty ministers, as advised by Dr. Fritz Kunkel.

"You should have no more than twenty," he said, "for you will find that the personal conferences will be the most important aspect of your work."

We did not quite believe this at the time. But it has turned out to be true. Ministers do not have a minister, for bishops, though they are fathers in God to their ministers and often greatly desire so to be, are usually kept so busy with diocesan affairs that they have no time for the healing of the soul. Ministers, moreover, are apt to need this healing of the soul or the deep mind or, as I call it, of the memories. They bear not only their own burdens, but the burdens of their congregation, and they must carry these burdens always with a serene and smiling face and must never disturb their little flock by loading upon them their own personal problems. So, from the very first, we found that there was need of counseling, confession, and personal prayer. This we did individually, never in a group, feeling that for the dignity of the individual soul, all that was told to one of the leaders must be surrounded with privacy and kept completely confidential. Indeed, this is the first principle of the confessional, whether formal or informal—anything told to a priest or other leader must never be told to any other person. This is a rule that I have always kept in all my work. Moreover, it is never necessary for me to say to one who comes to me, "I promise I won't tell anyone." This is so impressed in me that they know it, and I know it so completely that it would simply not occur to me to tell.

That first session was planned for ten days. Later we found this impractical and changed it to five days, often wishing that we could have twice the time! The first few days were a bit difficult. The foundation at this time was paying the way of all those attending, and this had its drawbacks, for one or two, I gathered, came rather to dispute and argue than to learn. It was several days before any unity was achieved. Then, about the time when the group entered into that "unity of the spirit in the bonds of love" through which comes power, the representative of the foundation came to appraise the situation. We had perforce agreed to this, but it disturbed that new-born unity, for no one knew why a strange face appeared among them.

From this time on, we made and held fast to the rule that the same people were to stay together during the entire conference and that no visitors would be permitted. For we discovered, somewhat to our surprise, that power emanated from the group as they entered into a wonderful unity of spirit, being indeed one body in Christ.

We did nothing to stir up this feeling of brotherhood and of divine love. There was no artificial stimulation of emotion. The hymns that we sang were out of the *Hymnal*, strong and stirring hymns, not sentimental ditties, for though the latter are quite suitable for certain groups, we did not feel them suitable for this meeting of ministers and clergy. It was and still is my conviction that there is life in the organized churches—a light that needs only to be lit with a new fire—a consecration of its ministers that needs only to be renewed and fanned into swift life by the winds of the Spirit—prayers and hymns and rituals honored by the centuries that need, not so much to be revised, as to be brought into new life by the illumination of the ageless meaning therein.

Knowing that strength comes from unity and not from division, we do not in the School of Pastoral Care encourage argument, but only study and the quiet contemplation of ideas that are ageless, but that to some may seem new. We have only one daily period of conversation and questions, and that we call a "hymn sing and question period" so that if any questions tend to be either belligerent or time-wasting, the leader can say, "Now who would like to suggest a hymn?" and thus turn the feeling of the meeting into a sense of peace. Strangely enough, this does not stifle broad speculation, but frees it. A minister once said, "This is amazing. I would not dare bring up these subjects anywhere else, or we would all be at each others' throats. But here we are discussing the most deep and varying concepts in an atmosphere of perfect love."

This unity does not always happen the first day! Once there was a very high-church Anglican monk among us and also a Pentecostal brother who posed a bit of a problem. In the midst of the question and hymn-sing period, the love of Christ so overwhelmed the group that the two of them, who had been at daggers' points, leaped up and hugged each other, laughing with heavenly joy! There was another occasion when among the ministers came one who is among my very best friends, the Reverend Olivia Henry, a Negro minister. (I refuse to call her "black," for, as she herself says, she is not black. "I'm only God's little brown cookie," says this fascinating woman.) She was welcomed by all without comment and with real Christian courtesy, but among the group was one very young minister from the Middle West who apparently had a problem about accepting her. He never mentioned this, but she told me that on the last day of the school he came to her and asked her to lay her hands on him and pray that God would help him to love everybody.

These two incidents, however, did not take place during the first school, which was a bit stiff and guarded. I do not know whether that fact influenced the final decision of the foundation. But in due time we were told that there were five directors instead of one as we had assumed there would be and that one of them did not approve of spiritual healing. Therefore, the original plan for the school would not be carried out, nor would any more funds be available except that rather small sum given us to start this work.

This was a terrible blow. Ted had resigned from his church, to the great grief of his congregation and to his own desolation, for a minister needs his own church as a ship needs an anchor. Moreover, he would not receive the munificent salary of ten thousand dollars a year that the foundation had offered—he would receive no salary. I was sure that we could get along without any salary, trusting to gifts given by missions and lectures and to royalties, but Ted did not share my spirit of adventure and felt that he must get another church. Therefore, Bishop Lawrence found him a little mission church in Millville, an hour's drive from our home. And we continued with the School of Pastoral Care.

Ted was in his element as a pastor to pastors. He was a trained and skilled teacher. His confirmation classes, in which he taught the reality of God, the redemptive work of Jesus Christ, and the power of the Holy Spirit, were attended by many who desired a refresher course in their faith, as well as by those seeking confirmation. Until the last two years of his life, when his energies began to wane, his lectures to young ministers were beyond compare. If every seminary had teaching like this, the kingdom of heaven would be right over the hill, and its sun would begin to rise upon us. For Ted taught "the cure of souls," as the ministry was called in the early church. And to many a minister who had never made a life confession, he was truly a doctor of the soul.

"This was my real ordination," said a young minister, after Ted prayed for him in our final blessing service. "I was never truly a minister until now."

Other ministers, of course, came to me with their problems, feeling less hesitation in telling certain things to a nonclerical "mother figure" than to a priest.

We have found it usually advisable to have three leaders in each session of the School of Pastoral Care, in order to provide a counselor for each minister, if he so desires. For the third leader, we often invited a psychologist who also believes in direct healing, or a Christian psychiatrist, or a minister versed in psychology. After Ted's departure into heaven, our son John sometimes helped in the School, not taking his father's place but his own more psychologically oriented one.

So even after Ted's death, the School of Pastoral Care survived and survives, directed by myself for a while (ridiculous, that, for I hate directing anything except a play, and I am by no means a "woman's lib" type of person), then by Dr. Francis Whiting, at that time Director of Evangelism of the Baptist Church in Michigan. Now, since Dr. Whiting has gone into other work, the School goes along under the leadership of regional directors, loosely held together by the central board in Massachusetts and by its secretary, Mrs. Walter Lewis. It owns nothing and is therefore accountable to no one. No one receives any salary except the secretary, for one cannot call the small gifts given to the leaders of each conference by any such exalted term as a salary. Those invited to lead are all busy people who can spare from their regular work only one week a year or perhaps two or three, and that is good. Thus the leaders have no chance to become one-sided or separated from real life, as some teachers and seminary professors are apt to become.

Lasell House is still the center of this work, but many sessions are now held in other places, by invitation of a minister, psychiatrist, or bishop, here and there across the United States from Florida to Washington—Massachusetts, Tennessee, and California now predominating. Sessions have also been held in Canada and England, Holland, New Zealand, and Australia.

Evidently this is the Lord's work, and He wants it to go on, even though He had to get it across to me in the first place by "trickery and snares," as Caesar used to say. For in those days I did not hear the Lord clearly, and it took first a foundation and then the failure of the foundation to get me off the ground!

The main purpose of the School of Pastoral Care is to teach ministers that area of the Christian faith that is not taught in seminaries: healing of soul, mind, and body through faith and prayer. The reason for making this a school for ministers (of religion or medicine) is obvious: these people are in positions of leadership, yet they very much need help themselves. And every one of them who learns the laws and acquires the power to pray for healing can help hundreds and thousands of lay people.

This is desperately needed, for churches lose members daily where ministers do not feed His sheep or feed His lambs with the Word of God which is truth and life. One can only grieve for them, for they are following that which they have been taught in their seminaries, and one may grieve all the more for the professors who teach them, in their ignorance, things which are not true. So they themselves were taught.

Presumably they do not dare to do their own research by trying the Lord to see whether His promises are true. Presumably they feel that they must be "mod," living up to the most recent fads in religion. But the winds of the Spirit blow so strongly that even while these learned ones are still intimating that God is dead, the young in heart are finding God through Jesus and through the Bible more and more every day—finding Him sometimes not in churches, but through other young people—being baptized, not in a font at a church door, but in the vastness of the ocean whose cold waters cannot freeze the flaming love of Christ within their hearts!

However, even upon some seminaries, thank God, the winds of the Spirit are blowing. There are seminaries wherein small prayer groups are filled with the Spirit and with power, and sooner or later that power is bound to break the shackles that try to bind it. I even know a few seminaries where healing prayer groups flourish and from which the light of the Spirit shines into the country round about.

For centuries people have been taught that this is a new dispensation and God does not heal today. In the School of Pastoral Care, we tell the ministers that He does. And we challenge them to make a decision concerning this by praying for healing themselves and seeing whether it works. In order to do this, they must revise and expand their understanding of the prayer of faith and of God and His universe permeated by His Holy Spirit.

"The trouble with this school," said one young man plaintively, "is that I have to re-think my whole theology."

"Of course," I said, "because the teaching of healing includes not only special instruction in certain areas, such as mental depression, obsessions, demon possession, etc., but also it includes a re-examination of one's beliefs concerning God and a deepened understanding of the mind of man."

Most of all, it includes stepping out on faith and trying the power of God. For this we have what we call, rather inadequately, a "prayer clinic," for the healing of minor ills. (Not major ills, for this School is most definitely not for sick people but for well people. The course requires an intense concentration of every faculty of mind and spirit, and a sick body cannot stand it.) In this session we ask those who need healing to state their need and then ask those who have never tried healing with the laying on of hands to come forward and lay hands on someone.

Thus they enter into the stream of faith of the leader who prays. They sense the power, either physically or spiritually. They become a part of the "Christian underground," and from this time forth when they pray for healing, they will not pray alone but as part of an unseen fellowship, the very body of Christ on earth; and so, as part of Our Lord Himself.

Now, inevitably, this requires not only a mental understanding of Christ's power to heal, but it also requires the actual power which proceeds today from the Holy Spirit through the Father and the Son. And the whole school is shaped toward an increase of the Holy Spirit. After instruction concerning God the Father, the Creator, God the Son, the Redeemer, and God the Holy Spirit, the Sanctifier, we close the School with a service of reconsecration. Two or three leaders lay hands on everyone who comes to the altar rail and pray that the gifts and power of the Spirit, already implanted in him through his ordination, will increase within him and set him on fire with holy love and power. We pray as moved by the Spirit, one beginning and sometimes another leader adding that which God gives him.

It is wonderful, indeed, how the Spirit works in these prayers! Often we say words that we cannot know concerning the healing of wounded memories of the past. Often we come forth with prophecies concerning the future which we could not know save by the grace of God, and later, having forgotten them, are amazed that they come true. And always the Spirit moves within the person, moving him to tears or to laughter or simply to a deeper peace within.

We do not at this time encourage the gift of speaking in tongues. Many who come have that gift but remain silent out of consideration for their brothers. Many others do not have it and are not yet prepared to receive it. They have come to this School seeking the power of God to heal, and we do not impose on them any gift that might distract their attention from this, our first objective. Remember that on my baptism in the Spirit I received a totally transforming rush of God's love, resulting in healing, in peace, and in joy, and in the understanding of truth. But I did not speak with tongues at that time.

Nevertheless, many a minister has received the gift of the Spirit, tongues and all, at a School of Pastoral Care, through instruction and prayer privately or in a small group.

All this was ten years ago, more or less. It is no longer necessary to have the smaller group, for now many have received tongues long before they come to the School. Also, one can always refer seekers to some of the many charismatic groups that are springing up from coast to coast.

Even in this day, however, the baptism in the Spirit and in particular the speaking in tongues is anathema to many rectors and bishops and senior wardens, to vestrymen and deacons and also to certain lay popes full of moneybags. Therefore, my advice to someone who is about to leave the School of Pastoral Care in a flame of holy joy and love and power is: "Keep still about it. It is not necessary to say to your congregation, 'Look at me: I have the gift of wisdom.' If you have the gift of wisdom, they will eventually know it. It is not necessary to say 'I now have the gift of healing.' Go to see those who are ill and in trouble and pray for them, and eventually they will know that the Spirit works through you to heal. It is not necessary to say to them, 'I have the gift of tongues!' This gift, like all the gifts, is merely a tool to help you build the kingdom of God on earth."

This was advice for ministers, not necessarily for everyone. Most of them heed these words and go home and let the light shine through them so that their churches are indeed filled with light, and yet remain protected from criticism. Thus their churches are more and more filled with power (and therefore also with people and with the money needed to support these churches). So it comes to pass that by the time people begin to know about the work of the Spirit in their lives, the fruits of this work speak so loudly that no unbelieving voice can drown out this testimony of fact.

There have been, however, a few, very few, who were so carried away that they did not heed my warnings and therefore lost their churches.

Now I am giving, as the reader will see, a summing up of the work of the School of Pastoral Care rather than a detailed history of it. But let me go back for a moment to the beginning and say that this latter aspect of the work of the School was for some years understood and undertaken by me alone. Ted was a magnificent teacher and a great comfort to the students, but he never ventured into the area of tongues. The students recognized in him a sound and conservative churchman and lifted up their heads and rejoiced. Ted and I were told time and again that we were a perfect team because we were so entirely different. Those who could not quite take my flights of mysticism took refuge under the shadow of Ted's wings and were content. How amazing that God uses us to complement one another and so build the Body of Christ!

The whole purpose of the service of reconsecration is that those who take part may have an *experience* of God. Most of the ministers have had such experiences but have lost the joy of them under the burden of life. For them the joy can be awakened, and they can once more enter into newness of life. The experience of rebirth can come to a person more than once in his walk through life.

Not without pain is this rebirth brought about. No baby comes into the world without some pain to the mother. Being apparently a mother to many ministers, I have found through the years that I am apt to follow a certain rather difficult cycle in my own feelings during a School of Pastoral Care. I dread the first day, due to a shyness that I have never been able to outgrow. On the second day, when we begin to feel at home with each other, the shyness disappears, and I am filled with joy at the sight of these men gathered together to receive the Lord's blessing and set forth on a healing adventure. But I become more and more tense and sometimes wake up on the third day with a migraine headache which gradually wears off as the day proceeds. On the fourth day I return to normal, and on the fifth, I am apt once more to be filled and swept with joy. It seems as though I have to go all the way down with them in order to lift them (those who can accept it) all the way up.

Yes, there is occasionally one who cannot accept it . . . until, usually at the last moment, the Lord succeeds in getting through to him. There was a Congregational minister once who did not believe any of what he considered my flight of fancy until the power of the Lord swept over him at the consecration service. Then the change was immediate, miraculous, and beautiful, and he has led a new life from that time on.

There was another minister who came only out of desperation because his two little girls were born with cystic fibrosis and there seemed no way to heal them save by a miracle. Though he tried for their sakes, he simply could not accept any of our instructions, so foreign were they to the mechanistic and "rational" theology that he had been taught. Even at the consecration service, his mind was closed to miracles, so no miracle could happen to him. But afterward, after our final meal, someone drew me excitedly into the chapel and I went, wondering who had fallen apart now. There were fourteen ministers standing around in awe and amazement because the chapel was filled with the fragrance of a kind of heavenly incense, more sweet than any that man can make. No incense had ever been used in that chapel.

And this minister was on his knees in front of the altar, bathed in tears of joy. He leaped up and flung his arms around everyone, laughing with exhilarated delight. Finally he drove away, still on cloud nine. He later sought and found the full baptism in the Spirit, and his daughters are getting well.

Since then I have often sensed the holy fragrance here and there in Lasell House, which, needless to say, no longer feels cold and sad but is filled with light and joy. When I mentioned this fragrance once to Tommy Tyson, one of our leaders, he simply said, "Naturally. Don't you see the angels?" And when I mentioned it to one of the cooks, she said, "Of course. As soon as your school is over, all three of us go into the chapel and just sit there to soak it up."

God has many ways of making His presence known.

After a School of Pastoral Care in Gilbulla, outside of Sydney, Australia, one of the ministers went back to the little chapel at the edge of the bush to take a snapshot. The altar was bare, the cross being high above it in the window that formed the reredos. There was no sunlight, no electric light in the chapel, and no flashlight on his camera. But the photograph showed a ball of gentle light softly gleaming in the center of the altar. When on my departure I showed this snapshot to a lady at the Sydney airport, she said simply, "Quite. I saw that light in the cathedral while you were lecturing."

As I look back over the years at the results of all this labor in the School of Pastoral Care, I am torn between joy and sorrow. For not all have carried through life the power then received—and of course not all received in the same measure, but varyingly according to their capacity and according to their desire.

There are churches, however, that rejoice my heart because they grow steadily in His love and healing power. His light shines through them and in them like a flame and like a fire. Those who enter sense His presence and fall on their knees with joy. The living witness of the church goes forth into the city, into the state, or even into the nation, a shining beacon proclaiming Jesus Christ and His salvation and love and healing.

Recently, the Rev. A. J. Glennon, canon of the Cathedral of Saint Andrew in Sydney, Australia, and leader of the Schools of Pastoral Care in that country, sent me a record of the service that celebrated the tenth anniversary of healing in Australia. There were twenty "elders" standing behind the altar rail and laying hands on the hundreds of people who filled the great cathedral, as they do once every week. Mr. Glennon conducted the service from the pulpit and called upon those who felt guided to act as elders on this occasion to come forward. So they came, men and women, and prayed in silence for those on whom they laid their hands as the canon prayed aloud from the pulpit. Every week this happens. A healing group that began with some twenty people now fills the cathedral. The record continued with testimonies from many and with the bishop's address of joy and encouragement.

Little candles of faith have also been lit in New Zealand and Canada, many of them in England, and more than I can count in the United States. All these lights that lighten the darkness of this world will help our Lord Jesus to bring forth His kingdom of heaven on earth.

19.

*H*AD it not been for the power of the Holy Spirit, with His wonderful gift of a mystic—and I might say magic—joy, I do not know how I could have come through the first eight years of the School of Pastoral Care which were also the last years of my husband's life. He had already suffered a slight heart attack, as I have mentioned. The canceling of the original plans for the school was a terrible shock to him. The effort of the hour's drive to the church in Millville was very difficult, especially in the winter with its horrors of snow and ice.

These things might have been overcome if Ted had been willing to follow doctors' orders and take care of his body—and if he had been willing to take care of his soul by permitting someone to pray for the healing of the memories, that great resource for the lifting of inner burdens. But he would not hear of it, being of a reticent and independent nature.

I do not blame him for this. Until the latter years of our marriage, I myself had not come to understand the tremendous healing available through the giving of our Lord's life for us. Nor did I understand until toward the end of his life that even in his idyllic childhood with six brothers and sisters, a saintly father and mother, and the whole of a Vermont countryside to roam in— even there—were certain old hurts and sorrows never revealed, never understood, never healed. By the time I came to know this, he was so stiffened and hardened in his resolution to row his own boat—to manage himself—that one could not break through his reserve. Indeed, there are people built after this pattern, and one can but respect them, for they are the strong ones who will stand erect in their own power or break under the load of life, but will never yield their minds to another's inspection.

The burden grew heavier, the heart weakened, and in time Ted was taken to the hospital with a heart attack from which the doctor said he would not recover. He did, for he was willing to accept prayer for healing of the body then, and he was surrounded by the prayers of many people who adored him. For indeed he was a father in God, first to his congregations, and later to many ministers of many churches; I have never known a man more deeply loved.

Recovering, he was able again to lecture in Schools of Pastoral Care. Occasionally, he even fulfilled an engagement to do a mission with me, though to these I went with fear and trembling overcome only by my faith in God. And, praise the Lord, Ted came safely home from these trips, stepping gladly off the train which was to him an amusement and a delight, and rejoicing in the new friendships made and the new healings begun. However, he had another serious heart attack, the prognosis unfavorable, and at this time I was doing a mission alone in Whittier, California. I had desired to cancel all such engagements, but he would not permit me to do so. First, he appreciated their value and had become very pleased and proud of my ventures in this line. Secondly, he felt that I would need this work both during his life and after it, since he had no salary.

Just as I was about to begin the first lecture, word came of his heart attack. My son who had reached him commanded me to come home immediately. I had to make a difficult decision. On holding it up to the Lord, I received guidance that if God had sent me on this trip (which we believed that He had), then God could hold Ted in His keeping until I had finished it. Therefore, saying no word to the congregation, I went into the pulpit and began my lectures. I called home every day and found Ted gradually improving. Indeed, God not only held him through the time of the mission, but actually quite miraculously so healed him that he was able to return home and resume a more or less active life.

He was now slow in thinking and in speech, but he had a young secretary who understood the situation and made of his morning's work on School of Pastoral Care letters and publicity a thing of gentleness and joy. This set me free for writing during the morning hours. I would go into my study, recently built on the other end of the house after Ted took over the little room off the kitchen. Here I was completely free for a few hours to live my own life. I would begin my meditation looking through the gardens and to the top of the little hill, and as I meditated on the light of God, I could often see a light like an aura around the birch trees, though what that light could be I did not know.

At this period I wrote *Dreams Are for Tomorrow*, a book that has possibilities, but whose ending has never satisfied me. One can see why that would be! For I would write a chapter or so, and then Ted would again be in such poor health that I could not collect myself sufficiently to write further, and then he would be better and I would write again. The writing was a lifeline from the Lord. In it, I could forget myself and stay in the kingdom of the Spirit, a world above a world, a world of meditation and creativity.

Ted was hardly strong enough to go to Alstead after that. In fact, he was never again to enter into Alstead with his former zest and delight. There were intermissions, however. There was a summer when Ted was almost his old self and when young Ted and his wife, Diana, and their tiny son, Timmy, spent the summer with us. This was in the period when Ted, a successful young lawyer on Wall Street, decided that the legal profession was too boring a way of life and changed into education. When Timmy was born, Ted was still living in a flat in Brooklyn, getting his M.A. at Columbia and teaching in a church school for boys in the New York area.

Our delight over the arrival of a first grandson was past all belief! In fact, I was so excited on hearing that Diana had gone to the hospital that I ran into a square bedpost barefooted and, of all the ridiculous things, broke my little toe! I would not go to a doctor for fear that he would put it in a cast and thus impede my activity. So I sought guidance, and on the strength of it, went and bought a tongue depressor, made a small splint, bound it on with adhesive tape and went to New York to help with the new baby, who was utterly adorable. Three weeks later the little family arrived in Alstead. Young Ted made himself a hideout in the loft of the barn and wrote his thesis, and all of us had a happy summer. I had just written *A Pasture for Peterkin* for children. Alstead breathes through every word of it, and many of the stories, such as that of Amanda learning prayer through praying for the baby bull, are true. I set Ted to drawing the illustrations.

"Go down to the Burroughs' barn," said I to my son, "and see if they have a newborn calf, for I need an illustration of one."

"Oh Mom, they won't! They have only two or three cows anyway."

But they did have a newborn calf. And Ted sat happily in the hay and drew the tiny calf still wet from being within his mother.

Later on, Timmy's little sister was born, a beautiful and delightful baby. But I must cease, or I will spend the rest of the book holding forth on my grandchildren, who now number nine. I do remember another summer, however, when for a week or so, not only Ted's family, but also Jack and his wife, Linny, and their little girl Katie were all at Alstead—and when the three of us women and the three babies would go to country auctions, the babies crawling delightedly in the dust and playing with baking pans and rocking chairs and manure spreaders and chamber pots and other bits of merchandise spread over the lawns and driveways in front of old barns. Our menfolk, in the meantime, stayed at home and occupied themselves, each in his own way, with writing and studying and mowing the hayfields and shingling the barn.

Alas, they are far away, those happy days in the little old farmhouse set upon a hill up rocky dirt roads that functioned as stream beds when the rains came. But I spend little time in dreaming of them, for I live in today and look toward a tomorrow of ever-opening horizons.

In time, Ted and his family moved to Tacoma, Washington, where he was the headmaster of the Charles Wright Academy. And Jack and his family went to the very town where I now live, Jack functioning as the assistant minister in St. Luke's Church, Monrovia. Tookie and Miles, meanwhile, were already in California and were adopting their first child, a beautiful little girl, through the help of a friend in Switzerland.

So Ted and I were alone. "No more More-Daddy," said Ted one day with a sigh, and my heart ached for him for I knew that it was true. He would never again see the charming little boy who called him "More-Daddy," trotting happily after him to barn or hayfield.

The next summer we went to Alstead again, but Ted was

weaker and could do little but sit by the stone wall and look wistfully over his fields and down to the lake. And the next summer he did not go at all.

The house was never rented. Somehow we could not so commercialize it. We lent it to relatives or to ministers who needed a vacation, and it was not entirely devoid of life, although I know it missed us. This sounds fanciful, and yet I sense a truth in it: the fields with no one to search in them for tiny flowers hid in the rough grass, the flower beds blooming unnoticed, the lawn growing up rough and dry.

"There is sorrow on the sea; it cannot be quiet" (Jer. 49:23). I felt a sorrow on the land that I trust will be someday healed as others cherish it and love it as we had done.

In the meantime, the flowers and gardens, the trees and the views in Westboro, were a comfort and joy to Ted. He could wander about the lawn or sit under the newly growing trees and find peace.

Except for the mornings when Ted's secretary-companion was with him, I was his companion and nurse, though in a very unobtrusive way, for he did not like any intimation of needing one! Perhaps it was not strange that it became more difficult for me to keep my carefully acquired confidence in my own health. With years of careful mind-training, I had built up a sense of immunity to colds and other germs. But I became overconfident, and it led to carelessness.

I visited young Ted's family, at that time in Watertown, Connecticut, immediately before making a lecturing trip west during one of Ted's times of comparative health. Both the little ones had flu, and having become completely oblivious to germs, I cuddled them and kissed them as usual, and found myself sickening with flu the very day I took the plane west. If I could have gone to bed and taken lemon juice and water, my favorite cure for all things, I would probably have been well in a day. But instead, I had to fly from here to there and to lecture everywhere, and I lost my voice! I would stand up in the pulpit and croak, "I've lost my voice! Pray for me!" and upheld by many prayers, would manage to gasp out a talk and then collapse. In the face of all this difficulty, I lost faith in my own power to claim healing for myself.

Nevertheless, I could still pray for others, and I did continually pray for Ted, and each time I did so he would breathe more easily and would feel better.

But complete healing did not come. So I asked for guidance. There is a time for everyone to depart, that I know, and he was approaching seventy. I said, "Lord, how long does he have?" And the answer came, "Three years."

His days were lengthened a little bit by continual prayer. He had three years and six months. But the last year and a half, after he was threescore years and ten, were truly, as Solomon said they would be, labor and sorrow. He had a massive stroke, was taken unconscious to the hospital, and the doctor told me that this was the end, that it would be a matter of a few hours. For nine years I had practiced holding myself taut and upright, for it was necessary to do so. I have wondered sometimes whether Ted would have felt more cherished and comforted if I had gone to pieces, weeping and wailing and collapsing on the bed. But if I had, who would have taken care of him? Therefore I did not fall apart when the doctor told me this—indeed, I could not, having so trained myself in bonds of restraint that it seemed impossible for me to untie them. But I believed him, and I did not pray for healing this time, for I knew that if Ted's life were prolonged it would be only to labor and sorrow. I prayed only for whatever was best, trusting God to take him at the right time.

However, others—all his people who loved him—did not consider these matters, but prayed definitely for healing. In all my books I counsel people to ask guidance before leaping into healing prayers, but few pay any attention. Ted did make a recovery, but indeed and truly he was not himself. With help and steady upholding, he could act and talk like his old self for a time, but he could not maintain it, nor could he understand why this was so.

During this period I thought it might be good to take him out of the winter cold into Florida, which he loved, and where his brother David lived. We actually tried it. He enjoyed the trip down on the train, and at first found pleasure in our little rented house by the Gulf. But his memory had failed. He would lift sofas and move garden seats in a spirit of gleeful showing off like a child, not remembering that it would hurt him. The weather, moreover, turned humid and dark, and we decided to come home. It was his last trip.

He knew on returning that his time here was not long, and he wanted me to promise that I would never again send him to a hospital. He hated hospitals and wanted to die at home. I told him that I could not make such a promise—that if the doctor were to say that a hospital was necessary to save his life, how could I excuse myself to his brothers and his children if I refused to send him there? He was afraid of it. And he was afraid of death. One time in Florida he told me with great wonderment that he had seen an angel standing in his doorway—did I suppose he was dreaming? I assured him that I believed there really was an angel standing at his door, and we rejoiced in the evidence of God's mercy. But he was still afraid of death until God in a most wonderful way took this fear from him.

He came down to breakfast one day with his eyes shining. Let not the reader think him bedfast all this time! He hated invalidism with a holy passion and was up and dressed and at his desk for a little while every morning.

"I had the most wonderful dream last night!" he said. "I was sitting in my chair in the living room. And then the room changed, and it was not this room, but my room in Vermont when I was a boy. Then it changed again, to the boardinghouse in Connecticut where I had my first job away from home. And then it became our first living room, in the house in Changshu. You were there, young and beautiful, and I saw the sofa we had, and everything in that room, just as it was. I had forgotten what it all looked like! Then the room became our living room in Moorestown, and you were there too, still beautiful but older, as you looked then. And finally I was back in this room. You came down the stairs at the same moment that the doctor walked in the front door. He came up to the back of my chair, put his hand on it and said, 'Oh, he's gone.' At that moment I looked at the clock on the mantelpiece. The hands went around and stopped at twelve o'clock, and then the wall behind the clock began to open. It opened wider and wider, and a shaft of bright light shone through it. I got up and walked out on the path of light."

"How beautiful!" I breathed, through tears that could not be shed.

"What do you think it means?" he asked.

"I think it means," I replied steadily, "that when you go, it will be just like that."

"Yes, I think so too," said he with great contentment. And that was the nearest that we ever came to speaking of the hour of his departure. We were both trained in the old school of self-control. We did not confront or share or indulge in dialogue. But we concealed nothing. We both knew that the time was short.

He lived five days more, and all that time he was relaxed and happy, nor would he ever take the role of an invalid. In fact, on the day he died, he was fully dressed and sat in a chair out of doors and instructed a carpenter as to how to mend the garage door! Ernestine came to dinner that night and was a gay and delightful companion as always. Taking her home, I said aloud, even as though my spirit knew it, "Anytime the Lord takes him now, it will be all right."

The Lord took him that night. He was ready for bed but wanted to sit up in the big chair and watch a baseball game on television, as he often did, for he would take a long nap after dinner and be wide awake until midnight. I was very tired, having been over to Lasell House to plan for a School of Pastoral Care that was supposed to take place on Monday. So in due time I went to bed, in the bedroom directly above him, the door open.

The next I knew it was early morning, before dawn, and the voice of an all-night station still spoke softly over the television set.

I ran downstairs. There he sat, his face as composed and peaceful as I had ever seen it, his attitude completely relaxed.

"He died instantaneously," the doctor said when he came. "He never knew when he went."

Indeed, he never saw death. But he had seen resurrection in the Spirit five days before, and he went in peace, in his own home, as he had so earnestly desired, sitting in his chair.

I called up our best Westboro friend, David Yates, and he promptly came and took charge of everything, sending many telegrams: to the children, to the thirty men who were planning on arriving at the School of Pastoral Care the next day, to the beloved new rector of Trinity Church, Moorestown, to the bishop . . .

Jack and I designed the tombstone: a tall rectangle with a

cross above Ted's name and rays of light streaming down from it, even like those rays that he had seen in his dream.

The church was full of friends and family and parishioners; the house was for days full of flowers; and life went on. I was upheld by the power of the Spirit. And for one moment, even in the midst of great sorrow, the Lord seemed to show me a new life waiting to be born.

And so there was. Perhaps I made a mistake in entering so soon into that new life: traveling and lecturing and praying and healing—but I had driven myself for so long that I could not let down. Only once did I break into a storm of tears, and then the telephone rang, and from long habit I pulled myself together and answered it. I thought, also, that if I took six months off to do nothing except be a heartbroken widow I would again sink into depression. And perhaps I would have done so. As it was, I buried my grief and went on working.

Between trips, I lived alone. Fortunately, I have never been afraid of sleeping alone in a house and was not now. True the house was full of sad memories, hiding around corners like rather pitiful ghosts, but it was also warmed with love. And it was home.

For the first time in my life I could begin each day with a meditation, and could enter high into the presence of God and fill myself with His light and life for the day's work. My study, even in the oncoming winter with its dark days and its skies heavy with coming snow, was filled with flowers that were the joy of my life. I remember especially a hibiscus that grew to the ceiling and opened in a New England winter its huge ruffled blossoms of creamy pink. And I still grieve for my passionflower vine that grew all the way across the picture window and from time to time electrified the air by the bursting into fragrant beauty of a fantastic blossom: five green sepals and five lavender petals opening out like a star, then a crown of delft blue stamens, and within it three outreaching pistils of gold and lilac. Is it a little thing to be comforted by the beauty of flowers? I do not think so. I could almost feel them smile at me when I came in of a morning, and my heart would lift up and I would greet them every one. As I meditated, lifting up my heart to the Lord, I would pray with open eyes, seeing the glory of God around my birch trees like a halo—like a light!

Three mornings a week Dorothy Lewis would come, and I would do with her the dictating and planning that Ted used to do, for the School of Pastoral Care was still going on. When the house was empty again, I would have lunch in the lovely little dining room overlooking the sloping lawn and the far meadows.

After lunch I would rest a while, a habit to which I have trained myself, for much of my work is done in the evening and I must be alert for it. Then came the hard time of the day: twilight creeping over the sad brown woods and filling the little house with shadows within which there lurked other shadows of wistful memories and of old sorrows too deep for tears. But the wonderful gift of the love of friends softened these evenings, for usually someone would invite me to dinner, and we would have a game of bridge, resting the soul and exercising the mind with gentle activity. Or Ernestine and I would take dinner time and time about with each other, going over a few letters afterward or simply cheering each other with the fellowship of old friends.

While in the West, I carried through a School of Pastoral Care planned long before. It may have been a mistake, for I was too sad and tired to do my best. But I was saved from making another mistake by a dream, having learned from my son Jack to notice and respect dreams. In the dream I was climbing a very steep black cliff covered with snow and ice, and one of my weakest friends, a man needing much prayer and calling on me continually for help, was trying to assist me. I reached for a handhold on a slab of black rock, and it came loose in my hands; and I said "I can't do it in the winter! If I wait until summer I can do it." And I awoke. Now there was the School of Pastoral Care canceled at Ted's death and still to be done, and I had planned it for February. But the Lord said in the dream, "It is too soon. And your heart is still covered with snow and ice. Wait until summer." So I waited.

Rufus Moseley used to say, "If the Lord can't make me listen any other way, He sometimes talks to me in dreams."

And so He does.

20

FTER the very small School of Pastoral Care in Los Angeles, I visited Jack and Tookie and their families, to my great comfort. Of all the joys and consolations in the world there is none so great as one's children, provided that one has sense enough to let them live their own lives. I never make my visits so long as to be boring to them. And I do thank God that I am not forced by circumstances to make my home with them and thus become a burden. Nevertheless, it pleases me very much that they might be willing to have me. Immediately after Ted's death, Miles wrote me a long letter inviting me to come and live with them, and it greatly comforted my heart.

Ted and Diana invited me to spend Christmas with them, so I went to Tacoma. We went to church together, processing up to the front seat in some embarrassment for there was no room in a less conspicuous place. Timmy took with him a new spyglass, the better to view the minister. Wendy, four years old, carried her doll. Diana carried a loaf of cranberry bread to give to the minister after church. There we sat right under his nose. He knew of my bereavement. So he spoke very kindly about God's love that follows us even through times of sorrow. Timmy leaned forward with his spyglass and listened eagerly. Wendy, however, sat perfectly still with her legs straight out in front of her and a dour expression on her face.

That evening we went to a little gathering of Ted's friends. We drove home through the rainy darkness of a Northwestern night, Timmy beside me on the back seat, Wendy in my lap.

"You do have pleasant people in this town," said I to Ted. "I like them."

"Sure," said Ted. "They're great. I don't know what people mean saying they don't like this one and that one. I like everybody."

Wendy who had been silent during the entire drive now spoke from the darkness of the back seat. "But I, particularly," said she, "do not like God."

"Why, Wendy?" asked Ted.

"Because He makes people die," said Wendy succinctly.

"Well, Nana," asked Ted, "what do you say to that?"

Nana had no reply.

In due time I flew back to Westboro to the little lonely house upon the hill, silent amid snow and ice. There were only my flowers to greet me, languishing in their pots on the windowsills awaiting my return.

Spring came again, and crocuses thrust their bright heads through the snow. And I prepared to set forth on a long-postponed trip to New Zealand.

A year before my husband's death, we had received invitations to conduct missions and lectures in Australia and New Zealand. Ted wistfully dreamed of a sea voyage to these far places, and of the joy of adventuring thither. But it was not to be. A year after his death in 1960, however, I went there alone, escaping the long New England winter and being snowbound alone in my little house, with dark coming down, blotting out the glittering beauty of the icy earth.

As soon as I was out of sight of the American continent, high in the sky amid dancing clouds over blue sea, the weight of years dropped from me, and I stepped forth into a new life. Somehow, I had always known that there would be a third period of my life when I would venture into the unknown to see what awaited me there.

So I rejoiced in New Zealand with its hills of blinding green, covered with white sheep, with volcanos old and new, resting comfortably in the midst of cities or smoking merrily into blue skies. All of its glorious and unbelievable beauty comforted my heart: tall ferns and towering trees, geysers and hot swimming pools, even mountains topped with ice and girded with golden poplars. And I rejoiced in the people with their charming accent based on English and Scots, with their honesty and their simplicity and their real gentleness. They looked upon me with some suspicion, as was only natural. I looked on myself with some suspicion, too, and often asked the Lord what He had in mind in sending a dumpy grandmother-type woman to the far reaches of the earth to proclaim the Gospel of healing.

It had appeared at one moment that I would not go on this trip, for I suffered with aching teeth just before leaving and was advised by the dentist that I had four impacted wisdom teeth and must proceed forthwith to a hospital and undergo oral surgery. I told the dentist that I could not do so because I was leaving on the morrow for New Zealand. When I reached Christchurch in South Island, the teeth had become really painful. So I said to a most extraordinary man who was in the parish house helping me with healing appointments, "Ben, you'd better put your hands on my face and pray for these teeth."

Whereupon this man, who had been healed through Dr. Christopher Woodard of a devastating illness, spoke to the teeth and said in his cockney New Zealand accent, "Naow, naow, teeth, quoiet daown."

And they did so. Moreover, they are still in my mouth and cause no trouble at all.

The most delightful visit was in Stratford, at the home of my friend Laurie Mulcock, editor of *Wholeness* magazine. I enjoyed his charming house and garden, his wife and daughter, and the mission in the Anglican church. Forty little girls from Saint Mary's School attended the first night of the mission, and more came every night until there were sixty. They sat on the edge of their pews and listened with utter absorption. I asked them after my meditation on the Redemption whether they had understood these holy mysteries, which I had not made any attempt to simplify.

"Oh, ra-*ther!*" they chorused, and proceeded to pray that I would arise in the cold grey dawn and come to their very early Communion service—which I did. I also went to Evening Prayer at a school for Maori girls and sang loudly in the Maori tongue, reading phonetically from their hymnbook. A lovely Maori had me in her charge, and if ever I stopped singing, she nudged me in the ribs with the hymnbook.

The assistant minister was a Maori gentleman, Te Pura Papana, and I later visited him and his charming wife, Princess Polly. She was discoursing on the arrival of the first English colonists, and she remarked "Some of us came to greet you and some of us came to eat you." (To be ceremoniously eaten was, I believe, a mark of honor in those days, although not one that I would particularly desire.)

After two weeks, I flew to Australia and entered a land more like the United States than like New Zealand. In fact, approaching Sydney and reading the signs: "Woolworth's," "Standard Oil" etc., one might think one was approaching Philadelphia. A School of Pastoral Care had been planned in St. Andrew's Cathedral, but it was startlingly different from those I had conducted and bore little resemblance to any of the plans suggested in letters. I was apparently the only teacher. There were not forty ministers, but eighty, and they met, not in a retreat center, but in the chapter house. Moreover, save for a few minutes of utter gasping exhaustion after lunch, I was busy in my hotel room the rest of the day with appointments for the healing of the memories: appointments desperately needed by men who had been for years in Japanese concentration camps, and by men holding missions in the outback and haunted by some aborigine curse—and that is no laughing matter. When the aborigine chief "points the bones" at someone, it takes all the powers of heaven to set that person free! This was the most difficult session that I ever held—and probably the most fruitful.

The weekend approached, full of engagements and appointments, and I was in a state of collapse. I called up Canon Glennon and said so. He replied, "Leave it to me. I will take you away, and no one will know where you are."

So he took me to a rather ramshackle hotel at Austinmeer, on top of cliffs overlooking the most gorgeous ocean I have ever seen —towering sapphire breakers rushing in from the Antarctic and breaking over volcanic rocks of ochre and orange and flame, so that the sea burned red and purple and green, unbelievable shades of turquoise and indigo. No one knew where I was. From morning until night I need not speak except to say "thank you" for the abounding meals served to me in the practically empty dining room—for this was not the season for making merry at the seashore. The bar, to be sure, did a roaring trade. But since this was conducted out-of-doors, the empty beer cans lightly hung upon trees, it concerned me but little. I could climb the cliffs and lie in a shallow shelf with the spray breaking far below and meditate in the sun—and I did. There, for the first time, I had a vision of heaven and of the heaven of heavens.

After this there was a CFO in the bush, with kookaburras waking me in the morning with their insane laughter, so infectious that one could but lie upon one's cot and laugh with them. Then there was a mission in the cathedral, open to anyone and filled every evening.

When I went home to Westboro, spring had come, and crocus and daffodils, scillas and bleeding hearts filled the tiny garden beyond my breezeway and my kitchen door. And all the plants within my study seemed to lift up their leaves on seeing me and returned to delighted life. For in my absence, even though they were watered and cared for by my secretary, they seemed to miss my love and to droop until I returned.

All that year and for another year I kept my schedule very full. I traveled to Canada, England, Scotland, and even Holland, where I did a School of Pastoral Care through an interpreter. Also, of course, I worked in many places in the United States. For there was no longer any reason why I should remain at home. This might have been the beginning of a new and quite satisfactory life for me, but for one thing: in my travels I met an attractive widower and permitted myself to respond to his affection and, in fact, to fall in love. No, I did not seek God's guidance. As a matter of fact, I did not want guidance. My emotions, held in stern check for many years, quite galloped away with me, and I did not want God to tell me anything. I knew what I wanted: this man. However, I wanted him in no other way save in honorable wedlock, and I was foolish enough to contemplate the possibility of his desiring the same thing.

But he did not. His heart might have said yes, but his mind said no.

From time to time I saw this man in my travels, and hope dies hard. But it died. And with it the desire for life faded away. It was two blows in the same place and too soon—losing the man I loved, twice. However, I forced myself to go on and refused to listen, any more than I was forced to listen, to the complaint of my body. I overcompensated by piling work on work, saying as it were to the unconscious: "More life! More life!" And in due time I found a lump in my breast. The body had responded in the only way it knew, by making more cells (which are in fact the bricks of which the house of life is built.)

After my first shock at finding this, I determined that God could heal it and told no one about it. This is precisely what I advise others *not* to do! Indeed, the lump did go away. Then I had to take a long trip, another one "down under" as I recall, and during the course of it, what with strain and weariness, the trouble returned. Nor did I have the spiritual power to cure it, for I was pouring out all I had on others. It is not too easy for the "healer" to be healed! One is geared to giving out, not to taking in!

As summer drew near, I knew that I should see a doctor and take his advice. But I felt that first I must finish my engagements, a School of Pastoral Care at Lasell House and a week's visit in Alstead from one of my young ministers who, I felt, particularly needed this respite. So I said nothing until my work was over. The school was rather a dull one, for so much of my energy was consumed in holding this secret within myself that I had little to give. The visit in Alstead did not work out as I had hoped, and before it was over, I had to tell my guests what was before me. I had not even advised my children of this, thinking to save them worry.

So, finally, I went to Ted's doctor in Bellows Falls, Vermont, David Stewart, a man whom I trusted and liked very much. He was extremely blunt with his patients (though most devoted) and always told them the truth. He told the truth to me, most furiously, and ordered me to come to the hospital not later than the very next morning.

Great was the consternation of my household when I told them this! For indeed I had a household at the time. It was an odd family, for they were all from Australia, my young minister having gone home. A young woman, Sheila McCarroll, had come to spend the summer with me as my helper and then to find work in the United States. Also a young minister, David Williams, and his wife were visiting me during a trip to the United States. I remember a few days before the hospital experience how we went up to my high meadow and picked blueberries while the birds sang overhead and the gentle wind lifted our hair, and there was not another sound anywhere in the whole world.

David was obliged to go to New York the day I went to the hospital, but Greta stayed to keep Sheila company, for she desperately needed it! On the day of the operation, David flew back, made the doctors equip him with gown and mask, and stood by me in prayer during the entire procedure. No wonder that although the operation was radical, my recovery was amazing, requiring not even one blood transfusion.

Now some readers might think that God gave me a "mountaintop" experience at this time. No, He didn't. Probably I was in no mood to experience such a thing, for I was much displeased with God and was not particularly happy that I had lived through the operation.

The Lord, however, did the best He could for me under these circumstances. He quickened my creative ability, so that I lay in my hospital bed and wrote poetry. To be sure, the sonnets that came from me were of a very rebellious nature, and if I ever get around to publishing my poems, these will probably be omitted. I was still annoyed with God and did not hesitate to tell Him so.

My sister, a trained nurse, came down from Burlington to help care for me the first week at home. If ever anyone recuperated in luxury, I did, there in my own lovely house with the autumn leaves flying like tongues of flame against a blue sky, all the meadows edged with gold and flame and crimson, tall pine trees rising like green exclamation marks here and there among them, as though nature herself were astounded by so much beauty. Before coming downstairs I would lie in bed looking out the dormer windows into the heart of flaming maples filled with the wistful murmurs of departing birds, for winter was nigh at hand, and I would hold notebook and pencil and say, "Lord, what shall I write?" (I might add that the Lord and I were friends again by this time.)

He replied, "Write of your own life in China."

So beginning that first day home from the hospital, I wrote the bits and pieces that later wove themselves into a story and became *The Second Mrs. Wu.*

Morton Kelsey, friend and rector, had told me long before that it would be good for me to "relive my old life."

"Heavens no!" I cried. "I haven't time for that. Besides it would be too boring."

But the Lord gave me time and gave me, moreover, a way of doing this that did not bore me but was utterly fascinating to me.

At this time there arose another problem. The doctor felt that I should have X rays up to the limit of tolerance, for eighteen days. I did not want this treatment and to this day wonder whether it was really necessary, but my children would have been terribly upset if I had not obeyed the doctor, and heaven knows they were sufficiently upset anyway when I called them and told them I was on the way to the hospital. They wanted me to cancel my plans and fly to Los Angeles and put myself in the care of Dr. Hawkins, Jack's wonderful doctor father-in-law. I thought of this wistfully, but I had Sheila there, and what would I do with her if I were to fly to Los Angeles?

So Sheila, who had just taken her driver's examination, drove me to Keene every day for these treatments. I will not dwell on their effects on my whole being, for they were far worse than the operation—painless, but most destructive, even of personality. However, I am grateful for all this, for the years have passed and I am well, and for that I now rejoice. I find that life, which I had thought not worth living, brought me more opportunities, more chance for creativity, more delight in the beauty and wonder of the world, than ever before.

Before starting on the X ray treatments, I had glimpses of this new life like a window opening upon a future world. Then, due to the mysterious effect of radiation, the shadows closed in again and I walked in semidarkness, only half-alive. I did not see the beauty of the fall about me when I returned to Westboro alone, Sheila going on to Washington to her new work in the Australian embassy. My friends were wonderfully patient with me, for I must have been a terrible bore! It wearied me to talk and caused me to cough uncontrollably—perhaps due to some injury to the vocal cords, following the X rays. My left arm was swollen and practically useless.

"Use it normally," the doctor had said, possibly failing to understand that normal use of it then meant trimming the bushes across my road in Alstead. So apparently it formed too much scar tissue, and adhesions set in, to add to all my other troubles. I felt unloved and unwanted and . . . But why continue? I was "a pain in the neck," and I am most grateful for the loyalty of friends who put up with me until the darkness began to lift.

The first ray of light came from one of the ministers of the School of Pastoral Care, Len LePoidevin, who called up from a neighboring parish to say that the Lord told him to come over and pray for me. My own minister in Westboro was a kind person and a good friend, but he did not understand healing. So Len came from time to time—my chaplain, I called him—and my spirits would lift a bit each time, as he conveyed to me a spark of hope in Christ. After his visit I noticed on walking down Mill Road a tiny flower in the grass—and realized that for months I had not *seen* these little messengers of God's love.

The Christmas season I spent visiting Jack, now rector of Trinity Church, Los Angeles. Neighbors kindly loaned him a small apartment on the second story of the house opposite the charming rectory on Melrose Hill. I could look down and see Katie, a delightful little red-haired girl, playing on the lawn with a friend—I could even see into the living room if I so chose—or I could look up and beyond and behold, far away and misty and as beautiful as a dream, the very mountains on which I now live. Deeply comforting was my relationship with Jack and Linny and Katie, and with my daughter Virginia and her husband, Miles Clark, who frequently came from his place of business and had a meal with me.

Christmas seemed strange and unnatural with no snow, but with an outdoor piñata party under the big pine tree on Christmas Eve. I was with my own, and was comforted. However, I was still not quite myself.

January saw me back in Westboro and deep in snow. In fact, during one snowstorm I was housebound for several days, unable to get the car out of the garage and drive down the silent, glittering street. It was lonely, but I was more and more becoming able to rise every morning into the light of God's love and to walk in that light.

Then an invitation came from a lovely lady, Francena Hart, who at that time was almost a stranger to me. Though she was younger than I, her husband had died some months before, leaving her in a twenty-eight-room mansion in Palm Beach that he had bought for investment purposes. She invited me to come to Florida and spend the rest of the winter with her there by the sea. I went, and it was indeed a paradise! There were coconut palms and hibiscus, instead of birch trees with their heads bent down and frozen into the ice! The ocean was just beyond the huge lawn, its blue thundering waves crashing against the sea wall! Back of the house was the tiled patio where we sat of an evening watching white clouds lit by the light of the city trailing across the soft skies, stars winking out between them, and always, now muted, now loud, the eternal cry of the sea!

My own dwelling place was a large bedroom, bath, and dressing room on the second floor, and adjoining it, a study with a balcony beyond. Stately ships steamed down the coast while pelicans solemnly flew just over the breaking waves, and the sun danced and glittered over the whole world. Here Ethel, the maid, brought my breakfast, and I spent the morning hours rewriting *The Second Mrs. Wu*. When ideas grew dim, I would go out to the sea wall, clad in bedroom slippers and muumuu, quite the thing in this area, and would walk and exult in the wind and the waves until the stream of creativity was mended. Then I would return, more or less wet (an unimportant detail) and work until lunch, which Francena and I had at one end of a vast carved Spanish table in the dim dining room.

Huge as it was, the house did not feel lonely. It was too full of love and life for that. In this place with my charming friend, life began to return to me. In the afternoons she would take me to the public beach to swim, for the ocean leaned too hard upon her beach and had engulfed the sand. She was a bit doubtful about swimming in the ocean, as many people were, claiming that pollution had come down the rivers and that even the vast sea was not clean. This I could not believe, and I waded and floated for hours in the sea, and in that healing element the use of my arm began to come back.

With some diffidence Francena found for me another way to regain this arm. She sent me to a chiropractor with a brilliant method of his own, working on the fascia to release adhesions and stimulate circulation. I am glad that I could have his treatments while he was still living, for he has now departed, and the empty place that he has left mourns him greatly.

With the utmost delicacy and tact, Francena managed to awake in me the desire to live; only a word here and a word there and an inspiring book, placed within my reach. She had a partner in this awakening: a small yellow bird, whom we called Mrs. Birdie. She lived in a cage with her husband, adjacent to two other cages inhabited by parakeets of different colors. Mrs. Birdie became ill.

One evening, we returned late from a movie and as usual, entered the back door and wended our way through shed, laundry, freezer room, pantry, and kitchen to the butler's pantry where the three large bird cages sat upon the counter. We were talking and laughing rather loudly, and Mrs. Birdie fell from her perch and lay immobile on the floor of the cage, her tiny claws curled up above her inert body. Whether she fell because she was ill or whether we startled her and so she fell, I do not know. But the next morning she was still there, not eating or drinking or moving, her little claws turned quite black and curled up like a tiny wizened baby's fists. We could not bear it. We would stand in front of the cage and tell her about Jesus and pray for her—but nothing happened.

Ethel said, "Mrs. Hart, I'm afraid Mrs. Birdie's gone."

"I don't think so," said Francena. "I think I saw a tiny movement." Again, and many times a day, we would stand before her cage and pray for her and speak to her words of hope and love. On the fourth day she began to move. She turned over, and little by little struggled her way to the side of the cage. Her feet were useless, so she used her wings and rowed herself, as it were, to the wires of her cage. Then she tried to climb up to the perch, hanging on with her little curved beak. She could not make it. She fell again to the floor of the cage, but she did not stay there. Again and again she tried, until her wings were streaked with tiny rivulets of blood. Finally she managed to crawl to her perch. Then, clinging precariously with those almost useless feet, she took her bill and pushed the claws into place on the perch! She could not maintain her balance very long, but the next day she tried again. And on achieving the perch with much labor, she lifted her head and managed very quaveringly a tiny song! As Francena said, "Unless one stands upon one's perch and sings, one is not a bird."

On the following day, when she reached the perch, her husband, Mr. Birdie, was there. So she bit him. We figured then that she must be well. It is noteworthy that a convalescent is apt to be cantankerous for a while.

As I stood by the cage and congratulated Mrs. Birdie, I thought, "If that little bird, weighing only an ounce and a half, can put up such a fight for life, so can I."

It was amazing to see the change in the personality of Mrs. Birdie. She got over her temporary crossness with her husband, and she developed a real love for human beings, particularly Francena, Ethel, and me. Up to this time, she had been antisocial, and when she heard footsteps, she would scurry to the rear of the cage and turn her back on life. But after this, when she heard footsteps anywhere in the house, she would set up a great twittering and calling until we came and stood by the cage and told her what a wonderful bird she was. Then she would listen, her head cocked first on one side and then on the other side, paying absolute attention to us as long as we talked to her. I do not know what traumatic experience had caused her for a season to be withdrawn and antisocial, but in order to be transformed into a new bird in Christ Jesus, she needed, not a psychiatrist (which is just as well), but only an experience of the healing love and power of Christ.

Although at this time I turned my face toward life rather than toward death, Satan was not through with me. I fell ill of a virus that was sweeping the area, and whether it was due to the pollution of the ocean I do not know. At any rate, the very day before flying to Virginia, where I was to make a visit and thence go to Westboro, I developed a severe cough. I was sure it could be healed by prayer, but it was not healed, and I might say that flying is not the best thing for a cough. I had no fever at the time, and evidently my cough was not too contagious, for my host and hostess did not catch it. I tried to demonstrate health by walking by the sea, but it did not work! When I reached home, I tried it still. I had been looking forward to the most exciting time of the whole year, the first breath of spring when I would take the dead leaves from my flower beds and ecstatically count all the little pale shoots of coming flowers beneath them. This I did, in faith, but without any noticeable amount of common sense, and my cough grew steadily worse; eventually I ran a degree or two of fever and felt terrible—not sick enough to impress a doctor but not well enough to do anything.

At a time like that it was not good to be alone.

I tried to lift my spirits by painting the lovely spring scene beyond my front door. But there was no joy in my picture. It actually looked sick! I finally realized that one cannot paint into a picture that which is not in oneself. Nor is there any use in painting a picture if one is not filled with the inner beauty of life. Those who paint merely in order to express their own turmoil and confusion commit an outrage against art and against life.

Summer came, and a mission in Monrovia, California, loomed before me, and still I coughed. However, on I went, by train rather than by air this time, stopping for a day to see the Grand Canyon and being to some small extent improved, although not healed, by the heart-shaking wild beauty of that indescribable work of nature.

My children were shocked at my condition, and pending the beginning of my work, put me in the Good Samaritan Hospital for observation. My friends Bert Hause and Dr. Hawkins were there, and to tell the truth, I enjoyed those four days of lying still and being in an oxygen tent from time to time to ease my cough. They found nothing wrong with me, but strange to say, during those four days I stopped coughing and was healed. So I went out in a wheelchair, the correct method of leaving such a place, and that night arose and did a mission in Saint Luke's Church, living with my friends Morton and Barbara Kelsey and being cared for most royally, with breakfast and the morning in bed and doing my lectures in the evening. In spite of all my coughing, God had evidently been working within me, for the mission went with the utmost success and power, and people speak of it to this day—this day when, strangely enough, I live in the mountains immediately above Saint Luke's Church.

I returned home improved in health but far from being really myself. However, I had made the decision: I would carry on with the work that was so very much needed in the world—the spreading of the word of healing. One of the most bitter elements of my own illness was knowing the shocking blow it would be to many another who did not understand that even though believing in healing, I was also human and could fall into error. Now I began to find that, on the other hand, every new step forward that I could take gave courage to others who had undergone surgery. As I learned to stand upon my feet, I could lift others to their feet. So I forever banished the thoughts of the desirability of death and of the possibility of hastening that end. I would live and not die. That much I decreed.

The decision could be made by me alone, and the quality that caused it to be made might be termed courage. This is to me the most important of all virtues—and the one of which we hear the least. Hand in hand with it goes obedience: the determination to do what God wants one to do, insofar as possible. Some counselors today sneer at this very thing.

"Still doing things because you think you *should?*" Even ministers have asked me that. What better reason could there be? Following every selfish desire leads to weakness, dims creativity, and dissipates joy. Thus I take sides against certain modern methods of counseling, for I consider the most important and the most joy-giving thing in life to be creativity: what one does with the talents that God has given. Creativity often comes through compensation for certain restrictions of one's inner life and of circumstances, rather than through the removal of those restrictions and a life of self-indulgence. Even my plants often bloom better if they are potbound, but when they are *too* constricted, I take them out of the pots and put them into a larger place—and so does God.

But He needs a gardener to do this transplanting.

He needed a gardener to transplant His love into my heart, for it was starved. Even in Alstead that summer I could not recapture the delight in my delphiniums growing tall beside my stone walls—in the old twisted apple tree scattering blossoms and fruit on the rocky road—in evening shadows blue upon the hills, while all the birds sang sleepy songs on their way to bed. There was sadness upon the fields and upon the hills, and there was sadness upon my heart, and it would not lift.

21.

HAT had happened all this time to the gift of the Holy Spirit and to the release and delight of speaking in tongues? Nothing. The gift was still there. Every morning I spoke in tongues and many a time thereafter; when driving the car alone, when communing with my beloved flowers. But I needed more than this. Many people think nowadays that this is all one needs—this one experience of the baptism in the Spirit in which they usually include speaking in tongues, and one who is not completely and permanently healed by this gift is often accused of having fallen from grace, of denying the Spirit, even of living in sin. I did not deny the Spirit, nor live in sin, though as for falling from grace, whatever that means, I probably did—but not intentionally. In fact, I strove more fervently than ever to arise into God's light and to live there. There were those, I might add, who advised me to go forth and have an affair. It is strange to think that such advice could be given by responsible people, even by Christian counselors. Do they not know that we are not merely flesh but also spirit, and that the spirit would be wounded by this breaking of the seventh commandment?

About this time, I lost all hope of ever again finding joy in this world. I would simply carry on my work as best I could while here. Meanwhile, God was looking about for the right person to help me, and finally, in the year 1962, that person came. He was a young minister whom I had met at a School of Pastoral Care and with whom I had corresponded sporadically ever since. His personality was warm and attractive, and his ideas were fascinating. He once wrote, for instance, "I feel that it is my duty to pray for the healing of the memories of my ancestors." I wanted to know what he meant by this and other far-out remarks. So I suggested that he and his wife might come the weekend before the School of Pastoral Care that they planned to attend that fall, and visit me in my home. His wife could not come, but John Sandford actually came, and my heart was warmed by his great, infectious smile and the light in his brown eyes.

He took one look at the house and proclaimed that it was full of dark spirits. So he went from room to room, blessing each one, making the sign of the cross in the air and commanding any contrary beings or thought-forms to depart. As a matter of fact, I have often so exorcised and blessed a house since then, and even, occasionally, a church. Indeed, is this not the purpose of the service of consecration of a church building?

John then ambled up the tiny path through thin birch woods to the top of the hill and stated that this bit of the earth had a good feeling. Indeed it did. The young people of today speak of places as having "bad vibes" and "good vibes" and they are quite right, even though some might object to the word vibrations, conveniently shortened. As a matter of fact, both Ted and I had felt the good feeling of the earth upon this little hillside even before our house was built.

As John and I talked and prayed together, the fact emerged that God had told him to go to Massachusetts and help me. He did not have money for the trip and did a bit of lumbering to earn it. He was warned in a dream that a tree would fall and kill him. A tree did fall, but being warned, he leaped aside and suffered only a cut on his head. He went to the doctor, had it sewed up, and went right on cutting down trees. Without this, I doubt whether he would have found the way to open my heart, so long closed and fortified, having found love too wounding a thing to be endured. This young man really cared for me as a person, not merely as a religious leader who might pray for him! So a bit of light began to dawn in me, but it was very dim.

Then we went to Lasell House, half-an-hour's drive away, and the burdens of praying for other people descended upon me. I tightened every nerve within that I might be able to carry that burden. John's ideas of past and future, of heaven and hell, were so interesting to me that I asked him to take one or two of my lectures, which he did. His lectures fascinated me, although they dismayed persons who could not follow in his deep interpretations of life on earth and in heaven. Giving the lectures, however, classed him among the leaders. So four of us met every morning for prayer, as the leaders usually did.

Every morning John prayed for me, but nothing happened. Indeed, I wearied of his prayers and of all prayers. One evening he followed me upstairs and suggested that we meet again that he might pray for me.

"No!" I said. "I don't *want* any more prayers. And I don't want any more of your visions and prophecies either. I'm tired and I just want to go to bed."

Nevertheless, in spite of my rudeness, he persisted. The last morning of the school, he and the two other leaders laid their hands on my head. John, as usual, prayed for the love of Christ to enter and heal me—and He came. It was as though I had been encased in a tight metal drum, and all of a sudden, the drum exploded! There I was, free. Light shone all around me, and Jesus stood before me in such a real way that I could see Him with my mind though not with my eyes! I laughed, I cried, I was utterly beside myself with joy and the feeling of being loved.

John had been healed through me of some physical difficulty long before the events of this chapter. Many a time since, he has prayed for me or I for him, for God uses each of us to help the other. Once, it seemed as though we might work together as partners, sharing the same missions. But I am apparently meant to be a pathfinder, not a partner. However, we have had some extraordinary experiences in prayer together.

Once I was a leader of a CFO in Oklahoma and John arrived, just for a day. He said I needed another prayer for the healing of the memories. This must have been guidance, for he had driven half the night and sat up in the train the other half in order to reach the conference center. I was not aware of any need for the healing of the memories, but I was always glad of a prayer with him.

"If anything comes into your mind as I pray, tell me," he said.

Something did come to mind several times. I pushed it down again, as I had for some twenty years, but it would not stay down. So I told him.

"It can't mean anything really," I said, "because this is only something that I read in a history book when I was eleven years old, studying the history of Sparta. But it's one of my horror pictures. It used to come up in my mind, and I could feel it coming and would break out in a cold sweat and think, 'Oh no—not that again,' but it would come."

"Then we had better pray about it," said he. "Tell me what it is."

It was a frightful effort to put into words this thing that exceeded all words in dreadfulness. I could hardly force my lips to frame that horror-picture of a human sacrifice. All these years it had lain dormant in my deep mind, only to leap out at me from time to time and awake me from sleep, sick with anguish yet held by a weird quirk of the being to the very thing that I so earnestly sought to forget.

I finally stumbled it out in words, and John prayed for the healing of that memory as naturally as he would pray for any other healing. And I felt nothing.

Before I left the camp, a young woman was inspired to pray for the opening in me of what she called the spiritual eye, or a quickening of the gift of discernment. I had learned through the years to be wary of unsought prayers, and when some beaming female advanced upon me with hands outstretched saying that the Lord had told her to say a little prayer for me, I would jump and run, saying that I was sorry but the Lord had not so advised me at the moment. Too many prayers lightly and casually said by too many people I find a distinct danger to the psyche. However, after consideration, I linked this young woman's suggestion with the prayer that John had made, and I consented. I did not feel anything at that time either, but I have learned that feeling is irrelevant. Sometimes one feels waves of heavenly heat or holy joy; sometimes one does not. One must trust, not one's feelings, but God!

Two days later, amazing things happened to me. Both prayers had apparently opened the door for my spirit to leap back through time. I don't know where I was in body when my spirit took this strange adventure. I am sure that I was not asleep. This was no dream. My body may have been in my study, waiting for me to come back from a meditation that became more than a meditation. But *I*, myself, was somewhere very far away. It was a deep, green valley, the surrounding folds not rocky but smooth and covered with low vegetation, something like the mountains on Oahu. There were neither flowers nor trees, only low soft bushes, none of which I recognized. This far valley was not on the planet earth, I feel sure. Nor was it "heaven" as we think of heaven. It seemed as though I was upon a new, uninhabited planet in some other solar system, around some other sun.

I was not in a body. I saw no living thing until Jesus walked down the valley past the folded hills, and as He came, every fold filled up with light. I saw Him with the eyes of the spirit, but not in bodily form. Then He spoke to me, though not in words, only in thought. What Spirit communicated to spirit was this: that He intended to send me down to the planet earth, not in a body, but in a spirit only. He would send an angel with me for protection. And He was sending me out like a spy going into a very far country, for a specific reason.

Then the scene changed instantly, as in a motion picture one scene flashes into another. I was in Sparta, Greece, and the sacrifice scene that had so often wakened me with horror was being enacted before my eyes.

The valley that I had seen was not vague, but somehow fluid, as though the life in it was not quite formed and set. But this scene in Sparta, before Christ was born—this scene was completely clear and sharp and bright. I could draw it in every detail, I could paint it: the marble temple at my right, with seven Corinthian columns and seven shallow marble steps leading down to the circular courtyard, paved with irregular stones of grey and pink and pale blue slate. People were standing in a semicircle looking at the altar. Beyond the altar, the hill dropped off sharply, and I could see past it another hill, with a marble building or two and trees that I recognized as belonging to this earth: cypress and a pale, feathery tree something like a pepper tree.

The people could not see me. I could see only their backs, draped in white or pastel colors, and I could hear nothing. I stood invisible behind the group, and I was aware, without seeing, that an angelic presence stood beside me. Strange that I could see the people so distinctly and could not see the angel!

The altar was something like a sundial. Upon the altar a boy was being sacrificed. But amazingly, as I actually looked upon this scene, the horror went away from it. I knew somehow that God had mercifully taken away the spirit of this youth, and in His own way was shielding it from a crime done in ignorance, with a vague desire to placate some sort of a deity. The boy was not suffering, although his body seemed to be suffering.

Then again the scene changed. I was once more in the valley and in deep grief, though it could not express itself in tears, for I was not in a body (II Cor. 12:2). Again Jesus came down the valley and spoke to me in thought, after this manner: "Now you have seen the very worst that can happen upon the planet earth. Would you then be willing to go down there, when I deem it best, and to be born and live on that planet for the purpose of relieving suffering? If so, I must tell you that it will be a hard life."

I do not remember my words, if they were words, but the sense of my heart was that I was willing. Thus I was healed in another manner. For I was never again bitter about the hardships of life nor angry with God, as I have confessed to being, remembering that this had happened long before my birth into this world. Once more I could "like God." For now I knew that I myself had consented to make this earthly pilgrimage for the sake of His Son Jesus Christ.

I am *not* expounding any theory. I am *only* stating what happened to me, as truthfully as I can. But I point out one very significant thing: *I was not in a body.* Many people have flashes of memory of places never seen in this life, or of something that could not have happened in their lifetime, and assume that this proves reincarnation—that is, being reborn in body after body upon this earth. I do not believe in this dreary theory. I do believe in immortality, and my experience when the consciousness was blanked out in this life and entered into the timelessness of heaven gives me a bit of comprehension of immortality.

Moreover, this calls to mind other memories. Did I not remember when I was a very small child, the glory of a life that I had known long before? Why else the waves of homesickness for "heaven" that would sweep over me? Why else the deep nostalgia that would come to me when singing hymns about heaven? Why was my favorite hymn an ancient one that my grandmother used to sing? "I'm but a pilgrim here, Heaven is my home. Earth is a desert drear, Heaven is my home."

Wordsworth must have thus remembered, for he said, "Trailing clouds of glory do we come, From God who is our home; Heaven lies about us in our infancy . . ."

All this may be upsetting to some people's theology, but experience comes before theology. Theology, as Evelyn Underhill says, is only man's attempt to explain his experience of God. At any rate, I am not propounding any theology. I am only telling the story of my life.

Of course I wrote to John of this experience, for he was at that time my mentor as well as my pupil, my spiritual father as well as my spiritual son. It seemed to make very little impression on him, possibly because he is often off in the clouds somewhere, and visions are commonplace in his life. They are not in mine, for my feet are all too closely planted upon the earth.

Frankly, I felt safer with my feet upon the earth! And John's wandering about in the heavens and picking up premonitions from all over the place were frightening to me. Sometimes his soul would make a rapport with more than his body could carry, and he would fall ill with a trouble that was not his own. Being his spiritual mother, therefore, I once wrote and urged him to try to close some of his spiritual centers or his psychic doors or whatever they were, lest he carry too heavy a burden. Whereupon he wrote back and said, "Why don't you try to open some of yours? I think you could see far more than you do see if you would only allow it."

Fair enough, I thought. So I began, and continue at times to practice, a way of meditation geared to a higher plane than this earth. This is not anything strange or "far out." I do not practice deep breathing or contemplate my navel! I merely give the Holy Spirit His way. I speak in tongues for a while, and if nobody else is in the house, I am apt to speak joyously with a loud voice and often with happy laughter. It isn't that I plan to shout or to laugh; in fact, the deliberate adopting of a certain manner of speaking or praying is to me offensive. I find it difficult to pray with certain people because the minute I start to pray they set up an "Oh Jesus" incantation. They turn it on like turning on a faucet, and it turns me off! Others moan, speaking in tongues with a high whimpering cadence. This disturbs me even more, for it is a ritual as definitely as, "The Lord be with thee" . . . "and with thy spirit," and of the two, I prefer the latter as being more pleasing to the ear. Therefore I seldom speak in tongues except alone in my own prayer place, and then I speak in the freedom of the Spirit, with forthright delight if so moved, or in a small, still voice. After a few moments of so speaking, I try my new venture and it is simply listening with the ears of the heart and with the eyes of the heart and with every sense alert . . . awaiting . . . expecting . . .

It is somehow easier for me to see than to hear. Even in Sparta I heard nothing, I only saw—and felt.

So I have apparently been, in spirit, through pastures green and beside still waters that are not of this earth. I have been in heavenly meadows where the flowers glow with an inner light and move and live as one looks upon them. I have been within the Holy City and have seen the inner appearances of the glories that Saint John describes in words somehow too concrete, too earthly. How can one describe a thing that is not a thing, that is not earthly but heavenly? I have seen the angels, their wings made, not of feathers, but of light, their robes woven, not of cloth, but of another substance like light, as indeed everything in that realm is made of light. I have even seen the Lord, though never upon this earth as some have seen Him. And I have seen many other heavenly pictures that it is "not lawful to utter" (II Cor. 12:4).

From this time forth, life in Westboro took on new glory and peace. My house was no longer filled with sorrow, but with light. I went away from home to take the light of God to cities far away, and I returned to find the light of God in my own house, even though at first it was still with the silence of emptiness, the only voices being the small unheard voices of my plants and flowers. My heart would lift up as I entered the study and saw them waiting for me, and their hearts would lift up too, for withering leaves would come back to life, and drooping flowers would stand straight and open wide their fragrant faces to the sunlight of my love and His love.

Almost every morning I would take my walk in the heavenly places, but not quite every morning. If I had a headache, for instance, I could not get off the ground, for this enterprise of the spirit demands a certain energy. After a while, when I did arise, my spirit would become weary, and I would simply find myself down on earth again with my eyes open. At other times the voice within me would say, "No. Not today." There were times apparently when He desired me, not to see visions, but simply to get to work with my writing. It was at this period that I wrote *The Healing Gifts of the Spirit*, and he who reads will be able to read through its lines, if he is sufficiently alert in spirit, the breathing of another world.

Nevertheless, there were many ways in which the life in Westboro, and the summers alone in Alstead were not satisfactory, and I felt more and more that I should move. In Alstead particularly, though I still loved it almost as one can love a person, I did not enjoy the old delight and comfort. Rather I felt that I should comfort the empty old house and the deserted fields. I was always more aware of the earth in Alstead than in Westboro and was less inclined to forget the earth and arise into the heavens. My study there was a little shack of bare unpainted wood, through whose cracks came various wasps and other creatures. It was high on a hill in my third field which we called "Jerry's field," since it had once belonged to Jerry White. Ted had made windows on its every side, and I had plastered it with pictures from *Arizona Highways*. So it was filled with the beauty of the near world, pine trees and field and far hill and high sky with white clouds trailing. And it was also filled with the beauty of the far world that the gentle New Hampshire hills had never seen: canyon and crag and desert and wild mountain peaks. This was my writing place, and when I entered with rejoicing into this rough shed with its table and typewriter, its straight wooden chair and an ancient upholstered relic leaking cotton—then my mind flew to writing and somehow would not dally with heavenly pastures.

In fact, I did not do my morning meditation here, for it was too far from the house to be sought in bathrobe and with coffee cup, on first arising. Therefore, I would take my coffee outside the door to the bit of garden between kitchen and dining room and there would look over the stone wall and down the hill and to the little flowers around my feet and would sense God's life entering into me from fragrant clover field and lemon lilies and hummingbirds. The delight of this world was so great that somehow I never quite arose into the mystic beauty of the other world. Possibly it was because about the time I was ready to "take off," an ant would crawl up my person or a mosquito would exhibit an undue interest in my ankles.

I still loved this little world, even though the days grew long and the evenings alone in my big living room opened the door to sorrows that would never be quite forgotten.

But my spirit was becoming restive, and I wondered whether I should move from a place that could no longer quite contain my soul. I greatly missed a church in which one could with unimpeded prayers and thoughts worship the Lord. For while one's private meditations are good, they still do not take the place of corporate worship and of partaking together of the body and blood of Christ.

The young rector was a good man and kind, but his mind was always on the relationship of man to man and never on the relationship of man to God. Certainly he did not believe that Jesus Christ moved or healed today and was at pains to say so. He even expressed a certain scorn for those who "used God instead of tranquilizers," whereas I would feel the same toward those who used tranquilizers instead of God. The minister, had I challenged him, would doubtless have said that God does not give us peace. My feeling is that He does, through Jesus Christ our Lord, who most definitely promised it, but that we do not accept it. The minister felt that we should look, not for peace, but for action, and to this I agree, but feel that the action can best be implemented by God filling our heart and mind and leading us in every possible way to do His will.

I had good and wonderful friends in Westboro who were most kind to me, and I did not want to leave them. But my children were on the West Coast, all of them.

"What are we supposed to do, Mom, when you get sick or something?" Ted once wrote me. "Fly three thousand miles to see you?"

I began to fear that my days in New England were coming to an end, yet I dreaded the thought of moving. I did not know whither I should flee and where I would find refuge. Long ago Ted had considered retiring to Raleigh, North Carolina, that gracious city where lived my kinfolks, "kissing cousins" unto the third and the fourth "removed." But my children would not like it if I seemed to prefer cousins to them, and I would not like it either, for I loved my children more than anyone else in the world. On the other hand, a widowed mother can become a burden and perhaps a difficulty to her children. Here, in this charming town, were trusted friends . . . and my pattern of life was set here, with Dorothy and Lillian, secretary and cleaning friend, with Lasell House but a short drive away, waiting for me to hold therein as many conferences as I desired. I had roots in this place, and even if they were given from time to time a bit of a tweak, they were still roots. The house was full of the presence of the Lord, sweet with the fragrance of my blossoming plants and warm with memories of love.

So I prayed for guidance and waited.

One winter I went on a trip to Texas to hold missions here and there. I remember particularly one in San Antonio, when an old friend, Reverend Jack De Forest, came to see me. He chatted about this and that, and I wondered what he had on his mind until at last he blurted out, "Agnes, do you speak in tongues or not? Some people say that you do."

"Of course I do," I replied. "I had that gift ten years ago, when I held a mission in your church."

"Thank the Lord!" breathed Jack, beaming with relief. "Then will you please come to my church again and tell them what it is all about before they all go into orbit?"

This was the beginning of a new era. I had become like a spiritual mother to this man. He could trust me to tell him about the Holy Spirit because for ten years I had had the baptism and the gifts, and yet had not swerved from the course that the Lord had laid out for me: the practice and teaching of healing.

The Lord has made us in different patterns and has called us to work for Him in different ways. My way seems to be to stay in the midst of the church and to minister to the more timid and cautious ones who yet do really desire to know more of God's truth.

So I finished my work in Texas, made a date with Jack De Forest for a forthcoming visit, and flew home, where my faithful friend Doug McLeod met me at the airport as he always did, provided I remembered to tell him exactly when and where I was arriving. There was a time when the Worcester airport was closed in by fog and I made a sudden change in plans, shouting out a message as I fled toward another plane. Apparently I omitted to give my name, for the message received by a somewhat stunned Mrs. McLeod read: "Your wife arriving Boston airport 11:00 P.M."

Doug drove me home through the titillating promise of early spring, snow melting under the pine trees, tiny gold and rosy leaflets coming out on the maples. I looked forward with eager expectancy to my own house, which would be warm and welcoming and fragrant, windows bright with begonias and geraniums.

True, there were no living things to welcome me, for I was away too much to keep a pet, but my flowers could speak with just as warm a welcome, although their little voices were not heard except in the heart.

So I entered the kitchen door and Doug brought in my suitcases and left. The house felt strange. I turned on the lights and went to my study, my heart sinking even as I walked. There was something wrong.

There was. Every plant drooped brown and dead, completely dead. The heat had gone off, pipes had burst, and the house had stood during three days of deadly cold before Dorothy found it and had the damage repaired. But the damage to my welcoming plants could never be repaired.

So in the year 1965, I knew that I would move.

22

*Y*ES, but where should I go?

I thought of Southern California, where Jack and Tookie lived. I recaptured the glory of towering mountains where tall yuccas marched solemnly up to the shattering cliffs of the summit. I remembered the perfumed air, orange blossoms and eucalyptus, and roses and the wild spicy fragrance of sagebrush. I also remembered looking down long streets in thick yellow smog, unable to see even the houses in the next block; I recalled the sting in the eyes, the smarting of the nose, the choking of the chest, and I thought, "But I can't live in that air! I can't breathe!"

Then my heart turned toward the South, with its gentle courtesy, its real love between black and white, between rich and poor; the South where Ted and I had longed to dwell upon retiring. But alone, with sons and daughter three thousand miles away? No, I could not do this.

My imagination ranged toward the Northwest, where Ted lived: Lakewood, near Tacoma, Washington, sublimely beautiful, shining with white snow on faraway Mount Rainier; the exclamation points of towering Douglas firs pointing to the heavens from every hilltop; the valleys filled with lakes through whose morning mist the wild ducks floated as out of dim air. (It was here that I had written the first chapter of *The Healing Gifts of the Spirit*, and I loved it.) But it rained there. Day after day a fine drizzle blotted out the beauty of the mountains and filled the air with dank moisture.

Somehow, as I meditated on the Northwest, fear gripped my heart—a vague heaviness which, as I have learned, often presages disaster. I lifted up my son and his family and prayed for them, and felt clear and serene. Then I prayed for John Sandford of

Idaho and his family, and again I felt no premonition of trouble. So I asked, "What is it, Lord?" and listened. And I felt that it was some disaster threatening the Northwest, the land itself. I asked, "Lord, may I pray for it to be fended off, just not to happen?"

The answer was "No." This answer did not come in words. In fact, I would not quite trust words unless they sounded very loud and clear within me, for it is all too easy to imagine "Yes" or "No" according to one's desires. The answer came in this way: when I tried to pray thus, the prayer did not rise. I could feel only heaviness. By this I knew that such a prayer project was too big for me.

So I asked, "Lord, may I pray for it to be minimized, so that it will not cause too much damage?"

And the answer was "Yes," for when I prayed after this pattern I could feel a lifting of my spirits and knew that the prayer was going forth. It is strange that I did not guess what the threatening danger was, but perhaps the Lord hid it from me lest I become frightened and lose my power in prayer. It was, of course, the earthquake, following hard upon the severe Alaska earthquake, but it just missed being a really destructive one and caused little or no damage. Of course, no one can prove that prayer had anything to do with this, but I felt sure that it did. For four days the prayer project lay heavy upon my heart, and after the earthquake came, it was lifted from me.

About this time I heard of various prophecies of earthquakes in Southern California, some prophecies such as Jeane Dixon's going so far as to name a date (I think the first one was in 1967, though when that one did not come to pass, she named other dates) and predicting that upon this day all of California would break off and slide into the ocean. Now, even though I had prayed about the Washington earthquake from a distance, still I felt that one could do better on the spot. I had found from experience that my friends and I could pray away a hurricane in an almost laughable manner if it were coming toward the East Coast, but that hurricanes far away in the Gulf did not seem to respond to our prayers. So I decided to move to Southern California.

During my frequent visits there with Jack and Tookie, I had looked a bit at houses for sale and had not seen anything that I liked. I knew God could guide me by my desires. Had He not done so in regard to the house on Mill Road and also to the little white house on the hill in Alstead? But no guidance came to me. I mentioned this to John Sandford once at a School of Pastoral Care where we were co-leaders. He said immediately, "In six months you will have your house."

The next Christmas I was with Tookie and Miles and there met a real-estate dealer, Margaret Sedenquist.

"Why don't you move to California?" said she.

I replied, "I would if I found exactly the right house."

"I'll find you a house!"

"But I don't want just any house. I couldn't bear to live in a little house on a flat street in line with lots of other little houses."

"I know just what kind of house you want," said she. "And when you come to Pasadena next June I will have your house."

She found it in March and was so sure of it that she did not even show it to anyone until I came. Then she drove me up a steep winding mountain road called appropriately, North Canyon Boulevard, to a split-level house high in the foothills, on the edge of a little canyon. It was protected from other houses by the curving sweep of the canyon on two sides, the steep hill across the road, and a thick bamboo hedge between this house and its neighbor. We went out on the balcony and looked up the mountains and down to the plains, as far as the spring mist would let us see. I said, "Yes, but where would I play? Where would I plant flowers and make gardens?"

"Come downstairs," she said. And we went down a staircase from the living room to a large room with fireplace and picture window that she called the rumpus room, though the only rumpus that goes on there now is the loud word of praise that from time to time ascends to the Lord when I am doing my morning meditation. Thence we stepped out upon a cement patio (which I have since carpeted and made into an outdoor living room) and went around the house upon a lawn bordered with irises and gladioli and many other flowers. All down the sides of the canyon were growing things: on the perpendicular side, ivy and bottle brush and oleanders; on the more gently sloping side, orchids and amaryllis of various kinds; on the upper level, sweet peas and roses; and in the formal border along the front of the house, various shrubs and gorgeous cactuslike plants with blossoms like water lilies, glowing crimson and orange and pink and flame.

"Oh!" I cried to the owner, Mrs. Gaines, bending down over one of them. "If I buy the house, may I have this plant?"

And she replied, "You may have all of them. I won't have room for them in the apartment complex that my husband and I are going to run."

That did it.

We departed to think it over, but I knew—then. And Mrs. Gaines had known before I did. I found out long afterward that she had dreamed of me the night before, and when I came to the front door, she recognized me as the one to buy the house!

"But it's too expensive!" I said, over lunch with Margaret. "Even when I sell my house on Mill Road, I won't have enough."

(Somehow I never can remember that one does not have to put down all the money immediately upon making a purchase!)

"Well, make them an offer," said Margaret. "They won't accept your first offer, of course, but you can dicker back and forth for a while and maybe you can agree upon something." I did so. "Now write a check," she said. "Just to hold it until you make up your mind."

"Oh, I don't think I should do that until I ask Jack about it," I replied. "And I can't get him on the phone."

"This check does not bind you," said Margaret. "You are not bound until they accept your offer and until you know that they have accepted it."

(This Margaret is a shrewd businesswoman as well as being a faithful servant of the Lord. And this is as it should be. There is no reason why a Christian should be stupid.)

So I wrote the check. Half-an-hour later, Mr. and Mrs. Gaines called up and accepted the offer.

Then I lay awake all night, more or less, in dismay at what I had done. How could I possibly take care of so big a house with its spacious cellar and all the grounds around it, even extending to the bottom of the canyon? How could I live there way up in the mountains all alone?

How wonderfully God works! For I did not know then that He had provided someone who also needed a new home and new work to come and live with me! I had not yet even met that person, except vaguely at a School of Pastoral Care, not even remembering her name! I came to know her during the long months when that unholy mystery, the escrow, was doing whatever it is that escrows do. Edith Drury invited me to drive with her down to North Carolina, where I was to lead a Camp Farthest Out. Usually an offer of this sort appalls me, for I think, "Then I'll have to talk all the way . . ." (One can become very tired of talking.) But the Lord must have inclined my heart to do His will, for I did.

I found her a gay and delightful companion. Indeed, we were brought up in much the same tradition, as Edith Drury's father was Dr. Samuel Drury of Saint Paul's School in Concord, New Hampshire, and she had read the same books and memorized the same poems and in general spoke the same language as I. It did not seem to matter that she was a New Englander of the New Englanders and I was Southern. But I am glad that we became acquainted in the South, for there her eyes were opened to some of the mysteries of that somewhat contradictory land. Being as full of curiosity as a cat, she explored the kitchen of the big shabby hotel where the conference met and became acquainted with the two beaming black cooks.

"But they're so happy!" she said. And on the drive through the piney woods of North Carolina she saw a little cottage covered with wild roses, and a Negro woman rocking contentedly upon the porch with a yellow cat beside her, and Edith said, "She's probably a lot happier than Negroes living in huge city buildings up North . . ."

And of course, she was. To be sure, up North she would have had an indoor bathroom and electric stove, and here there were only the fragrant piney woods dozing in the sun and a little outhouse on the edge of them—and starlight and quiet and the warm fragrance of pine trees and roses and yellow jasmine—and love and charity between her and her neighbors—only that infinite richness of life and nothing more.

All this happened during the spring before I bought the house.

When I returned from the West Coast, I went to Alstead, and as usual, swung between delight and loneliness. In this period, Edith invited me to visit her in her own summer home on Cranberry Island, Maine. She even sent her extraordinary friend, Celia Piper, in her little plane to pick me up at the Keene airport and fly me there. Celia was three hours late, and I envisioned her crashing in the bushes, until finally I saw a tiny plane land and bounce, land and bounce, and I said, "That will be Celia," and it was. She landed, bouncing once or twice more, at Bar Harbor. Edith met me and drove me to Southwest Harbor, and we went over on the ferry to Cranberry Island. There we drove in her ancient jeep to her little white cottage amid blueberry and cranberry fields.

It was immaculate and charming. Also, her forty-eight acres of outer Atlantic seashore were fascinating with their huge pink and cream "pebbles," as big as rocks but ground round by the surf, that scrunched when the tide rolled them up and down. Above the tide line were great bushes of a tough kind of wild rose that I have seen nowhere else except on the shore of Holland. Behind those, the ever-present spruce trees sent waves of perfume into the air, so that one delighted in the strong breath of the sea and the fragrance of evergreens and wild roses all at once. One delighted also in lobsters cooked on driftwood fires upon the beach, and in going down to the wharf and watching the sun set across the blue-green sea. All the island people knew Edith, and she knew them and loved them all. And I began to appreciate the great work this tall and rugged-looking woman had done for twenty-one years up and down the coast of Maine, her transportation often being a three-man cabin cruiser, the *Sunbeam*. She had been (and indeed still was) a missionary in the Maine Sea Coast Mission, working under great hardships of cold and loneliness. So had my parents worked in China. So had I begun my life upon this planet. And there developed a kinship and a respect that lasts until this day.

"If you ever need me, be sure to let me know," she said upon my departure. She has often said laughingly that that was the most fateful utterance she ever made! For I did need her, and soon.

I went to Winnipesaukee, driving there through the little twisting New Hampshire roads, and there gave a series of lectures on the power of Jesus Christ and His redeeming love. On the last night of this conference I said a healing-of-the-memories prayer for the whole group of some four hundred people. In this kind of praying, one must make a deep rapport with every one there, opening doors in every mind so that His redeeming love can come in and walk back through time in them, even to the day of birth.

This is a very dangerous thing to do. As I open doors in every mind so that Jesus Christ can come in, it is possible that through some open doors a destructive spirit can come in and attack me.

The danger is greatest where some of the group are indulging in spiritualism, attending séances, and other psychic meetings. Then their psychic centers are open to the psychic plane, which is not heaven, nor is it the abode of our Lord. Therefore He cannot enter in, and the way is left wide open to invasion and attack by the enemy.

Two days later, the blow fell. A dear friend, Beulah Dulaney, having attended the Camp, went home with me for a visit in Alstead. For two years Beulah had not been well. Her husband had died under circumstances that suggested to her a possible lack of understanding among his medical helpers, and ever since, dear Beulah had been quite understandably bitter toward the hospital and toward life in general. She had developed serious heart trouble, but the doctors had not diagnosed it, even though she had just had a complete physical examination. Her faith had been strong enough to smother or disguise the symptoms, but not strong enough to heal their cause. These symptoms showed themselves in intense pain in both hands and arms, and the doctors had concluded that it was from pressure in the upper spine.

Therefore, when she arrived in Alstead, we prayed with the laying on of hands for the healing of the spine and nerves, and also, with great earnestness, for her guidance as to her future life and work. However, the pain did not immediately decrease. Indeed, on the second day it became a little bit worse. Looking back from this vantage point, I realize that I should have insisted that she go to a hospital. True, I did mention this, but did not insist with sufficient energy. I am still not sure that this would have been better for her, though it would certainly have saved me from a dreadful shock. It might have prolonged life for a little while but not, as I was afterward told by her friends in Washington, for very long. In fact, they told me that she was planning a minor operation and that she could not possibly have survived it.

As it was, on the last night of her life, we prayed earnestly for guidance as to her future and for relief of the pain, and it was relieved. She felt quite gay, and we talked and went out of doors and enjoyed the starlight over the hills and the lovely smell of mown grass. But the next morning when I awoke out of uneasy dreams, I found her dead on the bathroom floor. The bathroom door was open, and the walls of the little house were very flimsy. If she had cried out, I would have awakened. It was evidently, as the doctor later said, an instantaneous death—and maybe it was the Lord's answer to her prayers for a happy home and for interesting and creative work. Maybe the time had come when her happiest home was to be in heaven and her most creative work was to be in the unseen rather than in the seen.

This was the greatest shock of my life. I had been prepared for Ted's death. Not for this.

I remembered Edith's words: "If you ever need me, let me know!" If I ever needed her it was now! I went rather dizzily to the telephone in the woodshed (an eminently suitable place for an instrument so demanding) and called her up. And she threw a few articles into a suitcase, leaped into her car, and came, not even stopping to tell anyone her destination.

It was a long drive. Neighbors, who were my dear friends, stayed with me all that grueling day. They informed me of the necessity of a death certificate and called Dr. Stewart, my physician from Bellows Falls. He told me, however, that he was not the coroner. He was from Vermont, and this happened in New Hampshire. It took a long time to locate the New Hampshire coroner, during which time the doctor related to me all the things that might happen if the coroner was not satisfied as to the cause of death: police, inquests, and so forth. At last we found him, and he appointed Dr. Stewart deputy coroner. Dr. Stewart was completely satisfied as to the cause of death. He wrote out the certificate and sent for the undertaker.

There remained the terrible duty of calling up Beulah's only son and breaking the news to him. Also, I had to pack her clothes and endure the long wait for the undertaker. I was unable to eat or drink, but was frozen and shriveled with anguish.

About two o'clock the undertaker came.

And at five o'clock Edith's red Volkswagen meandered up and down various country roads and at last turned into the little grassy drive between house and barn. She stayed with me for a week and then went back to Westboro with me and helped me prepare for a School of Pastoral Care in Michigan. She was used to emergencies after her years of missionary work up on the coast of Maine. She had helped haul coffins aboard the *Sunbeam* that they might be taken to islands and buried. She had even herself said the prayers for the departed and watched over the burial when no minister was available. She was not in the least daunted, and her whole demeanor was perfect—neither too distressed nor too flippant, but straightforward and practical, as though to say, "Here is life. It can be this way. Let's get on with it."

When I arrived at the School of Pastoral Care I was still deeply shaken. Morton Kelsey was co-leader, and he said to me, "This goes deeper than the shock of Beulah's death. There is something else weighing on the unconscious mind." After talking with me a bit he put his finger on it: "This awakens in your deep mind the memory of your father's death. You have told me that from that time on, your mother was not quite herself and eventually lapsed into senility. You have an unconscious fear that the same thing will happen to you."

He then prayed for the healing of the old memories about my father and mother, and I began to recover from shock.

My life at this time was crowded almost beyond endurance, yet it was good that it was so, for I could not possibly have relaxed into the placid routine of meditation and writing in Westboro. I had bought the California house in June, almost sight unseen, for it was a foggy day, and I never saw the glorious view that makes the place a bit of heaven. Someone from the West said to me, "You have a wonderful view from your new house!" And I replied, "Do I? I've never seen it."

The escrow was to be finished in October, and I planned to move in November as soon as my last School of Pastoral Care was over, so as to cross the country before the winter snows began. Unfortunately, I had a full schedule for the intervening months—Schools of Pastoral Care and missions.

Edith said, "You'll never make it. I will come down between your trips and help you pack." And so she did, with unparalleled efficiency. The house became filled with piles of this and that labeled "California," "Alstead," "Salvation Army," and "dump." Few things remained unlabeled, though some presented puzzles. Among these puzzling ones was a very holy bust in fine porcelain, residing in my study closet—for what can one do with a bust, no matter how holy? My house was always simple and cozy, and I had no use for such things. Edith and I were kneeling before the closet, the floor strewn with piles, and I cried, "What shall I do with this thing?"

Edith, meanwhile, was holding it. There was a crash and it shattered into a hundred pieces.

"Oh, dear!" cried Edith. "It just slipped out of my hand!"

Did I not say that she was the practical type? Her greatest value to me during this strenuous time was that she made me laugh. Once I went out to do errands, and she stayed at home to cope with matters of the kitchen. On my return she reported progress.

"I found the chicken bones," she said, "and I thought you might want to make soup of them, so I threw them out."

I laughed so hard that for a time I forgot all my troubles.

Meanwhile, I said a few healing-of-the-memories prayers for her, for who has lived without being wounded in the inner being? I was able to feel that our help was mutual and that I was not too heavily in debt. She came more than once and did practically all the packing and sorting. At last she offered to drive my car across the country.

"Oh, I can't let you do that!" I said. "But you can drive *with* me. Only, if you do, you had better take time off from your missionary work and spend the winter in California and really get some rest."

So then Edith reminded me of what she had told me a year before. She was thinking of retiring from this grueling mission work—fighting ice and storms and gales, sleeping in country houses without heat at temperatures ten below zero, climbing in and out of small boats and scrambling over ice cakes and through deep snow to hold a prayer meeting in a tiny country church or schoolhouse for the few people who might come.

"I am about ready to stop it," she said. "But I've been stalling because I did not know what I wanted to do. But now I think I will resign."

"Then come and spend the winter with me," I said. "And later on decide what to do next."

She is still here, and more and more the Lord finds prayer groups for her to lead and people for her to help. Every time she goes with me on a mission, I nearly lose her because the minister invites her to stay and help him. But she feels that her work and duty is here, helping me, for most of the year. In May, she goes back to Cranberry Island, opens her house, and plants her vegetable garden. And people come to see her from then to the time of her return in the fall.

I have often wondered whether God Himself maneuvered the tragic circumstances of Beulah's death in order to bring about this most unlikely partnership—for it is indeed unlikely, both of us being extremely independent, not to say "ornery" women. But I cannot think of it quite that way. Surely God could have accomplished it without so much heartbreak and shock. I think rather that Beulah's death was an attack of Satan, but that God overcame the enemy and turned it to a good purpose. He never promised that no trouble would come to us on this uncertain earth with its pall of evil and violent thinking. But we know that "All things work together for good to them that love God, to them who are called according to his purpose" (Rom. 8:28).

In other words, if we are faithful and endure to the end, He can take the very things that have caused us the most sorrow and can change the pattern and work them into good—perhaps into a more beautiful pattern than the original ones that we were following. A master craftsman in India makes the design for the Oriental rugs. They are hung high on a framework, and women and children sit behind them, pull the strands of many-colored wool in and out, and tie the knots. If someone makes a mistake, putting in, for instance, blue instead of red, the craftsman never makes him rip out the thread. Instead, he changes the pattern, weaving the thread often into a more intricate pattern and more beautiful design than the one he had first planned.

My last trip before making the long trek across the country was a ten-day stand: a School of Prayer in Minneapolis and then a School of Pastoral Care near Toronto.

Edith drove to Westboro during this time, left her car with relatives near Boston, and went to Westboro. There she packed the household effects marked "California," got all the furniture onto the moving van, cleaned the whole house from attic to cellar, put the suitcases in my car, and met me at the airport. So I did not go back to the house at all and was spared the last farewell to that beloved bit of our little earth. My friends had already bidden me farewell. A reception had been held in the parish house, and I received a check to be spent for plants and flowers for my new garden. Nothing could have pleased me more.

Thus we set forth from New England into the Far West. The trip on the whole was very pleasant. We got off our course only one time, just beyond Memphis, in gathering darkness and hard rain. We spent the night in a small motel where for supper we had catfish and hush puppies and okra pickle, much to Edith's amusement. We wandered about a bit in the morning, laughing over road signs reading "Marked Tree Road" and "Maggot Slough" and "Boggy Bottom" before we again found the through highway. These huge highways are wonderful, but one does not see the country from them. No matter where one drives, there are the same sweeping curves, the same grassy banks neatly mowed. What lies beyond no one can tell.

One other time we went aside into real life, this time by plan. We stopped at Birmingham and met an old friend. She drove us to her charming house, flower-smothered, on a quiet street shadowed by tall, ancient oak trees, so that all the world was the lacy green of filtered sunlight and warm shadow. One would never have known from the highway that such a world existed, just as one would never have seen the midcity section through which she led us the next day on our way back to the freeway.

"They are our friends," she said to me (for I rode with her and Edith followed). "When the riot-makers came down here and tried to stir them up, they refused. 'The white people are our best friends,' they said. And no one could get them to riot or demonstrate or anything. We have a black millionaire in this town," she went on, "a very fine man. He has done a great deal for the young people of the city."

"But I never heard of such a thing!" some of you may be thinking. No, you would not. Only love reveals the secrets of love.

We had planned to spend Thanksgiving Day in Albuquerque, hoping to enjoy that fascinating city, to visit Bill Lovekin, an old friend although young, and to have Thanksgiving dinner in the restaurant on top of the Sangre de Cristo mountain range. Instead, it rained; it poured! We went out under umbrellas to explore the city, but no stores were open, and it was dull and depressing. So finally about eleven o'clock, we decided that we might as well go on our way. All through the desert it rained. We grew hungry and found no restaurant wherein to have a Thanksgiving dinner, only signs gloating over rattlesnakes and Indian moccasins. Finally we entered the glaring new town of Grants where at least we could buy gas.

"Can you tell us," said we, being in the throes of hunger, "where we can find something to eat?"

And the youth replied, pointing to a drive-in, "Them brazier-burgers is real nice."

So we had our Thanksgiving dinner sitting in the car consuming chocolate milk shakes and brazier-burgers. And, indeed, they were real nice.

In the late afternoon the rain stopped, the sun came out, and all the world was a blaze of glory and of color unbelievable. We went our way with thanksgiving, eventually made our way to the house that I had so recently bought, and became Californians.

I might add that this purchase had seemed impossible a month earlier, for the bank did not get the escrow through in time. I do not know why. Possibly they were puzzled as they looked into my financial condition. Stocks? None. Bonds? None. (What are bonds?) Savings account? A very small amount, for I had not yet sold the house on Mill Road. At this juncture, Mr. Gaines personally lent me the money with which to buy his own house—no interest, provided I got it back to him in six months. How strange that many people think that all the world is in league to trick and defraud them! I have never in my life been tricked or defrauded, or if I was, I was too dumb to know it. I did get the money back to him—in four months to be exact, for I sold the Westboro house, refusing to wait for the higher price that my real-estate dealer expected, somewhat to her annoyance. The Westboro house sold for much less than I originally asked, but then, the Monrovia house sold for much less than the Gaineses had originally asked, so all is well. It rejoices me to go back and see the lovely young family who now live in the cottage on Mill Road, and I trust it is a blessing to them as it was to me.

It seemed strange that the very first morning in Monrovia, instead of looking forward eagerly to actually entering my new house, I should have sunk into depression. My spiritual eye was seeing a bit ahead in time, and there was something wrong. Sure enough, there was the house, repainted and repapered exquisitely, my own furniture charmingly arranged in an original and imaginative manner by Tookie and her friend, Betty Denning, who is now my very good friend also. There were children and grandchildren to meet me—but there was something wrong.

The house was redolent of paint, to which I am allergic, and of some other creeping odor that I could not identify. I came down with the most thundering migraine headache, which frightened Edith, though I could have told her, had I been able to speak with any clarity, that it would pass.

So it did, and with all windows open, the house was freed from the paint smell. Still, an odor remained on the lower floor of the house, in my study. I adore my study. It looks out directly onto patio and canyon. Birds dive-bomb and sing throughout all the trees (which trees, due to the plunging depths of the little canyon, are below me and not above.) But at that time I could not pray and work here more than an hour without again getting a headache. We summoned a plumber to find out whether there were any gas leaks, but he found nothing. We filled the room with fragrant iris and chrysanthemum and calla lilies out of my gardens. But even through the delicious fragrance of the purple iris and the spicy aroma of the white chrysanthemums and the fairy breath of callas, the undertone of an evil smell remained. Finally one day in my meditation I said, "What is it, Lord?" Now I must have prayed about this condition many a time during that first month. But this time I asked Him directly, with great urgency and with the definite expectancy of an answer.

And He said, in words as clear as any I have ever heard with my human ears, "You have a leak in your gas heater."

Why did He not tell me that before? I am sure He did, but the clouds of this life are thick about us, and the voices of the world tend to block out the voice of God. So it was only when I practically shouted my question and then listened with my whole heart that His message came through. Not a message of "Trust me, my child," but the simple, straightforward words: "You have a leak in your gas heater."

Therefore, we again summoned the perplexed plumber and told him that we had a leak in the gas heater and that he was to find it. He went below and emerged gloomily, stating that there was no leak.

"Yes, there is," said Edith, who was on deck at the time, for I was resting. "Go down again and find it."

After a considerable wait the plumber returned.

"Lady!" said he. "That could have been dangerous! Your water heater was pouring out gas all the time whether it was lit or not!"

So the house was healed. But there was still an unpleasant odor in the study even though the dizzy fumes were there no more. Edith therefore questioned the Lord about this with the same urgency that I had used, and according to her, He said, "Smell the rug."

So down on her haunches she went, and indeed the rug, having been saturated for so long with the odor of leaking gas, still smelled of it.

I am afraid that neither one of us is of the patient type. We did not try dry cleaning or wet cleaning or any other type of cleaning. We bundled up the rug, put it into the trash, went down to a secondhand store and bought another one to cover the midportion of the rather drab linoleum floor—for this room was meant for a rumpus room, remember, and did not rejoice in wall-to-wall carpeting as did the upstairs rooms. Possibly the Lord led me here too, for I found a mill-end of what I thought was a discreet dull gold and put it on the floor and found it to be a frank and lively orange. I love it! I had the picture window and the open stairway hung with a flower-garden chintz in green and purple and blue, had a mantlepiece built above the big fireplace, bought a huge secondhand desk for the middle of the large room, and filled the rest with bookcases and with my ancient chairs, and it is a delightful room, with my pastel paintings and my brother's oils brightening the white walls, and bits of treasures from all over the world enlivening the mantelpiece. I am the old-fashioned type, and my treasures have something of myself in them and I love them. Some people say that the more spiritual they become, the less they care for the earth and material things upon the earth. Not so with me. The more my spirit is absorbed in the kingdom of heaven, the more my heart delights in the earth that God has made and in the beautiful things that man has brought forth upon it.

23.

So here I am, surrounded and inundated with beauty on every side. When I awake in the morning I look from my bed to towering wild mountains, shining dimly through a veil of mist or starkly brilliant with the shadows of swift clouds ever changing their intoxicating pattern of beauty, mountains so rugged in their strength and yet so fragile, so delicately balanced, that from time to time tremors shake their steep slopes and small rocks fall tentatively upon the twisting mountain road that leads to these few houses.

I have become so attuned to mountains that I can often feel the tension within before the tremors come, and can gather them into God's love and comfort them and say to them, "Peace, be still. The love of God will help you to reduce your inner tensions easily, as you are doing now—just little quivers and you can rest again in His love. For He who created you in the first place is continuing His creation, and He can do so with gentleness, His love, through the love of those of us who trust Him, bringing to birth His kingdom of heaven on earth."

Recently, when I had finished a mission in Houston, two young women took me to the plane, and one of them said, "What is this about Southern California? The Lord spoke to our prayer group and said, 'Stop praying for sick people, and pray for Southern California!'"

The Lord had said this to me too, so loud and clear that much of my reason for moving to this unstable piece of earth was the better to pray for it. And this prayer concern has grown stronger with each passing day.

Since moving, the Lord has opened new doors of service to me. There are other doors opening—all over the land for His own feet to enter. His Spirit is breaking out among the young people in ways most dramatic and thrilling. I have seen the Jesus People. I have been to their meetings, and have been moved to tears of joy by the delight in the Lord that shines in their faces, and by the glory that nearly blasts the roof off their little meeting-places when they sing. My only fear for these wonderful young people is that, like generations of Christians before them, they will close the door to those of other Christian backgrounds than their own, proclaiming that theirs is the only way. *Jesus* is the only way, and He is so great that none of us can hold Him, contain Him, or keep the fullness of Him for ourselves alone.

These young people are a joy and delight to me, for they represent the hope of the world—the time when God will pour out His Spirit upon all flesh, and our sons and our daughters shall prophesy, our old men shall dream dreams, our young men shall see visions (Joel 2:28). Sharing with them, you know that that time has already begun!

They are also an indictment of the churches. True, here and there a church is awakening to its full power and responsibility, and is reaching out for the young ones, and showing them the living Jesus who can heal today. But for the most part, the churches have put God in a box of their own devising and have done their best to keep Him there. Their emphasis has been on the church's teaching and liturgical traditions—on forms and programs and finances—rather than on the power of the living Lord. Therefore they have seen the lost and little ones searching in all dark corners for something of life, and have had nothing to give them and no word to say to them.

But no matter what I am doing, it is never long out of mind that God sent me to Southern California to pray for the healing of the earth. As I write, the earth desperately needs rain. This morning a call came from the San Joaquin Valley asking prayers for rain and saying that unless the Lord thus heals the earth, all crops will be lost in that area. It is very difficult to pray for rain here because of the selfishness of most people. When I mention it, someone often says, "Oh, but not this weekend, because I am going on a trip." Nevertheless, I persist, and shall persist until the rains come.

Also, I pray continually for the healing of the San Andreas fault. I am praying for it now, as I look out my study window at the lovely mountains, dim in our California haze. I pray for the peace of God to enter into the San Andreas fault itself. I even pray for the "fire angels," not knowing what they may be, though presumably they are messengers of God, to enter in and accomplish a work of healing and adjustment so that this tremendous rift will settle its tensions gradually, without any totally destructive earthquake.

There are times when I feel great pressure to do this, when I wake in the night and sense tension in the mountains, when I pray an hour or two before going back to sleep. There are other times when this prayer burden seems light and easy.

However, perhaps to show me that prayer can indeed affect wind and waves and the earth itself, during this latter period of my life I have seen miracles over and beyond miracles of healing. I cannot explain them, nor will I attempt to. I merely state what I have seen and heard; the reader may believe or not as he likes.

A few years ago we held an excellent School of Pastoral Care at Yucaipa, California. We succeeded that time in limiting the enrollment according to the original plan. There were about forty-five ministers in the School. Our final Communion service was held informally in the lounge.

The Reverend Tod Ewald was the celebrant. We stood in a circle and he blessed an ordinary small dinner roll and gave it to his assistant, first taking a large chunk out of it himself. I remember glancing at it, as everyone began taking a piece, and thinking, "That will never do. He'll have to go back to the kitchen and get more bread."

But he did not go back to the kitchen. I forgot about this at the moment, but later I saw that the dinner roll had been passed all the way around the circle, and at the end of the service the minister had to call three others to come in back of his homemade altar table and help him consume it. (It is the rule in the Episcopal church that all remaining consecrated bread must be consumed.) There they stood, chewing as hard as they could, while we sang the final hymn!

This was all so quiet, and we were so deep in our devotions, that we did not even think about it at the time. Later, I mentioned it to one or two people and said, "Hey, what happened to that bread?" And with great awe, amazement, and wonder they exclaimed that it must have been a miracle!

Why did the Lord do this? I do not know, unless it was to show us that His word is true, and that He can move not only in the spirits and minds and bodies of people but also in bread, in wind, in the earth, in this very "creature," as St. Paul calls this world that God has created.

The next morning we held our final blessing service in the chapel, a large building with very tall windows. Just as we were about to pray for each one with the laying on of hands for the increase of the Holy Spirit, there came a sound like a rushing, mighty wind. The windows rattled so that we could not hear ourselves speak, yet the tall trees outside the windows were absolutely motionless. There was no wind out of doors. But energy, like a mighty, rushing wind, filled the chapel. Moreover, it was not an earthquake, because the floor did not move. One could see no motion at all. There was just a rushing, roaring sound of the power of the Holy Spirit.

And the chapel was filled with glory! One of the men arose and read from the second chapter of Acts about that wind of the Spirit that they had all heard. We continued our service of blessing with the laying on of hands, with great joy and power. However, we did not break into noise or pandemonium; the Lord had provided the noise! We simply continued our prayers that the Holy Spirit, already within His ministers, would be quickened into new life in every one of them.

On another occasion the Lord did a most amazing miracle. I am not quite sure that I approve of it, but at any rate it happened. We had been to a very difficult School of Pastoral Care in Northern California. At the end of it, I was quite exhausted with the effort of trying, under extreme tension, to do the Lord's work, and so I caught a cold. (Many years ago it came to me that if I wanted to maintain perfect health, I would have to cease doing such intensive work in the midst of other people. I would have to order my own life quietly and make my health my main endeavor. I concluded that my health was not of primary importance.)

Before my next mission in Scottsdale, Arizona, Edith and I spent the weekend in Tiburon on the seashore. We were sitting in our motel just inside a great picture-window. A tremendous wind arose which, the newspapers later reported, reached a hundred miles an hour. Actually, I was afraid that the plate-glass window would burst and explode into the room. It rattled and shook while small stones cracked against it. Feeling rather cross, I just shouted at the wind, as one might scold a naughty child: "Okay, *that's enough! Quiet down!*"

Suddenly, the wind was still. I cannot explain this, nor do I recommend it! It happened, that's all.

God does answer prayer, and His answers are not limited to healing of the body, but can also be the healing of the wind, and the showing forth of His glory in bread or in nature. And they can also include the healing of this terrestrial globe. "For we know," as Saint Paul said, "that the whole creation groaneth and travaileth in pain together until now" (Rom. 8:22).

A few verses earlier, Paul had said, referring also to the earth, "For the earnest expectation of the creature waiteth for the manifestation of the sons of God" (Rom. 8:19). We talk a great deal about waiting for the return of our Lord. I wonder sometimes whether He is waiting for us to become the sons of God. The bringing forth of the sons of God is surely God's will; there is no question about it. It is God's will that those who dare to become His sons, heirs to His power, shall exercise spiritual authority upon this earth. We are to stand between the sinning people and their Creator, even as did the prophets of old, and pray for forgiveness. Praying thus, we shall dare to accept God's forgiveness. And just as we have learned to picture a healed body when we pray for physical healing, we picture that healed earth that He called the kingdom of heaven.

Jesus warned us that there would be great tribulations, and so there have been, and how many more there will be we do not know. But although He warned us of tribulations, so that we would be prepared to meet them, He never told us to fix our gaze upon them. He gave us His command—absolute, straight, direct. He told us to pray, "Thy kingdom come, thy will be done, on earth as it is in heaven."

A number of California churches have fled the state—minister, congregation, everybody—because of prophecies that an earthquake would destroy the area completely. But this is not so surprising; any geologist who knows the area will tell you that Southern California is a dangerous place. We may as well either love it or leave it, and if we stay, either take what comes without complaint . . . or *do* something about it, with the greatest power of all—the miracle-working power of God!

Therefore I have continued in prayer for the San Andreas fault, and while nothing can be proved, there are some encouraging indications. Others guided by me have also started praying for the healing of the faults.

A group of young people whom I have never met heard about this concept of prayer, and with great joy worked out their own prayer-method. They go on long climbs up the mountains. That is no child's play. One 8,000-foot mountain took them two days to ascend. They climb without paths, scrambling over rocks as best they can, and sing to the mountains Christian hymns and songs. Sometimes they reach a place where they feel "bad vibrations." On reaching such a place, they erect a little wooden cross, though whether they pray out loud or merely sing I do not know.

Thus they carry the peace and the love of God to the very mountains themselves. The friend who told me this reported that the newspapers mentioned a certain mountain wherein there had been no tremors for a long time, and said that recently there had been there a number of small tremors, indicating release of tension. This was one of the mountains the young people had climbed.

I know that some earthquakes are bound to come that will be more than mere tremors. Therefore I pray that when, for geological reasons in the development of the earth, there must be a major earthquake, its center shall be in an unpopulated area where as little harm as possible will result. This has unquestionably happened.

One such earthquake had a lot of advance publicity because certain people with a gift of prophecy undoubtedly did foresee it. What they did not see was the power of prayer that could minimize it. They did not understand that in every prophecy there is an "if." "Yet forty days, and Nineveh shall be overthrown," cried Jonah to the people of Nineveh (Jon. 3:4). But it was not overthrown, because the people repented and turned to the Lord. The "if" in the prophecy was not expressed, but it was there. It is always there. In every prophecy of doom there is an "if."

In other words, God is stronger than fate. According to the mere working out of fate, this or that disaster will happen. But if someone with sufficient faith prays, or if a number of people pray and turn unto the Lord and cease from their evil ways, then, as God promised in II Chron. 7:14, He will hear them from His holy place, and He will come to them, and He will save their land.

In February, 1971, I awoke at six one morning with the bed bouncing in a most violent manner, and immediately I started talking to the earth. "Okay," I said to it. "That's enough. Come on now, quiet down. You're doing all right, but it is time to stop now. Quiet down—quiet down—quiet down!" Very quickly it did, with only the normal, more gentle after-shocks following.

The newspapers commented on three evidences of "great good luck" in connection with this earthquake. The first was that it occurred at six o'clock in the morning when most people were at home in bed. Freeways were destroyed, and some still stand there uncompleted—dramatic testimony to the power of this earth, and yet to my mind a greater testimony to the mercy of God. If the earthquake had come just two hours later, with the freeways full of cars, there would have been fearful carnage.

Another "lucky" fact was that the center of the earthquake was in a comparatively thinly populated area. If it had been in the middle of Los Angeles, the destruction would have been practically total, since its force measured eight plus on the Richter Scale.

The third piece of great "good luck" was reported to be that the earthquake stopped just exactly when it did. It would have done incalculably greater damage, had it continued even a second or two longer.

There was a time, as I have recounted in a former chapter, when the Lord opened to me the glory of the heavens, and from time to time my soul was deeply comforted by living briefly in His holy city and beholding, although dimly, His light there shining. My soul was greatly uplifted by arising—in dream or vision, in the body or not in the body, I know not—to the hill of the Lord, and beholding brief glimpses of the great white throne and the outer fringes of its glory.

Now that I have moved to California, these glimpses are few and far between. I have asked the Lord, "Why? I am drawing nearer every year to life in the many-dimensional kingdom of heaven. . . . Why do You not continue to uphold me with these far-shining visions?"

Insofar as I can tell, His answer is, "Not now. While you are on the earth, I desire that you help Me to be the light of the earth."

Jesus said, "As long as I am in the world, I am the light of the world" (John 9:5). Moreover, He commanded us, His followers, to be like a light, like a city set upon a hill whose light cannot be hid.

That is still my work here on this earth. It is not to escape into a visionary life. It is not to sit back longing for the "rapture," when I will be caught up to meet the Lord while all the wicked are destroyed. My work is to remain here, a person among people, and to be, as He said, like a lamp through whom His light shall shine into this earth. For He came down upon this earth, and died for us on the Cross, not to destroy us but to save us, not to wreck the little planet earth but to transform it into the kingdom of heaven.

Jesus commanded us to pray that the kingdom of heaven come upon earth, and that His will be done on earth even as it is done in heaven. In His holy word we are told how His will is done in heaven. In the twenty-first chapter of Revelation we read: "And God shall wipe away all tears from their eyes; and there shall be no more death, neither sorrow, nor crying, neither shall there be any more pain: for the former things are passed away."

For this tremendous, incomprehensible event we are told to pray—the time when the knowledge of God will cover the earth as the waters cover the sea—the time when one man will not say to another, "Know ye the Lord?" for all will know the Lord, from the least unto the greatest.

For the coming of this time, we are commanded to pray, and prayer without believing is of no avail. Prayer without faith accomplishes nothing. Therefore, as I pray this prayer, part of the

—— 312 ——

command of the Lord is that with the eyes of faith I see this earth becoming the kingdom of our God and of His Son, that by a tremendous leap of the imagination I look forward to the time when Jesus Himself, in ways that I do not know, shall reign upon this earth.

So He has commanded me, and while I remain here and obey Him, He comforts my soul, not with visions of heaven—heaven can wait—but with visions of God's glory upon this earth.

And yesterday morning for the first time, as I looked out to the misty hills (for though I am too high for smog, there is often a fog from the ocean), I could see the light around the trees. I do not know what this light is. But I cannot imagine it or dream it into reality. When it comes, it comes of itself, as though emanating from the very trees and not from me. Though I do not understand it, my heart is greatly rejoiced when I see it, for it testifies to my spirit of the Spirit of God permeating all His universe.

So may the light shine until the very creature—the earth itself—its ugliness turned into beauty, becomes indeed the kingdom of our God and of His Christ.